A Guide to Writing KANJI & KANA

Book 2

A Self-Study Workbook for
Learning Japanese Characters

Wolfgang Hadamitzky & Mark Spahn

TUTTLE PUBLISHING
Boston • Rutland, Vermont • Tokyo

This book has been typeset by Seiko Harada and Rainer Weihs, Trier, Germany, on a Macintosh® computer, using the Japanese Pagemaker®.

Published by Tuttle Publishing,
an imprint of Periplus Editions (HK) Ltd.,
with editorial offices at 153 Milk Street, Boston, Massachusetts 02109 and
130 Joo Seng Road, #06-01/03, Singapore 368357.

LCC Card No. 91-65055
ISBN 0-8048-3505-5

First edition, 1991
Seventh printing, 2004

Printed in Singapore

Distributed by:

Japan
Tuttle Publishing
Yaekari Building, 3rd Floor
5-4-12 Osaki, Shinagawa-ku
Tokyo 141-0032
Tel: (03) 5437 0171; Fax: (03) 5437 0755
Email: tuttle-sales@gol.com

North America, Latin America & Europe
Tuttle Publishing
Airport Industrial Park
364 Innovation Drive
North Clarendon, VT 05759-9436
Tel: (802) 773 8930; Fax: (802) 773 6993
Email: info@tuttlepublishing.com

Asia Pacific
Berkeley Books Pte. Ltd.
130 Joo Seng Road, #06-01/03
Singapore 368357
Tel: (65) 6280 1330; Fax: (65) 6280 6290
Email: inquiries@periplus.com.sg

CONTENTS

INTRODUCTION

The purpose of *A Guide to Writing Kanji and Kana* is to help students of Japanese master writing the two *kana* syllabaries (46 hiragana and 46 katakana) and the 1,945 basic characters (Jōyō Kanji) officially recommended for daily use.

With so many characters, it is important that you study them systematically, in a carefully thought-out progression. Most textbooks for learning Japanese, however, do not offer an introduction to Japanese script based on sound didactic principles. *A Guide to Writing Kanji and Kana* answers the need for a step-by-step presentation of characters by following the system developed in the book *Kanji & Kana* [1]. Also, up to three basic graphical elements (graphemes) indicating its meaning and/or pronunciation are listed for each kanji. Furthermore, the characters are taught not in isolation but as parts of important compounds that use only characters that have been introduced earlier.

Characters are presented in brush, pen, and printed forms. Each character in pen form is printed in light gray for you to trace over. These gray lines will guide your hand the first time you try writing a new character and will help you quickly develop a feel for the proper proportions.

When practicing writing the characters, don't forget that they should be written to fit into squares, either real or imaginary, of exactly the same size. *A Guide to Writing Kanji and Kana* has convenient, preprinted squares: large and normal size for all kana and the first 778 kanji, and normal size for kanji 779–1,945.

When memorizing kanji, use the same method as the one recommended in the Introduction of Book 1 for the syllabaries. For kanji, look at the **basic graphical elements** (graphemes) the entry character is made up of; you will soon notice that all kanji are constructed from relatively few basic elements. These elements often indicate the meaning and/or pronunciation of the kanji. Instead of following the order of kanji presented in this book, you can choose any order you like. You might, for example, select the order in which kanji are introduced in the textbook you're using in class. The disadvantage to this, however, is that the words and compounds will then contain characters that you have not yet learned.

The kanji are fully indexed by *on-kun* readings. The *Index* in Book 1 lists all kanji contained in that volume. The *General Index* at the end of Book 2 lists all kanji contained in both volumes, grouping together kanji that share the same reading and a common graphical element.

[1] Hadamitzky, Wolfgang and Mark Spahn: *Kanji & Kana: A Handbook and Dictionary of the Japanese Writing System,* Charles E. Tuttle Company, Rutland, VT and Tokyo, 1981.

EXPLANATION OF THE CHARACTER ENTRIES

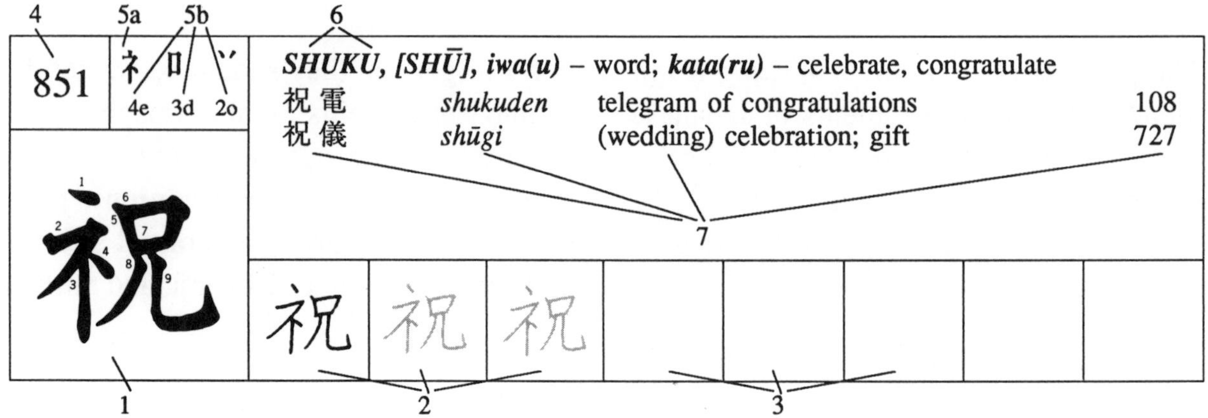

1. The kanji in brush form, with numbers showing stroke order positioned at the beginning of each stroke.

2. Three squares with the kanji in pen form, printed in light gray and serving as a practice template to trace over.

3. Empty squares in which to write the entry kanji and compounds.

4. Number of the kanji in these manuals.

5. a. Radical with its number-and-letter "descriptor", under which the kanji is listed in the *Japanese Character Dictionary* [2].

   b. Up to three graphemes (basic elements) with their number-and-letter "descriptor", under which the kanji can be retrieved in *SUNRISE Script.* [3]

   A numeral from 2 to 4 added to the descriptor indicates how many times that radical or grapheme is contained in the kanji. If the radical is not a grapheme, it is put in parentheses.

6. *On* readings, in capital italics; *kun* readings, in lowercase italics; readings that are infrequent or used only in special cases, in brackets; *okurigana* (part of a word that is written in kana), in parentheses; English meanings. All officially recognized readings of the kanji are listed.

7. Compounds, with romanization, meanings, and cross-reference numbers to the main entries for other kanji in the compound.

---

[2] Spahn, Mark and Wolfgang Hadamitzky: *Japanese Character Dictionary: With Compound Lookup via Any Kanji,* Nichigai Associates, Tokyo, 1989.

[3] Hadamitzky, Wolfgang and Mark Spahn: *SUNRISE Script: Electronic Learning and Reference System for Kanji,* JAPAN Media, Berlin, 1989. (With this computer program you can both hear and read the pronunciation of the characters.)

779	木 氵 一 (4a 3a 1a)	
染	***SEN, so(meru)*** – dye, color; ***so(maru)*** – be dyed, imbued; ***shi(miru)*** – soak into; be infected; smart, hurt; ***shi(mi)*** – stain, blot, smudge	
	(大気)汚染 *(taiki) osen* (air) pollution	26, 134, 693
	伝染病 *densenbyō* contagious disease	434, 380
	感染 *kansen* infection	262

780	艹 日 丷 (3k 4c 2o)	
黄	***KŌ, Ō, ki, [ko]*** – yellow	
	黄葉 *kōyō* (autumn) leaves	253
	黄熱(病) *(k)ōnetsu(byō)* yellow fever	645, 380
	黄金 *ōgon, kogane* gold	23
	黄色 *kiiro* yellow	204
	黄身 *kimi* egg yolk	59

781	木 日 艹 (4a 4c 3k)	
横	***Ō, yoko*** – side	
	専横 *sen'ō* arbitrariness, tyranny	600
	横道 *yokomichi* side street; side issue, digression	149
	横切る *yokogiru* cross, traverse	39
	横顔 *yokogao* profile	277
	横目 *yokome* side glance; amorous glance	55

782	一 土 冂 (1a3 3b 2r)	
再	***SAI, [SA], futata(bi)*** – once more, again, twice	
	再会 *saikai* meeting again, reunion	158
	再開 *saikai* reopening	396
	再編成 *saihensei* reorganization	682, 261
	再婚 *saikon* second marriage, remarriage	567
	再来週 *saraishū* week after next	69, 92

783	言 艹 土 7a 3k 3b			
講	***KŌ*** – club; lecture, study			
	講義	*kōgi*	lecture	291
	講演	*kōen*	lecture, address	344
	講師	*kōshi*	lecturer, instructor	409
	講堂	*kōdō*	lecture hall	496
	講和	*kōwa*	(make) peace	124

784	丷 厂 一 2o 2p 1a2			
兵	***HEI, HYŌ*** – soldier			
	兵器	*heiki*	weapon	527
	兵士	*heishi*	soldier	572
	歩兵	*hohei*	infantry; infantryman, foot soldier	431
	志願兵	*shiganhei*	a volunteer (soldier)	573, 581
	兵役	*heieki*	military service, conscription	375

785	氵 丷 厂 3a 2o 2p			
浜	***HIN, hama*** – beach			
	海浜	*kaihin*	seashore, beach	117
	京浜	*Kei-Hin*	Tokyo-Yokohama	189
	横浜	*Yokohama*	(port city near Tokyo)	781
	浜辺	*hamabe*	beach, seashore	775
	浜田	*Hamada*	(surname)	35

786	广 土 亻 3q 3b 2a2			
座	***ZA*** – seat; theater; constellation; ***suwa(ru)*** – sit down			
	座席	*zaseki*	seat	379
	座談会	*zadankai*	round-table discussion, symposium	593, 158
	(通信) 講座	*(tsūshin) kōza*	(correspondence) course	150, 157, 783
	口座	*kōza*	(savings) account	54
	銀座	*Ginza*	(area of Tokyo)	313

787 亠 亻 十 (2j 2a2 2k)

卒

SOTSU – soldier, private; end

卒業	*sotsugyō*	graduation	279
卒業試験	*sotsugyō shiken*	graduation examination	279, 526, 532
卒業証書	*sotsugyō shōsho*	diploma	279, 484, 131
卒中	*sotchū*	cerebral stroke, apoplexy	28
兵卒	*heisotsu*	a private, common soldier	784

788 亠 十 冫 (2j 2k 2b)

率

SOTSU, hiki(iru) – lead, command; ***RITSU*** – rate, proportion

率直	*sotchoku*	straightforward, frank	423
軽率	*keisotsu*	rash, hasty, heedless	547
能率	*nōritsu*	efficiency	386
倍率	*bairitsu*	(degree of) magnification	87
成長率	*seichōritsu*	rate of growth	261, 95

789 皿 丿 (5h 1c)

血

KETSU, chi – blood

血液	*ketsueki*	blood	472
血管	*kekkan*	blood vessel	328
(内)出血	*(nai)shukketsu*	(internal) hemorrhage	84, 53
止血剤	*shiketsuzai*	a hemostatic, styptic (agent)	477, 550
流血	*ryūketsu*	bloodshed	247

790 亻 十 (2a5 2k)

傘

SAN, kasa – umbrella

傘下	*sanka*	affiliated	31
日傘	*higasa*	parasol	5
雨傘	*amagasa*	umbrella	30
傘立て	*kasatate*	umbrella stand	121
こうもり傘	*kōmorigasa*	umbrella, parasol	

791 亻 土 口
2a 3b 3d

舎

SHA – house, hut, quarters

国民宿舎	*kokumin shukusha*	government-sponsored hostels	40, 177, 179
校舎	*kōsha*	schoolhouse, school building	115
兵舎	*heisha*	barracks	784
田舎	*inaka*	the country, rural areas	35

舎 舎 舎

792 皿 亻 ノ
5h 2a 1c4

衆

SHŪ, [SHU] – multitude, populace

公衆(電話)	*kōshū (denwa)*	public (telephone)	126, 108, 238
大衆文学	*taishū bungaku*	popular literature	26, 111, 109
民衆	*minshū*	the people, masses	177
アメリカ合衆国	*Amerika Gasshūkoku*	United States of America	159, 40

衆 衆 衆

793 口 厂 一
3d 2p 1a2

君

KUN – (suffix for male personal names); ruler; ***kimi*** – you (in masculine speech); ruler

和夫君	*Kazuo-kun*	Kazuo	124, 315
君主	*kunshu*	monarch, sovereign	155
立憲君主政(国)	*rikken kunshusei (koku)*	constitutional monarchy	121, 521, 155, 483, 40

君 君 君

794 口 王 丷
3d 4f 2o

群

GUN, mu(re), [mura] – group, herd; ***mu(reru)*** – crowd, flock

群衆	*gunshū*	crowd of people	792
群集	*gunshū*	crowd of people	436
群像	*gunzō*	group of people (in an artwork)	740
魚群	*gyogun*	school of fish	290
群島	*guntō*	group of islands, archipelago	286

群 群 群

795 阝 犭 丷
2d 3g 2o

隊

TAI – party, squad, unit

軍隊	*guntai*	troops, army, the military	438
部隊	*butai*	military unit, squad	86
兵隊	*heitai*	soldier, troops	784
探検隊	*tankentai*	expedition, expeditionary group	535, 531
楽隊	*gakutai*	(musical) band	358

隊 隊 隊

796 月 犭 一
4b 3g 1a

豚

TON, buta – pig

養豚	*yōton*	pig raising	402
豚カツ	*tonkatsu*	pork cutlet	
豚肉	*butaniku*	pork	223
豚小屋	*butagoya*	pigsty, pigpen	27, 167

豚 豚 豚

797 刂 ⺊ 厂
2f 2m 2p

劇

GEKI – drama, play

劇場	*gekijō*	theater, playhouse	154
演劇	*engeki*	drama, theatrical performance	344
歌劇	*kageki*	opera	392
劇的	*gekiteki*	dramatic	210
劇薬	*gekiyaku*	powerful medicine; virulent poison	359

劇 劇 劇

798 ⺊ ノ
2m2 1c

比

HI, kura(beru) – compare

比率	*hiritsu*	ratio	788
比例	*hirei*	proportion	612
対比	*taihi*	contrast, contradistinction	365
比重	*hijū*	specific gravity	227
見比べる	*mikuraberu*	compare	63

比 比 比

799 氵 日 ﾄ (3a 4c 2m2)

混

KON, ma(zeru) – mix; ***ma(zaru/jiru)*** – be mixed

混乱	*konran*	confusion, disorder, chaos	689
混雑	*konzatsu*	confusion, congestion	575
混合	*kongō*	mixture	159
混血の人	*konketsu no hito*	person of mixed race, half-breed	789, 1
混ぜ物	*mazemono*	adulteration	79

混 混 混

800 辶 艹 ﾞ (2q 3k 2o)

選

SEN, era(bu) – choose, select

当選	*tōsen*	be elected	77
改選	*kaisen*	reelection	514
精選	*seisen*	careful selection	659
予選	*yosen*	preliminary match; primary election	393
選手	*senshu*	(sports) player	57

選 選 選

801 ⺍ 扌 ﾞ (3n 3c 2o)

挙

KYO – all, whole; arrest, capture; name, give, cite; ***a(geru)*** – name, give, enumerate; arrest, apprehend; ***a(garu)*** – be apprehended; be found, recovered

選挙	*senkyo*	election	800
挙党	*kyotō*	the whole party	495
検挙	*kenkyo*	arrest, apprehension, roundup	531

挙 挙 挙

802 ⺍ 言 ﾞ (3n 7a 2o)

誉

YO, homa(re) – glory, honor

栄誉	*eiyo*	honor, glory	723
名誉	*meiyo*	honor	82
名誉職	*meiyoshoku*	honorary post	82, 385
名誉教授	*meiyo kyōju*	professor emeritus	82, 245, 602
名誉市民	*meiyo shimin*	honorary citizen	82, 181, 177

誉 誉 誉

803 亠 口 亻 (2j 3d 2a)

褒

HŌ, ho(meru) – praise

褒賞	*hōshō*	prize	500
褒美	*hōbi*	reward	401
過褒	*kahō*	excessive/undeserved praise	413
褒め上げる	*homeageru*	praise very highly, extol	32
褒め立てる	*hometateru*	admire, praise highly	121

褒 褒 褒

804 一 丨 ノ (1a3 1b 1c)

包

HŌ, tsutsu(mu) – wrap up

包容力	*hōyōryoku*	capacity; tolerance, catholicity	654, 100
包丁	*hōchō*	kitchen knife	184
小包み	*kozutsumi*	parcel	27
紙包み	*kamizutsumi*	parcel wrapped in paper	180
包み紙	*tsutsumigami*	wrapping paper, wrapper	180

包 包 包

805 扌 一 ノ (3b 1a3 1c)

均

KIN – equal, even

平均	*heikin*	average	202
均一	*kin'itsu*	uniform	2
均等	*kintō*	equality, uniformity, parity	569
均質	*kinshitsu*	homogeneous	176
均分	*kinbun*	divide equally	38

均 均 均

806 宀 心 山 (3m 4k 3o)

密

MITSU – close, dense, crowded; minute, fine; secret

機密	*kimitsu*	a secret	528
密輸	*mitsuyu*	smuggling	546
(人口)密度	*(jinkō) mitsudo*	(population) density	1, 54, 377
密接	*missetsu*	close, intimate	486
精密	*seimitsu*	minute, accurate, precision	659

密 密 密

807 禾 心 ノ (5d 4k 1c)

秘

HI, hi(meru) – keep secret

秘密	*himitsu*	a secret	806
極秘	*gokuhi*	strict secrecy, top secret	336
秘書	*hisho*	secretary	131
神秘	*shinpi*	mystery	310
便秘	*benpi*	constipation	330

秘 秘 秘

808 阝 一 | (2d 1a3 1b)

邦

HŌ – country; Japan

(在米)邦人	*(zaibei) hōjin*	Japanese (living in America)	268, 224, 1
邦字新聞	*hōji shinbun*	Japanese-language newspaper	110, 174, 64
連邦	*renpō*	federation, federal	440
連邦政府	*renpō seifu*	federal government	440, 483, 504

邦 邦 邦

809 阝 米 ヰ (2d 6b 2n)

隣

RIN, tonari – next door; ***tona(ru)*** – be neighboring

隣国	*ringoku*	neighboring country/province	40
隣席	*rinseki*	next seat, seat next to one	379
隣接	*rinsetsu*	border on, be contiguous, adjoin	486
隣人	*rinjin*	a neighbor	1
隣り合う	*tonariau*	adjoin/be next door to each other	159

隣 隣 隣

810 一 卄 ヰ (1a6 3k 2n)

舞

BU, ma(u) – dance, flutter about; ***mai*** – dance

舞台	*butai*	the stage	492
舞楽	*bugaku*	old Japanese court-dance music	358
歌舞き	*kabuki*	Kabuki	392
仕舞	*shimai*	end, conclusion	333
(お)見舞い	*(o)mimai*	visit, inquiry (after someone's health)	63

舞 舞 舞

811 夢 (radicals: 艹 3k, 罒 5g, 冖 2i)

MU, yume – dream

夢想	*musō*	dream, vision, fancy	147
悪夢	*akumu*	bad dream, nightmare	304
夢中	*muchū*	rapture; absorption, intentness; frantic	28
夢を見る	*yume o miru*	(have a) dream	63
夢にも	*yume nimo*	(not) even in a dream	

812 葬 (radicals: 艹 3k2, 歹 2n, ト 2m)

SŌ, hōmu(ru) – bury, inter

葬儀/式	*sō-gi/shiki*	funeral	727, 525
火葬	*kasō*	cremation	20
葬列	*sōretsu*	funeral procession	611
副葬品	*fukusōhin*	burial accessories	714, 230
改葬	*kaisō*	reburial, reinterment	514

813 鼻 (radicals: 田 5f, 目 5c, 廾 3k)

BI, hana – nose

耳鼻いんこう科医	*jibiinkōkai*	ear, nose, and throat specialist	56, 320, 220
鼻先	*hanasaki*	tip of the nose	50
鼻血	*hanaji*	nosebleed, bloody nose	789
鼻薬	*hanagusuri*	a bribe	359

814 違 (radicals: 辶 2q, 口 3d, 十 2k)

I, chiga(u) – be different; be mistaken; ***chiga(eru)*** – alter

相違	*sōi*	difference, disparity	146
違反	*ihan*	violation	324
違法	*ihō*	illegal	123
違憲	*iken*	unconstitutionality	521
間違い	*machigai*	mistake, error; accident, mishap	43

815 彳 口 十 3i 3d 2k

衛

EI – defend, protect

防衛	*bōei*	defense	513
自衛隊	*Jieitai*	(Japanese) Self-Defense Forces	62, 795
衛生	*eisei*	hygiene, sanitation	44
衛星	*eisei*	satellite	730
前衛	*zen'ei*	advance guard; avant-garde	47

衛 衛 衛

816 力 亠 丷 2g 2j 2o

効

KŌ, ki(ku) – be effective

効力	*kōryoku*	effectiveness, effect, validity	100
効果	*kōka*	effect, effectiveness	487
有効	*yūkō*	validity, effectiveness	265
無効	*mukō*	invalidity, ineffectiveness	93
時効	*jikō*	prescription (in statute of limitations)	42

効 効 効

817 阝 亠 丷 2d 2j 2o

郊

KŌ – suburbs, rural areas

近郊	*kinkō*	suburbs, outskirts	445
郊外	*kōgai*	suburbs, outskirts	83

郊 郊 郊

818 力 一 丨 2g 1a 1b

功

KŌ, [KU] – merits, success

成功	*seikō*	success	261
功労	*kōrō*	meritorious service	233
功業	*kōgyō*	achievement, exploit	279
功名	*kōmyō*	great achievement, glorious deed	82
年功	*nenkō*	long service/experience	45

功 功 功

819	攵 一 丨 4i 1a 1b	***KŌ, se(meru)*** – attack		
攻	攻勢	*kōsei*	the offensive	646
	攻防	*kōbō*	offense and defense	513
	攻守	*kōshu*	offense and defense	490
	攻城	*kōjō*	siege	720
	専攻	*senkō*	one's major (study)	600

820	糸 一 丨 6a 1a2 1b	***KŌ, [KU], kurenai*** – deep red; ***beni*** – rouge, lipstick		
紅	紅葉	*kōyō, momiji*	(autumn) leaves; maple tree	253
	紅茶	*kōcha*	black tea	251
	紅白	*kōhaku*	red and white	205
	真紅	*shinku*	crimson, scarlet	422
	口紅	*kuchibeni*	lipstick	54

821	氵 一 丨 3a 1a2 1b	***KŌ, e*** – inlet, bay		
江	江湖	*kōko*	the public, world	467
	入り江	*irie*	inlet, small bay	52
	江ノ島	*Enoshima*	(island near Kamakura)	286
	江戸	*Edo*	(old name for Tokyo)	152
	江戸っ子	*Edokko*	true Tokyoite	152, 103

822	⺍ 耳 攵 3n 6e 4i	***GEN, [GON], kibi(shii)*** – severe, strict, rigorous, intense; ***ogoso(ka)*** – solemn, grave, stately		
厳	厳重	*genjū*	strict, stringent, rigid	227
	厳格	*genkaku*	strict, stern, severe	643
	厳禁	*genkin*	strict prohibition	482
	尊厳	*songen*	dignity	704

823 舟 亠 几 (6c 2j 2s)

航

KŌ – navigation, sailing

航空便	*kōkūbin*	airmail	140, 330
航空券	*kōkūken*	flight/airplane ticket	140, 506
航路	*kōro*	sea route, course	151
航海	*kōkai*	sea voyage/navigation	117
巡航	*junkō*	a cruise	777

航 航 航

824 扌 亠 几 (3c 2j 2s)

抗

KŌ – resist

対抗	*taikō*	opposition, confrontation	365
抵抗	*teikō*	resistance	560
反抗	*hankō*	resistance, opposition	324
抗議	*kōgi*	protest	292
抗争	*kōsō*	contention, dispute	302

抗 抗 抗

825 广 車 (3q 7c)

庫

KO, [KU] – storehouse

車庫	*shako*	garage	133
金庫	*kinko*	a safe	23
国庫	*Kokko*	the (National) Treasury	40
文庫本	*bunkobon*	small cheap paperback	111, 25
在庫品	*zaikohin*	goods in stock, inventory	268, 230

庫 庫 庫

826 广 木 (3q 4a)

床

SHŌ, toko – bed; floor; ***yuka*** – floor

起床	*kishō*	rise, get up (from bed)	373
病床	*byōshō*	sickbed	380
温床	*onshō*	hotbed, breeding ground	634
床屋	*tokoya*	barber, barbershop	167
床の間	*tokonoma*	alcove in Japanese-style room	43

床 床 床

827	广 心 3q 4k
応	

Ō – reply, respond; comply with; fulfill, satisfy

反応	*hannō*	reaction	324
順応	*junnō*	adaptation, adjustment	769
相応	*sōō*	correspond, be suitable	146
応用	*ōyō*	(practical) application	107
応接間	*ōsetsuma*	reception room	486, 43

応 応 応

828	亠 丷 ノ 2j 2o 1c
充	

JŪ – fill; ***a(teru)*** – allot, allocate, apply (to)

充分	*jūbun*	enough, sufficient (cf. No. 38)	38
充満	*jūman*	fullness, abundance	201
充足	*jūsoku*	sufficiency	58
充実	*jūjitsu*	repletion, perfection	203
充血した目	*jūketsu shita me*	bloodshot eyes	789, 55

充 充 充

829	金 亠 丷 8a 2j 2o
銃	

JŪ – gun

銃器	*jūki*	firearm	527
小銃	*shōjū*	rifle	27
短銃	*tanjū*	pistol, revolver	215
機関銃	*kikanjū*	machine gun	528, 398
銃殺	*jūsatsu*	shoot dead	576

銃 銃 銃

830	糸 亠 丷 6a 2j 2o
統	

TŌ, su(beru) – govern, control

統制	*tōsei*	control, regulation	427
統治	*tōchi, tōji*	reign, rule	493
統一	*tōitsu*	unity, unification	2
統計	*tōkei*	statistics	340
伝統	*dentō*	tradition	434

統 統 統

831	亻 一 丨 (2a 1a2 1b)	令

REI – order, command

命令	*meirei*	an order	578
号令	*gōrei*	an order, command	266
訓令	*kunrei*	instructions, directive	771
政令	*seirei*	cabinet order, government ordinance	483
発令	*hatsurei*	official announcement	96

832	冫 亻 一 (2b 2a 1a2)	冷

REI, tsume(tai) – cold; ***hi(yasu), sa(masu)*** – chill, cool; ***hi(eru), sa(meru)*** – become cold; ***hi(ya)*** – cold water; cold saké; ***hi(yakasu)*** – poke fun at, tease; browse

冷水	*reisui*	cold water	21
冷戦	*reisen*	cold war	301
冷静	*reisei*	calm, cool, dispassionate	663

833	米 ⺊ 亻 (6b 2m 2a)	齢

REI – age

年齢	*nenrei*	age	45
学齢	*gakurei*	(of) school age	109
老齢	*rōrei*	old age	543
高齢	*kōrei*	old/advanced age	190
月齢	*getsurei*	phase of the moon; age in months	17

834	頁 亻 一 (9a 2a 1a2)	領

RYŌ – govern, rule

領土/地	*ryōdo/chi*	territory	24, 118
大統領	*daitōryō*	president	26, 830
領事	*ryōji*	consul	80
領収書/証	*ryōshū-sho/shō*	receipt	757, 131, 484
横領	*ōryō*	usurpation, embezzlement	781

835 臣 (匚 一 丨 — 2t 1a2 1b2)

SHIN, JIN – retainer, subject

大臣	*daijin*	(government) minister	26
総理大臣	*sōri daijin*	prime minister	697, 143, 26
臣民	*shinmin*	subject	177
臣下	*shinka*	subject, retainer	31
君臣	*kunshin*	sovereign and subject, ruler and ruled	793

臣 臣 臣

836 臨 (匚 口 一 — 2t 3d3 1a3)

RIN, *nozo(mu)* – face, confront; attend, assist at

臨時	*rinji*	temporary, provisional, extraordinary	42
臨床	*rinshō*	clinical	826
臨終	*rinjū*	one's last moments/deathbed	458
臨席	*rinseki*	attendance, presence	379
君臨	*kunrin*	reign, rule	793

臨 臨 臨

837 閣 (門 夂 口 — 8e 4i 3d)

KAKU – tower, palace; the cabinet

内閣	*naikaku*	the cabinet	84
閣議	*kakugi*	meeting of the cabinet	292
組閣	*sokaku*	formation of a cabinet	418
閣下	*kakka*	Your/His Excellency	31
金閣寺	*Kinkakuji*	Temple of the Golden Pavilion	23, 41

閣 閣 閣

838 額 (頁 夂 宀 — 9a 4i 3m)

GAKU – amount; framed picture; ***hitai*** – forehead

金額	*kingaku*	amount of money	23
額面	*gakumen*	face value, par	274
総額	*sōgaku*	total amount, sum total	697
差額	*sagaku*	the difference, balance	658
半額	*hangaku*	half the amount/price	88

額 額 額

839	艹 夂 氵 3k 4i 3a			
落	***RAKU, o(chiru)*** – fall; ***o(tosu)*** – drop; lose			
	転落	*tenraku*	a fall	433
	落第	*rakudai*	failure in an examination	404
	部落	*buraku*	village, settlement	86
	落語	*rakugo*	Japanese comic storytelling	67
	落ち着いた	*ochitsuita*	calm, composed	657

落 落 落

840	糸 夂 口 6a 4i 3d			
絡	***RAKU, kara(mu/maru)*** – get entangled			
	連絡	*renraku*	contact, liaison, communication	440
	連絡駅	*renraku-eki*	connecting station, junction	440, 284
	連絡線	*renraku-sen*	connecting line	440, 299
	絡み付く	*karamitsuku*	coil around, cling to	192
	絡み合う	*karamiau*	intertwine	159

絡 絡 絡

841	田 夂 口 5f 4i 3d			
略	***RYAKU*** – abbreviation, omission			
	省略	*shōryaku*	omission, abridgment, abbreviation	145
	略語	*ryakugo*	abbreviation	67
	略歴	*ryakureki*	brief personal history	480
	計略	*keiryaku*	plan, stratagem, scheme	340
	戦略	*senryaku*	strategy	301

略 略 略

842	口 一 3d 1a2			
司	***SHI*** – administer, conduct			
	司法	*shihō*	administration of justice, judicial	123
	司令	*shirei*	commandant, commanding officer	831
	司会者	*shikaisha*	master of ceremonies, chairman	158, 164
	司書	*shisho*	librarian	131
	上司	*jōshi*	one's superior (officer)	32

司 司 司

843	言 口 一 7a 3d 1a2			
詞	***SHI*** – words			
	品詞	*hinshi*	part of speech	230
	名詞	*meishi*	noun	82
	(他)動詞	*(ta)dōshi*	(transitive) verb	120, 231
	歌詞	*kashi*	lyrics, words to a song	392
	賀詞	*gashi*	congratulations, greetings	756

詞 詞 詞

844	丷 月 3n 4b			
肖	***SHŌ*** – resemble			
	肖像画	*shōzōga*	portrait	740, 343
	不肖	*fushō*	unlike/unworthy of one's father; (humble) I	94

肖 肖 肖

845	氵 月 丷 3a 4b 3n			
消	***SHŌ, ke(su)*** – extinguish; ***ki(eru)*** – go out; disappear			
	消防(車)	*shōbō(sha)*	fire fighting (engine)	513, 133
	消火器	*shōkaki*	fire extinguisher	20, 527
	消費者	*shōhisha*	consumer	749, 164
	消化	*shōka*	digestion	254
	消極的	*shōkyokuteki*	negative, passive	336, 210

消 消 消

846	辶 日 ノ 2q 4c 1c			
退	***TAI, shirizo(ku)*** – retreat; ***shirizo(keru)*** – drive away, repel			
	退職	*taishoku*	retirement, resignation	385
	退院	*taiin*	leave/be discharged from the hospital	614
	退学	*taigaku*	leave/drop out of school	109
	引退	*intai*	retire (from public life)	216
	進退	*shintai*	advance or retreat, movement	437

退 退 退

847	阝 2d	日 4c	ノ 1c

限

GEN, kagi(ru) – limit

無限	*mugen*	unlimited, infinite	93
制限	*seigen*	restriction, limitation	427
限度	*gendo*	a limit	377
期限	*kigen*	term, time limit, deadline	449
権限	*kengen*	authority, competence, jurisdiction	335

限 限 限

848	目 5c	日 4c	ノ 1c

眼

GAN, [GEN], manako – eye

両眼	*ryōgan*	both eyes	200
近眼	*kingan*	nearsightedness, shortsightedness	445
眼科医	*gankai*	eye doctor, ophthalmologist	320, 220
眼識	*ganshiki*	discernment, insight	681
千里眼	*senrigan*	clairvoyance, clairvoyant	15, 142

眼 眼 眼

849	目 5c	厂 2p	一 1a

眠

MIN, nemu(ru) – sleep; ***nemu(i)*** – tired, sleepy

不眠	*fumin*	sleeplessness, insomnia	94
安眠	*anmin*	a quiet/sound sleep	105
冬眠	*tōmin*	hibernation	459
居眠り	*inemuri*	a doze, falling asleep in one's seat	171
眠り薬	*nemurigusuri*	sleeping drug/pills	359

眠 眠 眠

850	氵 3a	口 3d	丷 2o

況

KYŌ – circumstances, situation

状/情況	*jōkyō*	conditions, situation	626, 209
現況	*genkyō*	present situation	298
実況	*jikkyō*	actual state of affairs	203
市況	*shikyō*	market conditions, the market	181
不況	*fukyō*	recession, economic slump	94

況 況 況

851 礻 口 丷 — 4e 3d 2o

祝

SHUKU, [SHŪ], iwa(u) – celebrate, congratulate

祝辞	*shukuji*	(speech of) congratulations	688
祝電	*shukuden*	telegram of congratulations	108
祝賀	*shukuga*	celebration; congratulations	756
祝日	*shukujitsu*	festival day, holiday	5
祝儀	*shūgi*	(wedding) celebration; gift	727

祝 祝 祝

852 立 口 丷 — 5b2 3d2 2o2

競

KYŌ, KEI, kiso(u) – compete, vie for; ***se(ru)*** – compete, vie; bid for

競争	*kyōsō*	competition	302
競走	*kyōsō*	race	429
競売	*kyōbai*	auction	239
競馬	*keiba*	horse racing	283

競 競 競

853 日 口 丷 — 4c 3d 3n

景

KEI – view, scene

景色	*keshiki*	scenery	204
風景	*fūkei*	scenery	29
景勝(地)	*keishō(chi)*	(place of) picturesque scenery	509, 118
景気	*keiki*	business conditions	134
不景気	*fukeiki*	hard times, recession	94, 134

景 景 景

854 彡 日 口 — 3j 4c 3d

影

EI, kage – light; shadow, silhouette; figure; trace

影像	*eizō*	image, shadow	740
人影	*hitokage, jin'ei*	silhouette, human figure	1
影法師	*kagebōshi*	person's shadow	123, 409
影絵	*kagee*	shadow picture, silhouette	345
面影	*omokage*	face, traces, vestiges	274

影 影 影

855 阝 日 ノ (2d 4c 1c3)

鄉

KYŌ – village, native place; ***GŌ*** – rural area, country

故郷	*kokyō*	one's hometown, native place	173
郷里	*kyōri*	one's hometown, native place	142
郷土	*kyōdo*	one's hometown	24
望郷の念	*bōkyō no nen*	homesickness, nostalgia	673, 579
近郷	*kingō*	neighboring districts	445

856 日 立 阝 (4c2 5b 2d)

響

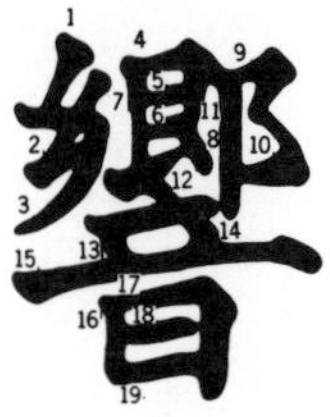

KYŌ, hibi(ku) – sound, resound, be echoed; affect

影響	*eikyō*	effect, influence	854
反響	*hankyō*	echo, response	324
音響	*onkyō*	sound	347
交響曲/楽	*kōkyō-kyoku/gaku*	symphony	114, 366, 358
響き渡る	*hibikiwataru*	resound, reverberate	378

857 立 日 十 (5b 4c 2k)

章

SHŌ – chapter; badge, mark

文章	*bunshō*	composition, writing	111
第三章	*daisanshō*	Chapter 3	404, 4
第三楽章	*daisan gakushō*	third movement	404, 4, 358
憲章	*kenshō*	charter, constitution	521
記章	*kishō*	medal, badge	371

858 阝 立 日 (2d 5b 4c)

障

SHŌ, sawa(ru) – hinder, interfere with; harm, hurt

保障	*hoshō*	guarantee, security	489
支障	*shishō*	hindrance, impediment	318
障害	*shōgai*	obstacle, impediment	518
故障	*koshō*	trouble, breakdown, out of order	173
障子	*shōji*	Japanese sliding paper door	103

859	艹 日 土 3k 4c 3b	*CHO, arawa(su)* – write, publish; *ichijiru(shii)* – marked, striking, remarkable, conspicuous		
著				
	著者	*chosha*	author	164
	著書	*chosho*	a (literary) work	131
	名著	*meicho*	a famous/great work	82
	著名	*chomei*	prominent, well-known	82

著 著 著

860	罒 日 土 5g 4c 3b	*SHO* – government office, station		
署				
	税務署	*zeimusho*	tax office	399, 235
	消防署	*shōbōsho*	fire station, firehouse	845, 513
	警察署	*keisatsusho*	police station	706, 619
	部署	*busho*	one's post/place of duty	86
	署名	*shomei*	signature, autograph	82

署 署 署

861	言 日 土 7a 4c 3b	*SHO* – all, various		
諸				
	諸国	*shokoku*	all/various countries	40
	諸島	*shotō*	islands	286
	諸説	*shosetsu*	various views/accounts	400
	諸事	*shoji*	various matters/affairs	80
	諸君	*shokun*	(Ladies and) Gentlemen!	793

諸 諸 諸

862	糸 日 土 6a 4c 3b	*SHO, [CHO]* – beginning; *o* – cord, strap, thong		
緒				
	緒戦	*shosen, chosen*	beginning of a war	301
	緒論	*shoron, choron*	introduction	293
	由緒	*yuisho*	history; pedigree, lineage	363
	情緒	*jōcho, jōsho*	emotion, feeling	209
	鼻緒	*hanao*	clog thong, *geta* strap	813

緒 緒 緒

863	金 立 日 8a 5b 4c	***KYŌ, kagami*** – mirror			
鏡		鏡台	*kyōdai*	dressing table	492
		三面鏡	*sanmenkyō*	a dresser with 3 mirrors	4, 274
		望遠鏡	*bōenkyō*	telescope	673, 446
		手鏡	*tekagami*	hand mirror	57
		眼鏡	*megane, gankyō*	eyeglasses	848

864	土 立 日 3b 5b 4c	***KYŌ, [KEI], sakai*** – boundary			
境		国境	*kokkyō*	border	40
		境界	*kyōkai*	boundary, border	454
		苦境	*kukyō*	distress, difficulties	545
		境内	*keidai*	precincts, grounds	84
		境目	*sakaime*	borderline; crisis	55

865	王 罒 口 4f 5g 3d	***KAN*** – ring, surround			
環		環境	*kankyō*	environment	864
		環状	*kanjō*	ring-shaped, annular	626
		光環	*kōkan*	corona	138
		一環	*ikkan*	a link, part	2

866	辶 罒 口 2q 5g 3d	***KAN*** – return			
還		返還	*henkan*	return, restoration; repayment	442
		帰還	*kikan*	return home, repatriation	317
		送還	*sōkan*	sending home, repatriation	441
		還元	*kangen*	restoration; reduction	137

867	阝 亻 一 2d 2a 1a3

陰

IN – negative, hidden; shadow, secret; ***kage*** – shadow; back; ***kage(ru)*** – get dark/clouded

陰陽	*in'yō*	yin and yang, positive and negative	630
陰性	*insei*	negative; dormant, latent	98
陰気	*inki*	gloomy, dismal, melancholy	134
日/木陰	*hi/ko-kage*	shade from the sun/of a tree	5, 22

陰 陰 陰

868	阝 心 ⺍ 2d 4k 3n

隠

IN, kaku(reru/su) – (intr./tr.) hide

隠者	*inja*	hermit	164
隠居	*inkyo*	retirement from active life	171
隠し芸	*kakushigei*	parlor trick, hidden talent	435
隠し引き出し	*kakushi hikidashi*	secret compartment (in a chest)	216, 53

隠 隠 隠

869	禾 心 ⺍ 5d 4k 3n

穏

ON, oda(yaka) – calm, quiet, mild, peaceful, moderate

穏和	*onwa*	mild, gentle, genial	124
平穏	*heion*	calmness, quiet, serenity	202
平穏無事	*heion-buji*	peace and quiet	202, 93, 80
穏当	*ontō*	proper, appropriate; gentle	77
穏便	*onbin*	gentle, quiet, amicable	330

穏 穏 穏

870	木 十 又 4a 2k 2h

枝

SHI, eda – branch

枝葉	*shiyō, edaha*	branches and leaves; digression	253
大枝	*ōeda*	bough, limb	26
小枝	*koeda*	twig	27
枝切り	*edagiri*	lopping off/pruning of branches	39
枝接ぎ	*edatsugi*	grafting	486

枝 枝 枝

871 扌 十 又 3c 2k 2h

技

GI, waza – technique; ability; feat

技術	*gijutsu*	technique, technology	187
技師	*gishi*	engineer	409
技能	*ginō*	technical skill, ability	386
演技	*engi*	acting, performance	344
競技	*kyōgi*	match, contest, competition	852

技 技 技

872 山 十 又 3o 2k 2h

岐

KI – forked road

分岐	*bunki*	divergence, branching	38
分岐点	*bunkiten*	point of divergence, junction	38, 169
岐路	*kiro*	fork in the road, crossroads	151

岐 岐 岐

873 虫 6d

虫

CHŪ, mushi – bug, insect

益/害虫	*eki/gaichū*	beneficial/harmful insect	716, 518
殺虫剤	*satchūzai*	insecticide	576, 550
毛虫	*kemushi*	hairy caterpillar	287
油虫	*aburamushi*	cockroach; hanger-on, parasite	364
虫歯	*mushiba*	decayed tooth, cavity	478

虫 虫 虫

874 虫 土 冂 6d 3b 2r

触

SHOKU, sawa(ru), fu(reru) – touch

触覚	*shokkaku*	sense of touch	605
接触	*sesshoku*	touch, contact	486
感触	*kanshoku*	the touch, feel	262
触角	*shokkaku*	feeler, antenna, tentacle	473
抵触	*teishoku*	conflict	560

触 触 触

875 騷

馬 虫 又
10a 6d 2h

SŌ, sawa(gu) – make noise

騷音	*sōon*	noise	347
騷動	*sōdō*	disturbance, riot	231
騷然	*sōzen*	noisy, tumultuous	651
大騷ぎ	*ōsawagi*	clamor, uproar, hullabaloo	26
騷ぎ立てる	*sawagitateru*	raise a great fuss/furor	121

876 戒

戈 艹
4n 3k

KAI, imashi(meru) – admonish, warn

警戒	*keikai*	caution, precaution, warning	706
訓戒	*kunkai*	admonition, warning	771
厳戒	*genkai*	strict watch/guard	822
戒律	*kairitsu*	(Buddhist) precepts	667
十戒	*jikkai*	the Ten Commandments	12

877 幾

戈 亻 ノ
4n 2a 1c4

KI, iku – how much/many, some

幾何学	*kikagaku*	geometry	390, 109
幾日	*ikunichi*	how many days, what day of the month	5
幾分	*ikubun*	some, a portion	38
幾つ	*ikutsu*	how much/many/old	
幾ら	*ikura*	how much/long/expensive	

878 倹

亻 口 一
2a3 3s 1a

KEN – thrifty, simple, modest

倹約	*ken'yaku*	thriftiness, economy	211
節倹	*sekken*	frugality, economy	464
勤倹	*kinken*	diligence and thrift	559

879 | 刂 口 亻 2f 3s 2a2

剣

KEN, tsurugi – sword

剣道	*kendō*	Kendo, Japanese fencing	149
刀剣	*tōken*	swords	37
短剣	*tanken*	short sword, dagger	215
剣劇	*kengeki*	swordplay/samurai drama	797
真剣	*shinken*	serious, earnest	422

剣 剣 剣

880 | ⺮ 木 冖 6f 4a 2i

策

SAKU – plan, means, measure, policy

政策	*seisaku*	policy	483
対策	*taisaku*	measure, countermeasure	365
具体策	*gutaisaku*	specific measure	420, 61
策略	*sakuryaku*	stratagem, scheme, tactic	841
術策	*jussaku*	artifice, stratagem, intrigue	187

策 策 策

881 | 刂 木 冖 2f 4a 2i

刺

SHI, sa(su) – pierce; ***sa(saru)*** – stick, get stuck

名刺	*meishi*	name/business card	82
風刺	*fūshi*	satire	29
刺し殺す	*sashikorosu*	stab to death	576
刺し傷	*sashikizu*	a stab; (insect) bite	633
刺身	*sashimi*	sashimi, sliced raw fish	59

刺 刺 刺

882 | 犭 一 丨 3g 1a 1b

犯

HAN, oka(su) – commit (a crime), violate, defy

犯人	*hannin*	criminal, culprit	1
犯行	*hankō*	crime	68
現行犯で	*genkōhan de*	in the act, red-handed	298, 68
共犯	*kyōhan*	complicity	196
防犯	*bōhan*	crime prevention/fighting	513

犯 犯 犯

883 狂 (犭 王 — 3g 4f)

KYŌ, kuru(u) – go crazy; run amuck; get out of order; ***kuru(oshii)*** – be nearly mad (with worry/grief)

狂言	*kyōgen*	play, drama; Noh farce	66
発狂	*hakkyō*	insanity, madness	96
狂気	*kyōki*	insanity, madness	134
狂乱	*kyōran*	frenzy, madness	689

884 獄 (犭 言 — 3g2 7a)

GOKU – prison

地獄	*jigoku*	hell	118
受験地獄	*juken jigoku*	the ordeal of examinations	260, 532, 118
獄舎	*gokusha*	prison, jail (building)	791
出獄	*shutsugoku*	release from prison	53
獄死	*gokushi*	die in prison	85

885 罪 (罒 ト 一 — 5g 2m 1a5)

ZAI, tsumi – crime, sin, guilt

犯罪	*hanzai*	crime	882
罪人	*zainin*	criminal	1
	tsumibito	sinner	
有罪	*yūzai*	guilty	265
罪業	*zaigō*	sin	279

886 罰 (罒 言 刂 — 5g 7a 2f)

BATSU – punishment, penalty; ***BACHI*** – (divine) punishment

罰金	*bakkin*	a fine	23
体罰	*taibatsu*	corporal punishment	61
厳罰	*genbatsu*	severe punishment	822
天罰	*tenbatsu*	punishment from God/Heaven	141
罰当たり	*bachiatari*	damned, cursed	77

887 刂 艹 一 (2f 3k 1a)

刑

KEI – penalty, punishment, sentence

刑事	*keiji*	criminal case; (police) detective	80
刑法	*keihō*	criminal law, the Criminal Code	123
刑罰	*keibatsu*	punishment, penalty	886
死刑	*shikei*	capital punishment	85
刑務所	*keimusho*	prison	235, 153

刑 刑 刑

888 土 艹 刂 (3b 3k 2f)

型

KEI, kata – model, form

類型的	*ruikeiteki*	stereotyped; typical	226, 210
原型	*genkei*	prototype, model	136
紙型	*kamigata, shikei*	papier-mâché mold	180
血液型	*ketsuekigata*	blood type	789, 472
大型トラック	*ōgata torakku*	large truck	26

型 型 型

889 衤 十 冂 (5e 2k 2r)

補

HO, ogina(u) – supply, make up for, compensate for

補給	*hokyū*	supply, replenishment	346
補正	*hosei*	revision, compensation	275
補助	*hojo*	assistance, supplement, subsidy	623
補充	*hojū*	supplement, replacement	828
補習教育	*hoshū kyōiku*	supplementary education	591, 245, 246

補 補 補

890 扌 十 冂 (3c 2k 2r)

捕

HO, to(ru/raeru), tsuka(maeru) – catch, grasp; *to(rawareru), tsuka(maru)* – be caught; hold on to

捕鯨	*hogei*	whaling	700
捕鯨船	*hogeisen*	whaling ship	700, 376
だ捕	*daho*	capture, seize	
生け捕り	*ikedori*	capturing alive	44

捕 捕 捕

891 辶 氵 一 2q 3a 1a3

逮

TAI – chase

逮捕	*taiho*	arrest	890
逮捕状	*taihojō*	arrest warrant	890, 626
逮夜	*taiya*	eve of the anniversary of a death	471

逮 逮 逮

892 辶 十 一 2q 2k 1a4

建

KEN, [KON], ta(teru) – build; ***ta(tsu)*** – be built

建設	*kensetsu*	construction	577
建立	*konryū*	erection, building	121
建物	*tatemono*	a building	79
二階建て	*nikaidate*	2-story	3, 588
建て前	*tatemae*	erection of the framework; principle	47

建 建 建

893 亻 辶 十 2a 2q 2k

健

KEN, suko(yaka) – healthy

保健	*hoken*	preservation of health, hygiene	489
穏健	*onken*	moderate, sound	869
強健	*kyōken*	robust health, strong physique	217
健在	*kenzai*	healthy, sound	268
健勝	*kenshō*	healthy	509

健 健 健

894 广 氵 一 3q 3a 1a2

康

KŌ – peace, composure

健康	*kenkō*	health	893
不健康	*fukenkō*	not healthy, unhealthful	94, 893
小康	*shōkō*	lull, brief respite	27

康 康 康

895	宀 丷 一 (3m 2o 1a)	**KYŪ, kiwa(meru)** – investigate thoroughly/exhaustively	
究明	*kyūmei*	study, investigation, inquiry	18
探究	*tankyū*	research, investigation	535
学究	*gakkyū*	scholar, student	109
究極	*kyūkyoku*	final, ultimate	336
論究	*ronkyū*	discuss thoroughly	293

究 究 究

896	石 艹 一 (5a 3k 1a)	**KEN, to(gu)** – whet, hone, sharpen; polish; wash (rice)	
研究	*kenkyū*	research	895
研究所	*kenkyūjo*	research institute	895, 153
研学	*kengaku*	study	109

研 研 研

897	宀 弓 丷 (3m 3h 2o)	**KYŪ, kiwa(maru)** – reach an extreme; come to an end; **kiwa(meru)** – carry to extremes; bring to an end	
窮極目的	*kyūkyoku mokuteki*	ultimate goal	336, 55, 210
窮地/境	*kyūchi/kyō*	predicament	118, 864
窮乏	*kyūbō*	poverty	754
困窮	*konkyū*	poverty	558

窮 窮 窮

898	宀 丷 亻 (3m 2o 2a)	**TOTSU, tsu(ku)** – thrust, poke, strike	
突然	*totsuzen*	suddenly	651
突破	*toppa*	break through, overcome	665
突入	*totsunyū*	rush in, storm	52
突き当たる	*tsukiataru*	run/bump into; reach the end	77
羽根突き	*hanetsuki*	Japanese badminton	590, 314

突 突 突

899	3m 2o
穴	

KETSU, ana – hole; cave

穴居人	*kekkyojin*	caveman	171, 1
落とし穴	*otoshiana*	pitfall, trap	839
穴あけ器	*ana akeki*	punch, perforator	527
送り穴	*okuriana*	(film) perforations, sprocket holes	441
穴子	*anago*	conger eel	103

穴 穴 穴

900	2k 1a4 1b
射	

SHA, i(ru) – shoot

発射	*hassha*	fire, launch	96
射殺	*shasatsu*	shoot dead	576
注射	*chūsha*	injection, shot	357
放射能	*hōshanō*	radioactivity	512, 386
反射	*hansha*	reflection; reflex	324

射 射 射

901	7a 2k 1a4
謝	

SHA – gratitude; apology; *ayama(ru)* – apologize

感謝	*kansha*	gratitude	262
謝礼	*sharei*	remuneration, honorarium	620
月謝	*gessha*	monthly tuition	17
謝罪	*shazai*	apology	885
代謝	*taisha*	metabolism (cf. No. 1405)	256

謝 謝 謝

902	3b 1a 1c
至	

SHI – utmost; *ita(ru)* – arrive, lead to

必至	*hisshi*	inevitable	520
至急	*shikyū*	urgency, urgent	303
夏至	*geshi*	summer solstice	461
至る所	*itaru tokoro*	everywhere	153
至東京	*itaru Tōkyō*	To Tokyo (at the edge of a map)	71, 189

至 至 至

903 攵土 一 4i 3b 1a

致

CHI, *ita(su)* – do (deferential, used like *suru*); bring about

一致	*itchi*	agreement, consistency	2
合致	*gatchi*	agreement, consistency	159
致命傷	*chimeishō*	fatal wound	578, 633
致死量	*chishiryō*	lethal dose	85, 411
風致地区	*fūchi chiku*	scenic area	29, 118, 183

致 致 致

904 刂土 一 2f 3b 1a

到

TŌ – arrive, reach

到着	*tōchaku*	arrival	657
到来	*tōrai*	arrival, advent	69
到達	*tōtatsu*	reach, attain	448
殺到	*sattō*	rush, stampede	576
周到	*shūtō*	meticulous	91

到 到 到

905 亻土 刂 2a 3b 2f

倒

TŌ, tao(reru) – fall over, collapse; ***tao(su)*** – knock down, topple, defeat

卒倒	*sottō*	faint	787
倒産	*tōsan*	bankruptcy	278
倒閣	*tōkaku*	overthrowing the cabinet	837
共倒れ	*tomodaore*	mutual destruction, common ruin	196

倒 倒 倒

906 言 口 丷 7a 3d 2o

誤

GO, ayama(ru) – err, make a mistake

誤解	*gokai*	misunderstanding	474
誤報	*gohō*	erroneous report/information	685
誤算	*gosan*	miscalculation	747
誤植	*goshoku*	a misprint	424
読み誤る	*yomiayamaru*	misread	244

誤 誤 誤

907 一 ノ 1a3 1c

互

GO, taga(i) – mutual, reciprocal, each other

相互	*sōgo*	mutual	146
交互	*kōgo*	mutual; alternating	114
互助	*gojo*	mutual aid	623
互選	*gosen*	mutual election	800
互い違いに	*tagaichigai ni*	alternately	814

互 互 互

908 糸 ノ 6a 1c

系

KEI – system; lineage, group

体系	*taikei*	system	61
系統	*keitō*	system; lineage, descent	830
日系	*nikkei*	of Japanese descent	5
直系	*chokkei*	direct descent	423
系図	*keizu*	genealogy, family tree	339

系 系 系

909 亻 糸 ノ 2a 6a 1c

係

KEI, kaka(ru) – relate to, concern; ***kakari*** – charge, duty; person in charge, clerk

関係	*kankei*	relation, relationship, connection	398
連係	*renkei*	connection, link, contact	440
係争	*keisō*	dispute, contention	302
係員	*kakariin*	clerk in charge, attendant	163

係 係 係

910 子 糸 ノ 2c 6a 1c

孫

SON, mago – grandchild

子孫	*shison*	descendant	103
皇孫	*kōson*	imperial grandchild/descendant	297
天孫	*tenson*	of divine descent	141
そう孫	*sōson*	great-grandchild	
ひ孫	*himago*	great-grandchild	

孫 孫 孫

911 心 糸 目 4k 6a 5c

懸

KEN, [KE], ka(karu) – hang; ***ka(keru)*** – offer, give

一生懸命	*isshōkenmei*	utmost effort, all one's might	2, 44, 578
懸案	*ken'an*	unsettled problem	106
懸賞	*kenshō*	offer of a prize	500
懸念	*kenen*	fear, apprehension	579
命懸け	*inochigake*	risking one's life	578

懸 懸 懸

912 氵 厂 ノ 3a 2p2 1c

派

HA – group, faction, sect, school (of thought)

宗派	*shūha*	sect	616
党派	*tōha*	party, faction	495
左/右派	*sa/uha*	the left/right wing	75, 76
派出所	*hashutsujo*	branch office; police box	53, 153
特派員	*tokuhain*	correspondent	282, 163

派 派 派

913 月 厂 ノ 4b 2p2 1c

脈

MYAKU – pulse, vein, blood vessel

動脈	*dōmyaku*	artery	231
静脈	*jōmyaku*	vein	663
山脈	*sanmyaku*	mountain range	34
文脈	*bunmyaku*	context	111
脈略	*myakuryaku*	logical connection, coherence	840

脈 脈 脈

914 貝 一 ノ 7b 1a2 1c2

貫

KAN, tsuranu(ku) – pierce; carry out

一貫	*ikkan*	consistency, coherence, integrated	2
貫通	*kantsū*	pass through, pierce	150
貫流	*kanryū*	flow through	247
突貫	*tokkan*	rush, storm	898
貫き通す	*tsuranukitōsu*	carry out (one's will)	150

貫 貫 貫

915	心 貝 一 4k 7b 1a2	**KAN, na(reru)** – get used (to); **na(rasu)** – make used (to); tame		
慣		習慣	*shūkan*	custom, practice	591
		慣習	*kanshū*	custom, practice	591
		慣例	*kanrei*	custom, convention	612
		見慣れる	*minareru*	get used to seeing	63

916	衤 日 夂 5e 4c 4i	**FUKU** – double, multiple, composite, again		
複		複雑	*fukuzatsu*	complicated	575
		複合	*fukugō*	composition, compound, complex	159
		重複	*chōfuku, jūfuku*	duplication, overlapping	227
		複製	*fukusei*	reproduction, duplicate, facsimile	428
		複数	*fukusū*	plural	225

917	彳 日 夂 3i 4c 4i	**FUKU** – return, be restored		
復		復習	*fukushū*	review	591
		反復	*hanpuku*	repetition	324
		復活	*fukkatsu*	revival	237
		復興	*fukkō*	reconstruction, revival	368
		回復	*kaifuku*	recovery, recuperation	90

918	彳 王 丶 3i 4f 1d	**Ō** – go		
往		往復	*ōfuku*	round trip	917
		往来	*ōrai*	comings and goings, traffic	69
		立ち往生	*tachiōjō*	standstill, getting stalled	121, 44
		右往左往	*uōsaō*	rush about in confusion	76, 75
		往年	*ōnen*	the past, formerly	45

919	火 口 土 4d 3s 3b	***EN, kemuri*** – smoke; ***kemu(ru)*** – smoke, smolder; ***kemu(i)*** – smoky			
煙		禁煙	*kin'en*	No Smoking	482
		煙突	*entotsu*	chimney	898
		発煙	*hatsuen*	emitting smoke, fuming	96
		黒煙	*kokuen*	black smoke	206

920	火 艹 十 4d 3k 2k	***SHŌ, ya(keru)*** – (intr.) burn; be roasted, broiled, baked; ***ya(ku)*** – (tr.) burn; roast, broil, bake			
焼		全焼	*zenshō*	be totally destroyed by fire	89
		焼(き)鳥	*yakitori*	grilled chicken	285
		日焼け	*hiyake*	sunburn, suntan	5
		夕焼け	*yūyake*	glow of sunset	81

921	辶 口 亻 2q 3s 2a	***SEN*** – move, change; climb			
遷		変遷	*hensen*	undergo changes	257
		左遷	*sasen*	demotion	75
		遷都	*sento*	transfer of the capital	188

922	礻 口 一 5e 3s 1a	***HYŌ*** – slip of paper, ballot, vote			
票		一票	*ippyō*	a vote	2
		得票	*tokuhyō*	votes obtained	374
		反対票	*hantaihyō*	no vote	324, 365
		開票	*kaihyō*	vote counting	396
		伝票	*denpyō*	slip of paper	434

923	木 ネ 口 4a 5e 3s	***HYŌ*** – sign, mark			
標		目標	*mokuhyō*	goal, purpose	55
		標語	*hyōgo*	slogan, motto	67
		標準語	*hyōjungo*	the standard language	778, 67
		標本	*hyōhon*	specimen, sample	25
		商標	*shōhyō*	trademark	412

標 標 標

924	氵 ネ 口 3a 5e 3s	***HYŌ, tadayo(u)*** – drift about, float			
漂		漂流	*hyōryū*	drift, be adrift	247
		漂着	*hyōchaku*	drift ashore	657
		漂白剤	*hyōhakuzai*	bleach	205, 550
		漂然	*hyōzen*	aimless; sudden, unexpected	651
		漂々	*hyōhyō*	light, buoyant	

漂 漂 漂

925	口 鳥 3d 11b	***MEI, na(ku)*** – (animals) cry, sing, howl; ***na(ru/rasu)*** – (intr./tr.) sound, ring			
鳴		共鳴	*kyōmei*	resonance; sympathy	196
		鳴動	*meidō*	rumble	231
		鳴き声	*nakigoe*	cry, call, chirping (of animals)	746
		海鳴り	*uminari*	rumbling/noise of the sea	117

鳴 鳴 鳴

926	鳥 〳 亻 11b 3n 2a	***KEI, niwatori*** – chicken, hen, rooster			
鶏		鶏肉	*keiniku*	chicken, fowl	223
		養鶏	*yōkei*	poultry raising	402
		鶏舎	*keisha*	chicken coop, henhouse	791
		鶏鳴	*keimei*	cockcrow, rooster's call	925
		鶏頭	*keitō*	cockscomb (flower)	276

鶏 鶏 鶏

927 口 丷 亻 3d 2o 2a

咲

sa(ku) – bloom

咲き出す	*sakidasu*	begin to bloom	53
咲き乱れる	*sakimidareru*	bloom in profusion	689
遅咲き	*osozaki*	blooming late	702
狂い咲き	*kuruizaki*	flowering out of season	883
返り咲き	*kaerizaki*	second bloom; comeback	442

咲 咲 咲

928 木 丷 女 4a 3n 3e

桜

Ō, sakura – cherry tree

桜花	*ōka*	cherry blossoms	255
八重桜	*yaezakura*	double-petal cherry blossoms	10, 227
桜んぼ	*sakuranbo*	cherry	
桜色	*sakurairo*	pink, cerise	204
桜肉	*sakuraniku*	horsemeat	223

桜 桜 桜

929 女 欠 冫 3e 4j 2b

姿

SHI, sugata – form, figure, shape, appearance, posture

姿勢	*shisei*	posture, stance	646
容姿	*yōshi*	face and figure, appearance	654
姿態	*shitai*	figure, pose	387
姿見	*sugatami*	full-length mirror	63
後ろ姿	*ushirosugata*	view (of someone) from behind	48

姿 姿 姿

930 女 丷 ノ 3e 3n 1c

妥

DA – peace, contentment

妥協	*dakyō*	compromise	234
妥結	*daketsu*	compromise, agreement	485
妥当	*datō*	proper, appropriate, adequate	77
妥協案	*dakyōan*	compromise plan	234, 106

妥 妥 妥

931	艹 木 ⺍ 3k 4a 3n	**SAI, na** – vegetable; rape, mustard plant			
菜		野菜	*yasai*	vegetable	236
		菜園	*saien*	vegetable garden	447
		菜食	*saishoku*	vegetarian/herbivorous diet	322
		山菜	*sansai*	edible wild plant	34
		菜種	*natane*	rapeseed, coleseed, colza	228

菜 菜 菜

932	彡 木 ⺍ 3j 4a 3n	**SAI, irodo(ru)** – color			
彩		色彩	*shikisai*	color, coloration	204
		彩色	*saishiki*	coloring, coloration	204
		多彩	*tasai*	colorful	229
		光彩	*kōsai*	luster, brilliancy	138
		水彩画	*suisaiga*	a watercolor painting	21, 343

彩 彩 彩

933	扌 木 ⺍ 3c 4a 3n	**SAI, to(ru)** – take (on), accept, employ; collect			
採		採用	*saiyō*	adopt; employ	107
		採決	*saiketsu*	voting	356
		採集	*saishū*	collecting (plants/butterflies)	436
		採録	*sairoku*	record (in a book)	538
		採算	*saisan*	a profit	747

採 採 採

934	口 ⺍ 亠 3d 3n 2j	**SHŪ, [JU], tsu(ku)** – take (a seat); engage (in an occupation); ***tsu(keru)*** – employ			
就		就職	*shūshoku*	find employment	385
		就任	*shūnin*	assumption of office	334
		就業時間	*shūgyō jikan*	working hours	279, 42, 43
		成就	*jōju*	accomplish, attain	261

就 就 就

935	氵 几 又 (3a 2s 2h)			
没	***BOTSU*** – sink, go down			
	没落	*botsuraku*	downfall, ruin	839
	没入	*botsunyū*	become immersed (in)	52
	出没	*shutsubotsu*	appear and disappear, frequent	53
	没収	*bosshū*	confiscation, forfeiture	757
	没交渉	*bokkōshō*	unrelated, independent	114, 432

936	氵 冖 丨 (3a 2i 1b2)			
沈	***CHIN, shizu(mu/meru)*** – (intr./tr.) sink			
	沈没	*chinbotsu*	sinking	935
	沈下	*chinka*	sinking, subsidence, settling	31
	沈静	*chinsei*	stillness, stagnation	663
	沈着	*chinchaku*	composed, calm	657
	沈思	*chinshi*	meditation, contemplation	99

937	氵 日 亻 (3a 4c 2a2)			
潜	***SEN*** – dive, hide; ***mogu(ru)*** – dive; crawl into; ***hiso(mu)*** – lurk, lie hidden			
	潜水	*sensui*	dive, submerge	21
	潜水夫	*sensuifu*	diver	21, 315
	潜在	*senzai*	hidden, latent, potential	268
	潜入	*sennyū*	infiltrate	52

938	氵 ⺍ 子 (3a 3n 2c)			
浮	***FU, u(kabu)*** – float, rise to the surface; ***u(kaberu)*** – set afloat; show; ***u(ku)*** – float, rise to the surface; ***u(kareru)*** – feel buoyant, be in high spirits			
	思い浮ぶ	*omoiukabu*	come to mind, occur to	99
	浮かぬ顔	*ukanukao*	dejected look	277
	浮世絵	*ukiyoe*	Japanese woodblock print	252, 345

939	乚 子 丨 (3n 2c 1b)	***NYŪ, chichi, chi*** – mother's milk, breast		
乳	牛乳	*gyūnyū*	(cow's) milk	281
	母乳	*bonyū*	mother's milk	112
	乳がん	*nyūgan*	breast cancer	
	乳首	*chikubi, chichikubi*	nipple	148
	乳母車	*ubaguruma*	baby carriage	112, 133

940	子 丨 (2c 1b)	***KŌ*** – hole; Confucius		
孔	気孔	*kikō*	pore	134
	通/空気孔	*tsū/kū-kikō*	air hole	150, 140, 134
	鼻孔	*bikō*	nostril	813
	多孔	*takō*	porous	229
	孔子	*Kōshi*	Confucius	103

941	子 一 丶 ((2c) 1a 1d)	***RYŌ*** – finish, complete; understand		
了	終了	*shūryō*	end, completion, expiration	458
	完了	*kanryō*	completion; perfect tense	613
	(任期)満了	*(ninki)manryō*	expiration (of a term of office)	334, 449, 201
	校了	*kōryō*	final proofreading	115
	了解	*ryōkai*	understanding; Roger! (on a radio)	474

942	子 一 ノ (2c 1a3 1c)	***SHŌ, uketamawa(ru)*** – hear, be told		
承	承知	*shōchi*	consent; be aware of	214
	承認	*shōnin*	approval	738
	承服	*shōfuku*	consent, acceptance	683
	了承	*ryōshō*	acknowledgment	941
	伝承	*denshō*	hand down (from generation to generation)	434

943	艹 火 氵 3k 4d 3a	***JŌ, mu(su)*** – steam; be sultry; ***mu(rasu)*** – steam; ***mu(reru)*** – be steamed; get hot and stuffy		
蒸		(水)蒸気	*(sui)jōki*	(water) vapor, steam	21, 134
		蒸発	*jōhatsu*	evaporate; disappear into thin air	96
		蒸し暑い	*mushiatsui*	hot and humid, sultry	638
		蒸し返す	*mushikaesu*	reheat; repeat, rehash	442

944	亻 一 丨 2a2 1a4 1b	***KŌ*** – season; weather; ***sōrō*** – (classical verb suffix)			
候		天候	*tenkō*	weather	141
		気候	*kikō*	climate	134
		測候所	*sokkōjo*	meteorological station	610, 153
		候補者	*kōhosha*	candidate	889, 164
		居候	*isōrō*	hanger-on, parasite	171

945	亻 夂 彡 2a 4i 3j	***SHŪ, [SHU], osa(meru)*** – study, master; ***osa(maru)*** – govern oneself			
修		修理	*shūri*	repair	143
		修業	*shūgyō*	pursuit/completion of one's studies	279
		修正	*shūsei*	revise, correct, retouch	275
		修行	*shugyō*	training, study	68

946	阝 夂 士 2d 4i 3b	***RYŪ*** – prosperity; high			
隆		隆盛	*ryūsei*	prosperity	719
		興隆	*kōryū*	rise, prosperity, flourishing	368
		隆起	*ryūki*	protuberance, rise, elevation	373
		隆々	*ryūryū*	prosperous, thriving; muscular	
		法隆寺	*Hōryūji*	(temple in Nara)	123, 41

947	阝 夂 十 2d 4i 2k	***KŌ, o(riru)*** – go down, descend, get off (a bus); ***o(rosu)*** – let off (a passenger), dismiss; ***fu(ru)*** – fall (rain/snow)		
		降雨量 *kōuryō*	(amount of) rainfall	30, 411
		降下 *kōka*	descent, fall, landing	31
		以降 *ikō*	since, from … on	46
		飛び降りる *tobioriru*	jump down (from)	530

降 降 降

948	雨 目 木 8d 5c 4a	***SŌ, shimo*** – frost		
		霜害 *sōgai*	frost damage	518
		霜柱 *shimobashira*	ice/frost columns	598
		霜解け *shimodoke*	thawing	474
		霜焼け *shimoyake*	frostbite	920
		霜降り *shimofuri*	marbled (meat), salt-and-pepper pattern	947

霜 霜 霜

949	雨 一 8d 1a3	***SETSU, yuki*** – snow		
		雪害 *setsugai*	damage from snow	518
		新雪 *shinsetsu*	new-fallen snow	174
		初雪 *hatsuyuki*	first snow of the year/winter	679
		大雪 *ōyuki*	heavy snowfall	26
		雪合戦 *yukigassen*	snowball fight	159, 301

雪 雪 雪

950	雨 夂 力 8d 4i 2g	***MU, kiri*** – fog		
		五里霧中 *gori-muchū*	in a fog, mystified	7, 142, 28
		霧雨 *kirisame*	misty rain, drizzle	30
		朝霧 *asagiri*	morning mist/fog	469
		夕霧 *yūgiri*	evening mist/fog	81
		黒い霧 *kuroi kiri*	dark machinations	206

霧 霧 霧

951	雨 足 夂 8d 7d 4i	**RO, [RŌ]** – open, public; ***tsuyu*** – dew			
		露天で	*roten de*	outdoors, in the open air	141
		露店	*roten*	street stall, booth	168
		露出	*roshutsu*	(indecent/film) exposure	53
		露見	*roken*	discovery, detection, exposure	63
		朝露	*asatsuyu*	morning dew	469
露		露 露 露			

952	雨 田 8d 5f	**RAI, *kaminari*** – thunder			
		雷鳴	*raimei*	thunder	925
		落雷	*rakurai*	thunderbolt, bolt of lightning	839
		雷雨	*raiu*	thunderstorm	30
		地雷	*jirai*	(land) mine	118
		魚雷	*gyorai*	torpedo	290
雷		雷 雷 雷			

953	雨 厂 一 8d 2p 1a2	**SHIN, *furu(eru/u)*** – tremble, shake			
		地震	*jishin*	earthquake	118
		震動	*shindō*	tremor, vibration	231
		震度 5	*shindo go*	magnitude 5 (on the Japanese scale of 7)	377
		震央/源	*shin'ō/gen*	epicenter	351, 580
		身震い	*miburui*	shivering, trembling	59
震		震 震 震			

954	扌 厂 一 3c 2p 1a2	**SHIN, *fu(ruu)*** – swing, wield; flourish; ***fu(ru)*** – wave, shake			
		振興	*shinkō*	advancement, promotion	368
		振動	*shindō*	swing, oscillation, vibration	231
		不振	*fushin*	inactivity, stagnation, slump	94
		振り替え	*furikae*	transfer	744
		振り返る	*furikaeru*	turn one's head, look back	442
振		振 振 振			

955 女 士 ノ 3e 3p 1c

妊

NIN – pregnancy

妊婦	*ninpu*	pregnant woman	316
妊婦服	*ninpufuku*	maternity dress	316, 683
不妊	*funin*	sterile, infertile	94
妊産婦	*ninsanpu*	expectant and nursing mothers	278, 316

妊 妊 妊

956 女 厂 一 3e 2p 1a2

娠

SHIN – pregnancy

妊娠	*ninshin*	pregnancy	955
妊娠中絶	*ninshin chūzetsu*	abortion	955, 28, 742

娠 娠 娠

957 氵 日 厂 3a 4c 2p

濃

NŌ, ko(i) – dark, thick, heavy, strong (coffee)

濃度	*nōdo*	(degree of) concentration	377
濃厚	*nōkō*	thickness, richness, strength	639
濃霧	*nōmu*	dense fog	950

濃 濃 濃

958 口 丷 一 3d 2o 1a2

豆

TŌ, [ZU], mame – bean, pea; (prefix) miniature

大豆	*daizu*	soybean	26
小豆	*azuki*	adzuki bean	27
枝豆	*edamame*	green soybean	870
コーヒー豆	*kōhīmame*	coffee bean	
豆本	*mamehon*	miniature book, pocket edition	25

豆 豆 豆

959	口 日 丷 3d 4c 2o
豊	***HŌ, yuta(ka)*** – abundant, rich

豊富	*hōfu*	abundance, wealth	713
豊作	*hōsaku*	good harvest	360
豊漁	*hōryō*	good catch (of fish)	699
豊年	*hōnen*	fruitful year	45
豊満	*hōman*	plump, voluptuous, buxom	201

960	口 丷 一 3d 2o 1a3
登	***TŌ, TO, nobo(ru)*** – climb

登山	*tozan*	mountain climbing	34
登場	*tōjō*	stage entrance; appearance	154
登記	*tōki*	registration	371
登録	*tōroku*	registration	538
登用	*tōyō*	appointment; promotion	107

961	广 艹 一 3q 3k 1a2
廃	***HAI, suta(reru/ru)*** – become outmoded, go out of fashion, be on the wane

廃止	*haishi*	abolition, abrogation	477
廃業	*haigyō*	going out of business	279
退廃	*taihai*	degeneracy, decadence	846
廃人	*haijin*	cripple, invalid	1

962	亠 木 艹 2j 4a 3k
棄	***KI*** – abandon, throw out, give up

廃棄物	*haikibutsu*	waste (matter)	961, 79
放棄	*hōki*	give up, renounce, waive	512
棄権	*kiken*	abstention, nonvoting; renunciation	335
自棄	*jiki*	self-abandonment	62
破棄	*haki*	destruction; annulment, revocation	665

963 巾 艹 冖 (3f 3k 2i)

帯

TAI – belt, zone; ***obi*** – belt, sash; ***o(biru)*** – wear; be entrusted (with)

包帯	*hōtai*	bandage	804
地帯	*chitai*	zone, area, region, belt	118
熱帯	*nettai*	the tropics	645
所帯	*shotai*	household	153

964 氵 艹 巾 (3a 3k 3f)

滞

TAI – stay, stopping over; ***todokō(ru)*** – be left undone; fall into arrears, be overdue, be left unpaid

滞在	*taizai*	stay, sojourn	268
遅滞	*chitai*	delay, procrastination	702
滞納	*tainō*	delinquency (in payment)	758
沈滞	*chintai*	stagnation, inactivity	936

965 糸 丨 丿 (6a 1b3 1c)

純

JUN – pure

純毛	*junmō*	pure/100 percent wool	287
純益	*jun'eki*	net profit	716
純文学	*junbungaku*	pure literature, belles lettres	111, 109
純日本風	*junnihonfū*	classical Japanese style	5, 25, 29
単純	*tanjun*	simple	300

966 金 丨 丿 (8a 1b3 1c)

鈍

DON, nibu(i) – dull, thick, slow-witted, sluggish, blunt, dim; ***nibu(ru)*** – become dull/blunt, weaken

鈍感	*donkan*	obtuse, thick, insensitive	262
鈍重	*donjū*	dull-witted, phlegmatic, stolid	227
鈍角	*donkaku*	obtuse angle	473
鈍器	*donki*	blunt object (used as a weapon)	527

967	⻌ 米 2q 6b	**MEI, mayo(u)** – be perplexed, vacillate; get lost; go astray		
		迷宮/路	*meikyū/ro*	maze, labyrinth	721, 151
		迷信	*meishin*	superstition	157
		迷彩	*meisai*	camouflage	932
		低迷	*teimei*	be low, in a slump (market prices)	561
		迷子	*maigo*	lost child	103

迷 迷 迷

968	⻌ 木 丶 2q 4a 1d	**JUTSU, no(beru)** – state, mention, refer to, explain		
		供述	*kyōjutsu*	testimony, deposition	197
		記述	*kijutsu*	description	371
		上述	*jōjutsu*	above-mentioned	32
		口述	*kōjutsu*	oral statement; dictation	54
		著述家	*chojutsuka*	writer, author	859, 165

述 述 述

969	心 戈 口 4k 4n 3d	**WAKU, mado(u)** – go astray, be misguided, be tempted		
		迷惑	*meiwaku*	trouble, inconvenience	967
		当惑	*tōwaku*	puzzlement, confusion	77
		思惑	*omowaku*	opinion, intention, expectation	99
		惑星	*wakusei*	planet	730
		戸惑い	*tomadoi*	become disoriented/flurried	152

惑 惑 惑

970	土 戈 口 3b 4n 3d	**IKI** – region, area		
		地域	*chiiki*	region, area, zone	118
		区域	*kuiki*	boundary, zone, district	183
		領域	*ryōiki*	territory, domain	834
		流域	*ryūiki*	(river) basin, valley	247
		聖域	*seiiki*	sacred ground	674

域 域 域

971 亻 貝 ⺍ 2a 7b 3n

償

SHŌ, *tsuguna(u)* – make up for, compensate, indemnify, atone for

補償	*hoshō*	compensation, indemnification	889
弁償	*benshō*	compensation, reimbursement	711
報償	*hōshō*	compensation, remuneration	685
無償	*mushō*	free of charge, gratis	93

償 償 償

972 囗 口 十 3s 3d 2k

固

KO, *kata(i)* – hard; ***kata(maru/meru)*** – (intr./tr.) harden

固体	*kotai*	a solid	61
固有	*koyū*	own, peculiar, characteristic	265
固定	*kotei*	fixed	355
固執	*koshitsu*	hold fast to, persist in, insist on	686
強固	*kyōko*	firm, solid, strong	217

固 固 固

973 亻 囗 口 2a 3s 3d

個

KO – individual; (counter for various objects)

個人	*kojin*	an individual	1
個体	*kotai*	an individual	61
個性	*kosei*	individuality	98
個別的	*kobetsuteki*	individual, separate	267, 210
一個	*ikko*	1 piece	2

個 個 個

974 木 口 十 4a 3d 2k

枯

KO, *ka(reru)* – wither; ***ka(rasu)*** – blight, let wither

枯死	*koshi*	wither away, die	85
栄枯	*eiko*	ups and downs, vicissitudes	723
枯れ木	*kareki*	dead/withered tree	22
枯れ葉	*kareha*	dead/withered leaf	253
木枯らし	*kogarashi*	cold winter wind	22

枯 枯 枯

975 又 厂 丨 (2h 2p 1b) 皮

HI, kawa – skin, hide, leather, pelt, bark, rind

皮肉	*hiniku*	irony	223
皮相	*hisō*	superficiality, shallowness	146
毛皮	*kegawa*	fur	287
皮細工	*kawazaiku*	leatherwork	695, 139
皮切り	*kawakiri*	beginning, start	39

皮 皮 皮

976 衤 厂 又 (5e 2p 2h) 被

HI, kōmu(ru) – incur, suffer, receive

被害者	*higaisha*	victim	518, 164
被告(人)	*hikoku(nin)*	defendant	690, 1
被選挙資格	*hisenkyo shikaku*	eligibility for election	800, 801, 750, 643
被服	*hifuku*	covering, coating	683

被 被 被

977 彳 厂 又 (3i 2p 2h) 彼

HI – he; that; **kare** – he; **[kano]** – that

彼岸	*higan*	equinoctial week; goal	586
彼ら	*karera*	they	
彼氏	*kareshi*	he; boyfriend, lover	566
彼女	*kanojo*	she; girlfriend, lover	102

彼 彼 彼

978 禾 ⺌ 一 (5d 3n 1a) 称

SHŌ – name, title

名称	*meishō*	name, designation	82
愛称	*aishō*	term of endearment, pet name	259
尊称	*sonshō*	honorific title	704
称号	*shōgō*	title, degree	266
相/対称	*sō/taishō*	symmetry	146, 365

称 称 称

979 食 巾 一 8b 3f 1a

飾

SHOKU, kaza(ru) – decorate, adorn

修飾	*shūshoku*	embellishment; modify (in grammar)	945
飾り付け	*kazaritsuke*	decoration	192
飾り気	*kazarike*	affectation, love of display	134
首飾り	*kubikazari*	necklace, choker	148
着飾る	*kikazaru*	dress up	657

飾 飾 飾

980 阝 日 丨 2d 4c 1b

郎

RŌ – man, husband; (suffix for male given names)

新郎新婦	*shinrō-shinpu*	bride and groom	174, 316
郎等/党	*rōtō/dō*	vassals, retainers	569, 495
野郎	*yarō*	guy	236
太郎	*Tarō*	(male given name)	629
二/次郎	*Jirō*	(male given name)	3, 384

郎 郎 郎

981 广 日 阝 3q 4c 2d

廊

RŌ – corridor, hall

廊下	*rōka*	corridor, hall	31
回廊	*kairō*	corridor, gallery	90
画廊	*garō*	picture gallery	343

廊 廊 廊

982 日 丨 4c 1b

甲

KŌ – A, No. 1 (in a series); shell, tortoise shell; **KAN** – high (voice)

甲鉄	*kōtetsu*	armor, armor plating	312
甲状せん	*kōjōsen*	thyroid gland	626
甲種	*kōshu*	Grade A, first class	228
甲高い	*kandakai*	high-pitched, shrill	190

甲 甲 甲

983 一 1a

乙

OTSU – B, No. 2 (in a series); the latter; duplicate; bass (voice); strange; stylish; fine

甲乙	*kō-otsu*	A and B; discrimination, gradation	982
乙女	*otome*	virgin, maiden	102
乙な味	*otsu na aji*	delicate flavor	307

乙 乙 乙

984 一 冂 亻 1a 2r 2a

丙

HEI – C, No. 3 (in a series)

甲乙丙	*kō-otsu-hei*	A, B, C; Nos. 1, 2, 3	982, 983
丙午	*hinoeuma*	(year in the Chinese 60-year cycle; it is said a woman born in such a year [1906, 1966 ...] will be domineering and will lead her husband to an early grave)	49

丙 丙 丙

985 木 冂 亻 4a 2r 2a

柄

HEI, gara – pattern, design; build; character; ***e*** – handle

横柄	*ōhei*	arrogance	781
身柄	*migara*	one's person	59
人柄	*hitogara*	character, personality	1
事柄	*kotogara*	matters, affairs	80
間柄	*aidagara*	relation, relationship	43

柄 柄 柄

986 扌 日 丨 3c 4c 1b

押

Ō, o(su) – push; ***o(saeru)*** – restrain, hold in check, suppress

押収	*ōshū*	confiscation	757
押韻	*ōin*	rhyme	349
押し入れ	*oshiire*	closet, wall-cupboard	52
後押し	*atooshi*	push, support, back	48
押し付ける	*oshitsukeru*	press against; force (upon)	192

押 押 押

987 扌 日 丨 3c 4c 1b

抽

CHŪ – pull, extract

抽出	*chūshutsu*	extraction, sampling	53
抽象	*chūshō*	abstraction	739
抽象的	*chūshōteki*	abstract	739, 210
抽せん	*chūsen*	drawing, lottery	
抽せん券	*chūsenken*	lottery/raffle ticket	506

988 車 日 丨 7c 4c 1b

軸

JIKU – axis, axle, shaft; (picture) scroll

車軸	*shajiku*	axle	133
地軸	*chijiku*	earth's axis	118
自転軸	*jitenjiku*	axis of rotation	62, 433

989 扌 日 又 3c 4c 2h

捜

SŌ, saga(su) – look/search for

捜査	*sōsa*	investigation	624
家宅捜査	*kataku sōsa*	search of the house/premises	165, 178, 624
捜査本部	*sōsa honbu*	investigation headquarters	624, 25, 86
捜し回る	*sagashimawaru*	search around for	90
捜し当てる	*sagashiateru*	find out, discover, locate	77

990 宀 十 一 3m 2k 1a

宇

U – heaven

宇内	*udai*	the whole world	84
気宇広大	*kiukōdai*	magnanimous	134, 694, 26
宇都宮	*Utsunomiya*	(capital of Tochigi Prefecture)	188, 721

991 宙 (宀 3m, 日 4c, 丨 1b)

CHŪ – midair; space, heaven

宇宙	*uchū*	space, the universe	990
宇宙旅行	*uchū ryokō*	space flight	990, 222, 68
宇宙飛行士	*uchū hikōshi*	astronaut	990, 530, 68, 572
大宇宙	*daiuchū*	macrocosm, the universe	26, 990
宙返り	*chūgaeri*	somersault	442

992 届 (尸 3r, 日 4c, 丨 1b)

todo(ku) – reach, arrive; ***todo(keru)*** – report, notify; send, deliver

欠席届け	*kessekitodoke*	report of nonattendance	383, 379
欠勤届け	*kekkintodoke*	report of absence	383, 559
届け先	*todokesaki*	where to report; receiver's address	50
無届け	*mutodoke*	(absence) without notice	93

993 択 (扌 3c, 尸 3r, 丶 1d)

TAKU – selection, choice

選択	*sentaku*	selection, choice	800
選択科目	*sentaku kamoku*	an elective (subject)	800, 320, 55
採択	*saitaku*	adoption, selection	933
二者択一	*nisha takuitsu*	either-or alternative	3, 164, 2

994 沢 (氵 3a, 尸 3r, 丶 1d)

TAKU, sawa – swamp, marsh

光沢	*kōtaku*	luster, gloss	138
ぜい沢	*zeitaku*	luxury, extravagance	
毛沢東	*Mōtakutō*	Mao Zedong, Mao Tse-tung	287, 71
金沢	*Kanazawa*	(capital of Ishikawa Prefecture)	23

995 刂口 2f 3d

召

SHŌ, me(su) – (honorific) summon; wear; take (a bath)

召集	*shōshū*	convene (the Diet)	436
応召	*ōshō*	be drafted, called up	827
召し上がる	*meshiagaru*	eat, drink, have	32
お気に召すまま	*O-ki ni Mesu Mama*	(As You Like It—Shakespeare)	134

996 氵口刂 3a 3d 2f

沼

SHŌ, numa – swamp, marsh

沼沢	*shōtaku*	marsh, swamp, bog	994
湖沼	*koshō*	lakes and marshes	467
沼地	*numachi*	marshland, swampland	118
沼田	*numata*	marshy rice field	35

997 日口刂 4c 3d 2f

昭

SHŌ – bright, clear

昭和	*Shōwa*	(Japanese era, 1926-1989)	124
昭和63年	*Shōwa rokujūsannen*	1988	124, 45
昭和年間	*Shōwa nenkan*	the Showa era	124, 45, 43
昭和元年	*Shōwa gannen*	first year of the Showa era (1926)	124, 137, 45

998 火日口 4d 4c 3d

照

SHŌ, te(ru) – shine; ***te(rasu)*** – shine on; ***te(reru)*** – feel embarrassed

照明	*shōmei*	illumination, lighting	18
対照	*taishō*	contrast	365
参照	*sanshō*	reference	710
東照宮	*Tōshōgū*	(shrine in Nikko)	71, 721

999 焦 (隹 8c, 火 4d)

SHŌ – fire; impatience; yearning; ***ko(gasu)*** – scorch, singe; pine for; ***ko(geru)*** – get scorched; ***ko(gareru)*** – yearn for; ***ase(ru)*** – be in a hurry, hasty, impatient

焦点	*shōten*	focal point, focus	169
焦熱地獄	*shōnetsu jigoku*	an inferno	645, 118, 884
黒焦げ	*kurokoge*	charred, burned	206

焦 焦 焦

1000 超 (土 3b, 口 3d, 刂 2f)

CHŌ, ko(su/eru) – cross, go over, exceed

超過	*chōka*	excess	413
超音速	*chōonsoku*	supersonic speed	347, 502
超大国	*chōtaikoku*	a superpower	26, 40
超満員	*chōman'in*	crowded beyond capacity	201, 163
超人	*chōjin*	a superman	1

超 超 超

1001 越 (戈 4n, 土 3b, ⺊ 2m)

ETSU, ko(su/eru) – cross, go over, exceed

超越	*chōetsu*	transcendence	1000
越権	*ekken*	overstepping one's authority	335
越境	*ekkyō*	jumping the border	864
引っ越す	*hikkosu*	move, change residences	216
勝ち越し	*kachikoshi*	a net win, being ahead	509

越 越 越

1002 趣 (耳 6e, 土 3b, 又 2h)

SHU, omomuki – purport, gist; taste, elegance; appearance

趣味	*shumi*	interest, liking, taste; hobby	307
趣向	*shukō*	plan, idea	199
趣意	*shui*	purport, meaning; aim, object	132
情趣	*jōshu*	mood; artistic effect	209
野趣	*yashu*	rural life and beauty, rusticity	236

趣 趣 趣

1003	辶 方 子 (2q 4h 2c)	***YŪ, [YU], aso(bu)*** – play, enjoy oneself, be idle		
	遊歩道	*yūhodō*	promenade, mall, boardwalk	431, 149
	周遊(券)	*shūyū(ken)*	excursion (ticket)	91, 506
	遊説	*yūzei*	speaking tour, political campaigning	400
	遊休	*yūkyū*	idle, unused	60
	遊び相手	*asobiaite*	playmate	146, 57

遊

1004	方 一 丨 (4h 1a2 1b2)	***SHI, SE, hodoko(su)*** – give, bestow; carry out, perform, conduct		
	施設	*shisetsu*	facilities, institution	577
	施行	*shikō*	enforce; put in operation	68
	実施	*jisshi*	carry into effect, enforce, implement	203
	施政	*shisei*	administration, governing	483

施

1005	方 ⺊ 亻 (4h 2m 2a)	***SEN*** – go around, revolve, rotate		
	旋回	*senkai*	turning, revolving, circling	90
	周旋	*shūsen*	good offices, mediation	91
	旋律	*senritsu*	melody	667
	旋風	*senpū*	whirlwind, cyclone, tornado	29
	あっ旋	*assen*	good offices, mediation	

旋

1006	方 艹 丷 (4h 3k 2o)	***KI, hata*** – flag, banner		
	国旗	*kokki*	flag (of a country)	40
	校旗	*kōki*	school banner/flag	115
	半旗	*hanki*	flag at half-mast	88
	星条旗	*seijōki*	the Stars and Stripes (U.S. flag)	730, 564
	旗色	*hatairo*	the tide of war; things, the situation	204

旗

1007	一 口 丨 (1a 3s 1b)	***RI*** – an official			
		官吏	*kanri*	an official	326
		吏員	*riin*	an official	163
		能吏	*nōri*	capable official	386
		吏党	*ritō*	party of officials	495

吏 吏 吏

1008	一 日 丨 (1a 4c 1b)	***KŌ, sara*** – anew, again, furthermore; ***fu(kasu)*** – stay up till late (at night); ***fu(keru)*** – grow late			
		変更	*henkō*	alteration, change, modification	257
		更衣室	*kōishitsu*	clothes-changing room	677, 166
		更年期	*kōnenki*	menopause	45, 449
		更生	*kōsei*	rebirth, rehabilitation	44

更 更 更

1009	石 日 一 (5a 4c 1a)	***KŌ, kata(i)*** – hard, firm			
		硬質	*kōshitsu*	hard, rigid	176
		硬度	*kōdo*	(degree of) hardness	377
		硬化	*kōka*	hardening	254
		硬貨	*kōka*	coin; hard currency	752
		強硬	*kyōkō*	firm, unyielding	217

硬 硬 硬

1010	木 艹 冂 (4a 3k 2r)	***KŌ, kama(eru)*** – build, set up; assume a posture/position; ***kama(u)*** – mind, care about; meddle in; look after			
		機構	*kikō*	mechanism, structure, organization	528
		構成	*kōsei*	composition, makeup	261
		構想	*kōsō*	conception, plan	147
		心構え	*kokorogamae*	mental attitude, readiness	97

構 構 構

1011	貝 7b	艹 3k	冂 2r

購

KŌ – buy, purchase

購入	*kōnyū*	purchase	52
購入者	*kōnyūsha*	purchaser, buyer	52, 164
購買	*kōbai*	purchase	241
購読	*kōdoku*	subscription	244
購読料	*kōdokuryō*	subscription price/fee	244, 319

購 購 購

1012	氵 3a	艹 3k	冂 2r

溝

KŌ, mizo – ditch, gutter, groove

下水溝	*gesuikō*	drainage ditch, sewage pipe	31, 21
海溝	*kaikō*	an ocean deep, sea trench	117
日本海溝	*Nippon Kaikō, Nihon Kaikō*	Japan Deep/Trench	5, 25, 117

溝 溝 溝

1013	言 7a	艹 3k	亠 2j

譲

JŌ, yuzu(ru) – transfer, assign; yield, concede

譲歩	*jōho*	concession, compromise	431
割譲	*katsujō*	cede (territory)	519
互譲	*gojō*	mutual concession	907
譲り渡す	*yuzuriwatasu*	turn over, transfer	378
親譲り	*oyayuzuri*	inheritance from a parent	175

譲 譲 譲

1014	日 4c	氵 3a	艹 3k

暴

BŌ, aba(reru) – act violently, rage, rampage, run amuck; ***[BAKU], aba(ku)*** – disclose, expose, bring to light

暴力団	*bōryokudan*	gangster syndicate	100, 491
暴風	*bōfū*	high winds, windstorm	29
乱暴	*ranbō*	violence, roughness	689
暴露	*bakuro*	expose, bring to light	951

暴 暴 暴

1015 火 日 氵 4d 4c 3a

爆

BAKU – explode

爆発	*bakuhatsu*	explosion	96
爆発的	*bakuhatsuteki*	explosive	96, 210
原爆	*genbaku*	atomic bomb	136
被爆者	*hibakusha*	bombing victim	976, 164
爆薬	*bakuyaku*	explosives	359

爆 爆 爆

1016 扌 車 几 3c 7c 2s

撃

GEKI, u(tsu) – attack; fire, shoot

攻撃	*kōgeki*	attack	819
反撃	*hangeki*	counterattack	324
爆撃	*bakugeki*	bombing raid	1015
撃沈	*gekichin*	(attack and) sink	936
目撃者	*mokugekisha*	eyewitness	55, 164

撃 撃 撃

1017 氵 攵 日 3a 4i 4c

激

GEKI, hage(shii) – violent, fierce, strong, intense

過激派	*kagekiha*	radicals, extremist faction	413, 912
感激	*kangeki*	deep emotion/gratitude	262
激情	*gekijō*	violent emotion, passion	209
激動	*gekidō*	violent shaking; excitement, stir	231
激流	*gekiryū*	swift current	247

激 激 激

1018 言 十 丶 7a 2k 1d

討

TŌ, u(tsu) – attack

検討	*kentō*	examination, investigation, study	531
討論	*tōron*	debate, discussion	293
討議	*tōgi*	discussion, deliberation, debate	292
討ち死に	*uchijini*	fall in battle	85
討ち取る	*uchitoru*	capture; kill	65

討 討 討

1019 言 一 丨 7a 1a 1b

訂

TEI – correcting

訂正	*teisei*	correction, revision	275
校訂	*kōtei*	revision	115
改訂	*kaitei*	revision	514
増訂	*zōtei*	revised and enlarged (edition)	712

1020 扌 一 丨 3c 1a 1b

打

DA, u(tsu) – hit, strike

打開	*dakai*	a break, development, new turn	396
打算的	*dasanteki*	calculating, selfish, mercenary	747, 210
打楽器	*dagakki*	percussion instrument	358, 527
打ち合わせ	*uchiawase*	previous arrangement	159
打ち消し	*uchikeshi*	denial; negation	845

1021 扌 几 又 3c 2s 2h

投

TŌ, na(geru) – throw

投票	*tōhyō*	vote	922
投書	*tōsho*	letter to the editor, contribution	131
投資	*tōshi*	investment	750
投機	*tōki*	speculation	528
投影	*tōei*	projection	854

1022 欠 匚 ノ 4j 2t 1c

欧

Ō – Europe

欧州	*Ōshū*	Europe	195
欧州共同体	*Ōshū Kyōdōtai*	the European Community	195, 196, 198, 61
西欧	*Seiō*	Western Europe	72
欧米	*Ō-Bei*	Europe and America/the U.S.	224

1023 木 匚 ノ 4a 2t 1c

枢

SŪ – pivot

枢軸	*sūjiku*	pivot, axis, center	988
中枢	*chūsū*	center	28
枢要	*sūyō*	important	419
枢密	*sūmitsu*	state secret	806

枢 枢 枢

1024 米 厂 一 6b 2p 1a

断

DAN – decision, judgment; ***kotowa(ru)*** – decline, refuse; give notice/warning; prohibit; ***ta(tsu)*** – cut off

決断	*ketsudan*	(prompt) decision, resolution	356
油断	*yudan*	inattention, negligence	364
横断	*ōdan*	crossing	781
断念	*dannen*	abandonment, giving up	579

断 断 断

1025 糸 米 丨 6a 6b 1b

継

KEI tsu(gu) – follow; succeed to, inherit

後継	*kōkei*	succession	48
継承	*keishō*	succession, inheritance	942
継続	*keizoku*	continuance	243
中継	*chūkei*	(radio/TV) relay, hookup	28
受け継ぐ	*uketsugu*	inherit, succeed to	260

継 継 継

1026 刂 十 一 2f 2k 1a

判

HAN – stamp, seal; ***BAN*** – (paper) size

判断(力)	*handan(ryoku)*	judgment	1024, 100
判決	*hanketsu*	a decision, ruling	356
判事	*hanji*	a judge	80
公判	*kōhan*	(public) trial	126
判明	*hanmei*	become clear, be ascertained	18

判 判 判

1027	亻 十 一 2a 2k 1a	***HAN, BAN, tomona(u)*** – go with, accompany; entail, be accompanied by, be associated with	
伴			
同伴	*dōhan*	keep (someone) company	198
伴りょ	*hanryo*	companion, comrade, partner	
相伴う	*aitomonau*	accompany	146

伴 伴 伴

1028	言 十 一 7a 2k 1a	***HYŌ*** – criticism, comment	
評			
評論	*hyōron*	criticism, critique, commentary	293
論評	*ronpyō*	criticism, comment, review	293
評価	*hyōka*	appraisal	421
評判	*hyōban*	fame, popularity; rumor, gossip	1026
書評	*shohyō*	book review	131

評 評 評

1029	扌 ⺊ 3c 2m2	***HI*** – critique	
批			
批判	*hihan*	critique	1026
批判的	*hihanteki*	critical	1026, 210
批評	*hihyō*	critique, criticism, review	1028
批評眼	*hihyōgan*	critical eye	1028, 848
文芸批評	*bungei hihyō*	literary criticism	111, 435, 1028

批 批 批

1030	戈 一 4n 1a3	***NI*** – two (in documents)	
弐			
弐万円	*niman'en*	20,000 yen	16, 13

弐 弐 弐

1031 戈 ト 一 (4n 2m 1a)

武

BU, MU – military

武器	*buki*	weapon, arms	527
武力	*buryoku*	military force	100
武道	*budō*	military arts	149
武士	*bushi*	samurai, warrior	572
武者	*musha*	warrior	164

武 武 武

1032 夂 心 冖 (4i 4k 2i)

憂

YŪ, ure(eru) – grieve, be distressed, be anxious; ***ure(e/i)*** – grief, distress, anxiety; ***u(i)*** – unhappy, gloomy

憂国	*yūkoku*	patriotism	40
物憂い	*monoui*	languid, weary, listless	79
憂き目	*ukime*	grief, misery, hardship	55
憂い顔	*ureigao*	sorrowful face, troubled look	277

憂 憂 憂

1033 亻 心 夂 (2a 4k 4i)

優

YŪ, sugu(reru) – excel; ***yasa(shii)*** – gentle, tender, kindhearted

優勢	*yūsei*	predominance, superiority	646
優勝	*yūshō*	victory, championship	509
優先	*yūsen*	priority	50
優柔不断	*yūjūfudan*	indecision, vacillation	774, 94, 1024
女優	*joyū*	actress	102

優 優 優

1034 心 ト 一 (4k 2m 1a5)

悲

HI, kana(shii) – sad; ***kana(shimu)*** – be sad, lament, regret

悲劇	*higeki*	tragedy	797
悲恋	*hiren*	disappointed love	258
悲鳴	*himei*	shriek, scream	925
悲観	*hikan*	pessimism	604

悲 悲 悲

1035 亻 ⺊ 一 (2a 2m 1a5)

俳

HAI – actor

俳優	*haiyū*	actor	1033
俳句	*haiku*	haiku, 17-syllable Japanese poem in 5-7-5 form	337
俳人	*haijin*	haiku poet	1

俳 俳 俳

1036 扌 ⺊ 一 (3c 2m 1a5)

排

HAI – exclude, reject, expel

排気ガス	*haikigasu*	exhaust gas/fumes	134
排液	*haieki*	drainage (in surgery)	472
排撃	*haigeki*	reject, denounce	1016
排日	*hai-Nichi*	anti-Japanese	5
排他的	*haitateki*	exclusive, cliquish	120, 210

排 排 排

1037 車 ⺊ 一 (7c 2m 1a5)

輩

HAI – fellow, colleague, companion

先輩	*senpai*	one's senior (at school/work)	50
後輩	*kōhai*	one's junior, younger people	48
年輩	*nenpai*	age, elderliness	45
同年輩の人	*dōnenpai no hito*	someone of the same age	198, 45, 1
輩出	*haishutsu*	appear one after another	53

輩 輩 輩

1038 彳 罒 心 (3i 5g 4k)

徳

TOKU – virtue

道徳	*dōtoku*	morality, morals	149
公徳	*kōtoku*	public morality	126
人徳	*jintoku*	one's natural virtue	1
不徳	*futoku*	lack of virtue, vice, immorality	94
徳川	*Tokugawa*	(historical surname)	33

徳 徳 徳

1039 耳 罒 心 6e 5g 4k

聴

CHŌ, ki(ku) – hear, listen

聴取	*chōshu*	listening	65
聴衆	*chōshū*	audience	792
聴講	*chōkō*	attendance at a lecture	783
公聴会	*kōchōkai*	public hearing	126, 158
聴覚	*chōkaku*	sense of hearing	605

聴 聴 聴

1040 日 ト 4c 2m

旨

SHI, mune – purport, content, gist; instructions

趣旨	*shushi*	purport, content, gist	1002
要旨	*yōshi*	gist, essential points	419
本旨	*honshi*	main purpose, true aim	25
論旨	*ronshi*	point/drift of an argument	293

旨 旨 旨

1041 扌 日 ト 3c 4c 2m

指

SHI, yubi – finger; ***sa(su)*** – point to

指導	*shidō*	guidance, leadership	703
指令	*shirei*	order, instruction	831
指名	*shimei*	nomination, designation	82
指定席	*shiteiseki*	reserved seat	355, 379
人さし指	*hitosashiyubi*	index finger, forefinger	1

指 指 指

1042 月 日 ト 4b 4c 2m

脂

SHI, abura – (animal) fat

油脂	*yushi*	oils and fats	364
脂身	*aburami*	fat (of meat)	59
脂っ濃い	*aburakkoi*	greasy, rich (foods)	957

脂 脂 脂

1043 卩 厂 一 (2e 2p 1a2)

印

IN – seal, stamp; ***shirushi*** – sign, mark

印象	*inshō*	impression	739
調印	*chōin*	signing, signature	342
印税	*inzei*	a royalty (on a book)	399
印紙	*inshi*	revenue stamp	180
矢印	*yajirushi*	(direction) arrow	213

印 印 印

1044 刂 尸 巾 (2f 3r 3f)

刷

SATSU, su(ru) – print

印刷	*insatsu*	printing	1043
印刷物	*insatsubutsu*	printed matter	1043, 79
増刷	*zōsatsu*	additional printing, reprinting	712
刷新	*sasshin*	reform	174
刷り直す	*surinaosu*	reprint to correct mistakes	423

刷 刷 刷

1045 亠 一 丨 (2j 1a 1b)

片

HEN – part; ***kata-*** – one (of two)

破片	*hahen*	broken piece, fragment, splinter	665
断片	*danpen*	fragment, piece, snippet	1024
木片	*mokuhen*	block/chip of wood, wood shavings	22
片目	*katame*	one eye	55
片道	*katamichi*	one way, each way	149

片 片 片

1046 亠 厂 又 (2j 2p 2h)

版

HAN – printing block/plate, printing; edition

出版社	*shuppansha*	publishing house	53, 308
版権	*hanken*	copyright	335
初版	*shohan*	first edition	679
改訂版	*kaiteiban*	revised edition	514, 1019
版画	*hanga*	print, woodblock print	343

版 版 版

1047 木 厂 又 4a 2p 2h

板

HAN, BAN, ita – a board

甲板	*kanpan, kōhan*	deck (of a ship)	982
合板	*gōban, gōhan*	plywood	159
黒板	*kokuban*	blackboard	206
床板	*yukaita*	floorboard	826

板 板 板

1048 貝 厂 又 7b 2p 2h

販

HAN – sell

販売	*hanbai*	sales, selling	239
販売値段	*hanbai nedan*	selling price	239, 425, 362
自動販売機	*jidō hanbaiki*	vending machine	62, 231, 239, 528
市販	*shihan*	marketing	181
販路	*hanro*	market (for goods), outlet	151

販 販 販

1049 亻 厂 又 2a 2p 2h

仮

KA, [KE], kari – temporary, provisional, tentative, supposing

仮説	*kasetsu*	hypothesis, supposition	400
仮定	*katei*	supposition, assumption, hypothesis	355
仮面	*kamen*	a mask	274
仮名	*kamei*	fictitious name	82
仮病	*kebyō*	pretended illness, malingering	380

仮 仮 仮

1050 宀 目 艹 3m 5c 3k

寛

KAN – leniency, generosity

寛大	*kandai*	magnanimity, tolerance, leniency	26
寛容	*kan'yō*	magnanimity, generosity, forbearance	654
寛厚	*kankō*	generous, large-hearted	639
寛厳	*kangen*	severity and leniency	822

寛 寛 寛

1051	力 隹 一 2g 8c 1a2	*KAN, susu(meru)* – recommend, offer, advise, encourage		
勧	勧告	*kankoku*	recommendation, advice	690
	勧業	*kangyō*	encouragement of industry	279
	勧進	*kanjin*	soliciting religious contributions	437

勧 勧 勧

1052	欠 隹 一 4j 8c 1a2	*KAN* – joy, pleasure		
歓	歓待	*kantai*	hospitality	452
	歓談	*kandan*	pleasant chat	593
	歓声	*kansei*	shout of joy, cheer	746
	歓楽街	*kanrakugai*	amusement center	358, 186
	歓心を買う	*kanshin o kau*	curry favor	97, 241

歓 歓 歓

1053	亻 口 十 2a 3d 2k	*I, era(i)* – great, eminent, extraordinary, excellent		
偉	偉大	*idai*	great, mighty, grand	26
	偉人	*ijin*	great man	1
	偉才	*isai*	man of extraordinary talent	551
	偉業	*igyō*	great achievement	279
	偉観	*ikan*	a spectacular sight	604

偉 偉 偉

1054	糸 口 十 6a 3d 2k	*I* – woof (horizontal thread in weaving); latitude		
緯	緯度	*ido*	latitude	377
	緯線	*isen*	a parallel (of latitude)	299
	北緯	*hokui*	north latitude	73
	南緯	*nan'i*	south latitude	74
	経緯	*keii*	longitude and latitude; the details	548

緯 緯 緯

1055 辶 厂 卩 2q 2p 2e

迎

GEI, muka(eru) – go to meet, receive; invite, send for

歓迎	*kangei*	welcome	1052
迎合	*geigō*	flattery	159
送迎	*sōgei*	welcome and sendoff	441
出迎え	*demukae*	meeting (someone) on arrival, reception	53

迎 迎 迎

1056 亻 厂 卩 2a 2p 2e

仰

GYŌ, [KŌ], ao(gu) – look up at; look up to, respect; ask for, rely (on); **ō(se)** – what you say, (your/his) wish

仰視	*gyōshi*	look up (at)	606
仰天	*gyōten*	be astonished, frightened	141
信仰	*shinkō*	faith, religious conviction	157
仰向け	*aomuke*	facing upward, on one's back, supine	199

仰 仰 仰

1057 扌 厂 卩 3c 2p 2e

抑

YOKU, osa(eru) – hold down/in check, suppress, control

抑制	*yokusei*	control, restrain, suppress	427
抑留	*yokuryū*	detention, internment	761
抑止	*yokushi*	deter, stave off	477
抑揚	*yokuyō*	rising and falling of tones, intonation	631

抑 抑 抑

1058 卩 厂 丨 2e 2p 1b

卵

RAN, tamago – egg (cf. No. 295)

鶏卵	*keiran*	(hen's) egg	926
産卵	*sanran*	egg-laying, spawning	278
卵黄	*ran'ō*	yolk	780
卵管	*rankan*	Fallopian tube, oviduct	328
卵形	*tamagogata, rankei*	egg-shaped, oval	395

卵 卵 卵

1059 十 糸 冖 2k 6a 2i

索

SAKU – rope, cord; search for

索引	*sakuin*	an index	216
捜索	*sōsaku*	search	989
家宅捜索	*kataku sōsaku*	search of the house/premises	165, 178, 989
探索	*tansaku*	search, inquiry, investigation	535
思索	*shisaku*	thinking, speculation, contemplation	99

1060 田 糸 5f 6a

累

RUI – involvement, trouble; accumulation; continually

累加/増	*ruika/zō*	acceleration, successive increase	709, 712
累積	*ruiseki*	accumulation, cumulative	656
累計	*ruikei*	(sum) total	340
係累	*keirui*	family encumbrances, dependents	909
累進	*ruishin*	successive/progressive promotions	437

1061 田 艹 丷 5f 3k 2o

異

I, koto – be different

異常	*ijō*	unusual, abnormal	497
異質	*ishitsu*	heterogeneity	176
異国	*ikoku*	foreign country	40
異議	*igi*	objection	292
異教	*ikyō*	heathenism, paganism, heresy	245

1062 丷 田 艹 2o 5f 3k

翼

YOKU, tsubasa – wing

左翼	*sayoku*	the left wing, leftist	75
右翼	*uyoku*	the right wing, rightist	76
両翼	*ryōyoku*	both wings	200
比翼の鳥	*hiyoku no tori*	happily married couple	798, 285

1063 亻 木 一 (2a 4a 1a)

余

YO, ama(ru) – be left over, in excess; ***ama(su)*** – leave over

二十余年	*nijūyonen*	more than 20 years	3, 12, 45
余命	*yomei*	the rest of one's life	578
余計	*yokei*	too much, unwanted, uncalled-for	340
余地	*yochi*	room, margin	118
余波	*yoha*	aftereffect	666

余 余 余

1064 日 ト 又 (4c 2m 2h)

暇

KA, hima – free time, leisure

休暇	*kyūka*	holiday, vacation, time off	60
余暇	*yoka*	leisure, spare time	1063
暇つぶし	*himatsubushi*	a waste of time, killing time	
暇取る	*himadoru*	take a long time, be delayed	65
暇な時	*hima na toki*	leisure time, when one is free	42

暇 暇 暇

1065 阝 木 亻 (2d 4a 2a)

除

JO, [JI], nozo(ku) – get rid of, exclude

解除	*kaijo*	cancellation	474
除名	*jomei*	remove (someone's) name, expel	82
除外	*jogai*	except, exclude	83
免除	*menjo*	exemption	733
取り除く	*torinozoku*	remove, rid	65

除 除 除

1066 彳 木 亻 (3i 4a 2a)

徐

JO – slowly

徐々に	*jojo ni*	slowly, gradually	
徐行	*jokō*	go/drive slowly	68
徐歩	*joho*	walk slowly, saunter, mosey	431

徐 徐 徐

1067	又 木 亻 2h 4a 2a	*JO* – narrate, describe			
叙		叙述	*jojutsu*	description, narration	968
		叙景	*jokei*	description of scenery	853
		叙情詩	*jojōshi*	lyric poem/poetry	209, 570
		叙事詩	*jojishi*	epic poem/poetry	80, 570
		自叙伝	*jijoden*	autobiography	62, 434

叙 叙 叙

1068	刂 木 艹 2f 4a 3k	*JŌ* – surplus			
剰		剰余(金)	*jōyo(kin)*	a surplus	1063, 23
		(出生)過剰	*(shussei) kajō*	surplus, excess (of births)	53, 44, 413
		余剰	*yojō*	surplus	1063
		剰員	*jōin*	superfluous personnel, overstaffing	163

剰 剰 剰

1069	亻 木 十 2a 4a 2k	*SHA, nana(me)* – slanting, diagonal, oblique			
斜		斜面	*shamen*	a slope, slant, incline	274
		斜線	*shasen*	slanting line, slash [/]	299
		斜辺	*shahen*	oblique side, hypotenuse	775
		斜陽	*shayō*	setting sun	630
		斜視	*shashi*	squint	606

斜 斜 斜

1070	一 土 艹 1a 3b 3k	*SUI, ta(reru/rasu)* – (intr./tr.) hang down, dangle, drip			
垂		垂直	*suichoku*	perpendicular, vertical	423
		垂線	*suisen*	a perpendicular (line)	299
		懸垂	*kensui*	suspension, dangling; doing chin-ups	911
		虫垂	*chūsui*	the appendix	873
		雨垂れ	*amadare*	raindrops	30

垂 垂 垂

1071 目 土 艹
5c 3b 3k

睡

SUI – sleep

睡眠	*suimin*	sleep	849
睡眠不足	*suimin-busoku*	lack of sleep	849, 94, 58
午睡	*gosui*	nap, siesta	49
熟睡	*jukusui*	sound/deep sleep	687
こん睡(状態)	*konsui (jōtai)*	coma	626, 387

睡 睡 睡

1072 辶 木 亻
2q 4a 2a

途

TO – way, road

途中	*tochū*	on the way, midway	28
前途	*zento*	one's future, prospects	47
途絶える	*todaeru*	come to a stop	742
帰途	*kito*	one's way home	317
(開発)途上国	*(kaihatsu) tojōkoku*	developing country	396, 96, 32, 40

途 途 途

1073 土 木 氵
3b 4a 3a

塗

TO, nu(ru) – paint

塗料	*toryō*	paints, paint and varnish	319
塗布	*tofu*	apply (salve)	675
塗り物	*nurimono*	lacquerware	79
塗り立て	*nuritate*	freshly painted	121
塗り替える	*nurikaeru*	repaint, put on a new coating	744

塗 塗 塗

1074 艹 十 一
3k2 2k 1a2

華

KA, [KE], hana – flower, florid, showy, brilliant

華道	*kadō*	(Japanese) flower arranging	149
華美	*kabi*	splendor, pomp, gorgeousness	410
中華料理	*chūka ryōri*	Chinese food/cooking	28, 319, 143
中華人民共和国	*Chūka Jinmin Kyōwakoku*	People's Republic of China	28, 1, 177, 196, 124, 40

華 華 華

1075	艹 口 十 (3k 3s 2k)	**KAKU** – reform; **kawa** – leather	
革	革命	*kakumei*	revolution	578
	革新	*kakushin*	reform	174
	改革	*kaikaku*	reform, reorganization	514
	変革	*henkaku*	reform, innovation, revolutionize	257
	皮革	*hikaku*	leather	975

革 革 革

1076	艹 口 亻 (3k 3s 2a)	**KA, kutsu** – shoe	
靴	製靴	*seika*	shoemaking	428
	革靴	*kawagutsu*	leather shoes	1075
	靴下	*kutsushita*	socks, stockings	31
	靴屋	*kutsuya*	shoe store	167
	靴一足	*kutsu issoku*	1 pair of shoes	2, 58

靴 靴 靴

1077	亻 冖 又 (2a 2i 2h)	**SHIN, oka(su)** – invade; violate, infringe on; damage	
侵	侵略	*shinryaku*	aggression, invasion	841
	侵入	*shinnyū*	invasion, raid, trespass	52
	侵害	*shingai*	infringement	518
	不可侵条約	*fukashin jōyaku*	nonaggression pact	94, 388, 564, 211
	侵食	*shinshoku*	erosion, weathering	322

侵 侵 侵

1078	氵 冖 又 (3a 2i 2h)	**SHIN, hita(ru)** – be soaked, steeped; **hita(su)** – dip, immerse	
浸	浸水	*shinsui*	inundation, submersion	21
	浸出	*shinshutsu*	exuding, oozing out, percolation	53
	浸食	*shinshoku*	erosion, corrosion	322
	水浸し	*mizubitashi*	submersion, inundation	21

浸 浸 浸

1079	宀 氵 冖 3m 2b 2i	**SHIN, *ne(ru)*** – go to bed, sleep; ***ne(kasu)*** – put to bed		
寝				
	寝室	*shinshitsu*	bedroom	166
	寝台	*shindai*	bed	492
	寝具(類)	*shingu(rui)*	bedclothes, bedding	420, 226
	昼寝	*hirune*	nap, siesta	470
	寝苦しい	*negurushii*	unable to sleep well	545

1080	扌 巾 冖 3c 3f 2i	***SŌ, ha(ku)*** – sweep		
掃				
	(大)掃除	*(ō)sōji*	(general) housecleaning	26, 1065
	清掃夫	*seisōfu*	street sweeper, cleaning man	660, 315
	掃除婦	*sōjifu*	cleaning lady	1065, 316
	掃討	*sōtō*	sweeping, cleaning, mopping up	1018
	一掃	*issō*	sweep away, eradicate, stamp out	2

1081	ソ 十 一 2o 2k 1a2	**KEN, *ka(neru)*** – combine, double as; ***-ka(neru)*** – cannot		
兼				
	兼業	*kengyō*	a side business	279
	兼任	*kennin*	hold 2 posts (simultaneously)	334
	首相兼外相	*shushō ken gaishō*	prime minister who is also foreign minister	148, 146, 83
	待ち兼ねる	*machikaneru*	cannot wait, wait impatiently for	452

1082	口 十 一 3d 2k 1a4	***JIN, tazu(neru)*** – search for; ask, inquire		
尋				
	尋問	*jinmon*	questioning, interrogation	162
	尋常	*jinjō*	normal, ordinary	497
	尋ね人	*tazunebito*	person being sought, missing person	1

1083	禾 冂 一 (5d 2r 1a3)			
粗	***SO*** – crop tax, tribute			
	租税	*sozei*	taxes	399
	地租	*chiso*	(obsolete) land tax	118
	租借	*soshaku*	lease (land)	766
	租界	*sokai*	(foreign) settlement, concession	454
	租借地	*soshakuchi*	leased territory	766, 118

Stroke order: 1–10

1084	米 冂 一 (6b 2r 1a3)			
粗	***SO, ara(i)*** – coarse, rough			
	粗末	*somatsu*	coarse, plain, crude, rough, rude	305
	粗暴	*sobō*	wild, rough, rude, violent	1014
	粗野	*soya*	rustic, loutish, vulgar, ill-bred	236
	粗悪	*soaku*	coarse, crude, base, inferior	304
	粗食	*soshoku*	coarse food, plain diet	322

Stroke order: 1–11

1085	阝 冂 一 (2d 2r 1a3)			
阻	***SO, haba(mu)*** – hamper			
	阻止	*soshi*	obstruct, impede	477
	阻害	*sogai*	check, impediment, hindrance	518
	険阻	*kenso*	steep, precipitous, rugged	533

Stroke order: 1–8

1086	宀 冂 一 (3m 2r 1a3)			
宜	***GI*** – good, all right			
	便宜	*bengi*	convenience, expediency	330
	便宜上	*bengijō*	for convenience/expediency	330, 32
	時宜	*jigi*	right time/opportunity	42
	適宜	*tekigi*	suitable, appropriate, fitting	415

Stroke order: 1–8

1087 田 冖 冂 5f 2i 2r

畳

JŌ, tatami – tatami, straw floor-mat; ***tata(mu)*** – fold up

四畳半	*yojōhan*	4½-mat room	6, 88
畳表	*tatami-omote*	woven covering of a tatami	272
畳替え	*tatamigae*	replacing *tatami-omote*/tatami	744
畳屋	*tatamiya*	tatami maker/store	167

畳 畳 畳

1088 扌 爫 又 3c 3n 2h

援

EN – help, assistance

援助	*enjo*	assistance, aid	623
応援	*ōen*	aid, support, backing, cheering	827
後援	*kōen*	support, backing	48
声援	*seien*	shout of encouragement, cheers, rooting	746
援軍	*engun*	reinforcements	438

援 援 援

1089 糸 爫 又 6a 3n 2h

緩

KAN, yuru(mu) – become loose, abate, slacken; ***yuru(meru)*** – loosen, relieve, relax, slacken; ***yuru(i)*** – loose; generous; lax; gentle (slope); slow; ***yuru(yaka)*** – loose, slack; magnanimous; gentle, easy, slow

緩和	*kanwa*	relieve, ease, lighten	124
緩急	*kankyū*	fast and slow speed; emergency	303

緩 緩 緩

1090 ⺮ 月 力 6f 4b 2g

筋

KIN, suji – muscle, tendon; blood vessel; line; reason, logic; plot (of a story); coherence; source (of information)

筋肉	*kinniku*	muscle	223
筋道	*sujimichi*	reason, logic, coherence	149
筋違い	*sujichigai, sujikai*	a cramp; illogical, wrong	814
筋書き	*sujigaki*	synopsis, outline, plan	131

筋 筋 筋

1091 ⺮ 目 木 6f 5c 4a

hako – box

本箱	*honbako*	bookcase	25
貯金箱	*chokinbako*	savings box, (piggy) bank	762, 23
重箱	*jūbako*	nested boxes	227
豚箱	*butabako*	police lockup, jail, hoosegow	796
箱根	*Hakone*	(resort area near Mt. Fuji)	314

箱

1092 ⺮ 車 一 6f 7c 1a

HAN – example, model, pattern; limit

範例	*hanrei*	example	612
師範	*shihan*	teacher, master	409
規範	*kihan*	norm, criterion	607
広範	*kōhan*	extensive, wide, far-reaching	694

範

1093 一 冂 丶 1a 2r 1d

TAN – red

丹念	*tannen*	application, diligence	579
丹誠	*tansei*	sincerity; efforts, diligence	718
丹精	*tansei*	exertion, diligence, painstaking care	659
丹前	*tanzen*	man's padded kimono	47

丹

1094 舟 6c

SHŪ, fune, [funa] – boat

小舟	*kobune*	boat, skiff	27
舟遊び	*funaasobi*	boating	1003
舟歌	*funauta*	sailor's song, chantey	392

舟

1095	舟 6c	日 4c	ノ 1c

舶

HAKU – ship

船舶	*senpaku*	ship, vessel; shipping	376
舶来	*hakurai*	imported	69
舶来品	*hakuraihin*	imported article/goods	69, 230

舶 舶 舶

1096	舟 6c	几 2s	又 2h

般

HAN – carry; all, general

一般的	*ippanteki*	general	2, 210
一般化	*ippanka*	generalization, popularization	2, 254
全般	*zenpan*	the whole	89
全般的	*zenpanteki*	general, overall	89, 210
先般	*senpan*	recently, some time ago	50

般 般 般

1097	皿 5h

皿

sara – plate, dish, saucer

皿洗い	*saraarai*	washing dishes	692
サラダ一皿	*sarada hitosara*	1 plate of salad	2
大皿	*ōzara*	large dish, platter	26
小皿	*kozara*	small plate	27
受け皿	*ukezara*	saucer	260

皿 皿 皿

1098	皿 5h	舟 6c	几 2s

盤

BAN – (chess/go) board, tray, platter, basin

基盤	*kiban*	basis, foundation	450
円盤	*enban*	disk; discus	13
空飛ぶ円盤	*soratobu enban*	flying saucer	140, 530, 13
水盤	*suiban*	basin	21
終盤戦	*shūbansen*	end game	458, 301

盤 盤 盤

1099 盆

丷 皿 刂
2o 5h 2f

BON – Buddhist Festival of the Dead; tray

盆地	*bonchi*	basin, valley	118
盆景	*bonkei*	miniature landscape on a tray	853
(お)盆	*(O)Bon*	the Bon Festival	
	(o)bon	tray	

1100 盗

皿 欠 冫
5h 4j 2b

TŌ, nusu(mu) – steal

強盗	*gōtō*	burglar, robber	217
盗難(保険)	*tōnan (hoken)*	theft (insurance)	557, 489, 533
盗用	*tōyō*	embezzlement; surreptitious use, plagiarism	107
盗作	*tōsaku*	plagiarism	360
盗品	*tōhin*	stolen goods, loot	230

1101 塩

土 皿 口
3b 5h 3d

EN, shio – salt

食塩	*shokuen*	table salt	322
塩分	*enbun*	salt content, salinity	38
塩酸	*ensan*	hydrochloric acid	516
塩水	*ensui*	salt water, brine	21
塩入れ	*shioire*	saltshaker	52

1102 凡

几 丶
2s 1d

BON, [HAN] – common, ordinary

凡人	*bonjin*	ordinary person, man of mediocre ability	1
平凡	*heibon*	commonplace, mediocre	202
凡例	*hanrei*	introductory remarks	612
凡才	*bonsai*	common ability, mediocre talent	551

1103 巾 几 丶 3f 2s 1d

帆

HAN, ho – sail

出帆	*shuppan*	sailing, departure	53
帆走	*hansō*	sailing	429
帆船	*hansen*	sailing ship, sailboat	376
帆柱	*hobashira*	mast	598

1104 日 目 4c 5c

冒

BŌ, oka(su) – risk, brave, defy, dare; desecrate

冒険	*bōken*	adventure	533
冒険小説	*bōken shōsetsu*	adventure novel	533, 27, 400
冒頭	*bōtō*	beginning, opening, lead	276
感冒	*kanbō*	a cold	262
冒とく	*bōtoku*	blasphemy, sacrilege, defilement	

1105 巾 日 目 3f 4c 5c

帽

BŌ – cap, hat, headgear

帽子	*bōshi*	hat, cap	103
宇宙帽	*uchūbō*	space helmet	990, 991
赤帽	*akabō*	redcap, luggage porter	207
無帽	*mubō*	hatless, bareheaded	93
帽章	*bōshō*	badge on a cap	857

1106 弓 卜 一 3h 2m 1a3

張

CHŌ, ha(ru) – stretch, spread

主張	*shuchō*	insistence, assertion, contention	155
出張	*shutchō*	business trip	53
出張所	*shutchōjo*	branch office, agency	53, 153
引っ張る	*hipparu*	pull, tug at	216
見張る	*miharu*	keep watch, be on the lookout	63

1107 巾 ⺊ 一 3f 2m 1a3

帳

CHŌ – notebook, register; curtain

手帳	*techō*	(pocket) notebook	57
電話帳	*denwachō*	telephone book/directory	108, 238
(貯金) 通帳	*(chokin) tsūchō*	bankbook, passbook	762, 23, 150
帳面	*chōmen*	notebook, account book	274
帳消し	*chōkeshi*	cancellation, writing off (debts)	845

帳 帳 帳

1108 亻 日 丨 2a 4c 1b

伸

SHIN, no(biru) – stretch, lengthen, grow; ***no(basu)*** – stretch out, lengthen, extend

伸張	*shinchō*	extend, expand	1106
二伸	*nishin*	postscript, P.S.	3
伸び伸び	*nobinobi*	at ease, relieved, refreshed	

伸 伸 伸

1109 糸 日 丨 6a 4c 1b

紳

SHIN – gentleman

紳士	*shinshi*	gentleman	572
紳士用	*shinshiyō*	men's, for men	572, 107
紳士服	*shinshifuku*	men's clothing	572, 683
紳士協定	*shinshi kyōtei*	gentleman's agreement	572, 234, 355

紳 紳 紳

1110 糸 日 宀 6a 4c 3m

縮

SHUKU, chiji(maru/mu) – shrink, contract; ***chiji(meru)*** – shorten, condense; ***chiji(rasu/reru)*** – make/become curly

伸縮	*shinshuku*	expansion and contraction, flexibility	1108
短縮	*tanshuku*	shortening, reduction	215
縮図	*shukuzu*	reduced/scaled-down drawing	339
軍縮	*gunshuku*	arms reduction	438

縮 縮 縮

1111 廴 士 丿 2q 3p 1c

廷

TEI – imperial court; government office

宮廷	*kyūtei*	imperial court	721
法廷	*hōtei*	(law) court	123
開廷	*kaitei*	holding (law) court	396
出廷	*shuttei*	appearance in court	53
廷臣	*teishin*	court official, courtier	835

廷 廷 廷

1112 广 士 廴 3q 3p 2q

庭

TEI, niwa – garden

家庭	*katei*	home, family	165
校庭	*kōtei*	schoolyard, school grounds	115
庭球	*teikyū*	tennis	726
庭園	*teien*	garden	447
前庭	*maeniwa, zentei*	front garden	47

庭 庭 庭

1113 扌 广 丿 3c 3q 1c

拡

KAKU – extend, expand

拡大	*kakudai*	magnification, expansion	26
拡張	*kakuchō*	entension, expansion	1106
拡充	*kakujū*	expansion, amplification	828
拡散	*kakusan*	diffusion	767
拡声機/器	*kakuseiki*	loudspeaker	746, 528, 527

拡 拡 拡

1114 彳 卜 一 3i 2m 1a2

征

SEI – conquer

征服	*seifuku*	conquer, subjugate	683
征服者	*seifukusha*	conqueror	683, 164
出征	*shussei*	going to the front, taking the field	53
遠征	*ensei*	(military) expedition; playing tour	446
長征	*chōsei*	the Long March (in China)	95

征 征 征

1115 ⻌ ⺊ 一 2q 2m 1a

延

EN, no(basu/beru) – lengthen, prolong, postpone; *no(biru)* – be postponed, delayed, prolonged

延長	*enchō*	extension	95
延期	*enki*	postponement, extension	449
遅延	*chien*	delay, being behind time	702
引き延ばす	*hikinobasu*	draw out, prolong, enlarge	216

延 延 延

1116 言 ⻌ ⺊ 7a 2q 2m

誕

TAN – birth

誕生	*tanjō*	birth	44
誕生日	*tanjōbi*	birthday	44, 5
誕生祝い	*tanjōiwai*	birthday celebration	44, 851
生誕(百年)	*seitan (hyakunen)*	(centenary of someone's) birth	44, 14, 45

誕 誕 誕

1117 糸 貝 土 6a 7b 3b

績

SEKI – achievements; spinning

成績	*seiseki*	performance, results	261
成績表	*seisekihyō*	list of grades, report card	261, 272
業績	*gyōseki*	work, achievements; business performance	279
功績	*kōseki*	meritorious service	818
実績	*jisseki*	record of performance, actual results	203

績 績 績

1118 亻 貝 土 2a 7b 3b

債

SAI – debt, loan

負債	*fusai*	debt, liabilities	510
国債	*kokusai*	national debt, public loan	40
債券	*saiken*	bond, debenture	506
債権(者)	*saiken(sha)*	credit(or)	335, 164
債務(者)	*saimu(sha)*	debt(or)	235, 164

債 債 債

1119	口 厂 一 3d 2p 1a
后	***KŌ*** – empress

皇后	*kōgō*	empress	297
皇后陛下	*kōgō-heika*	Her Majesty the Empress	297, 589, 31
皇太后	*kōtai-gō/kō*	the empress dowager	297, 629

后 后 后

1120	禾 口 亠 5d 3d2 2j
稿	***KŌ*** – manuscript, draft

原稿(用紙)	*genkō (yōshi)*	manuscript (paper)	136, 107, 180
草稿	*sōkō*	rough draft, notes	249
投稿	*tōkō*	contribution (to a periodical)	1021
稿料	*kōryō*	fee for a manuscript/article/artwork	319

稿 稿 稿

1121	禾 ⺈ 丶 5d 2n2 1d2
移	***I, utsu(ru)*** – move (one's residence), change, be catching; ***utsu(su)*** – move (one's residence/office), transfer, infect

移動	*idō*	moving, migration	231
移転	*iten*	move, change of address	433
移(住)民	*i(jū)min*	emigrant, immigrant	156, 177
移植	*ishoku*	transplant	424

移 移 移

1122	山 月 3o 4b2
崩	***HŌ, kuzu(reru)*** – fall to pieces, collapse; ***kuzu(su)*** – demolish; change, break (a large bill); write (cursive simplified kanji)

崩御	*hōgyo*	death of the emperor	708
山崩れ	*yamakuzure*	landslide	34
荷崩れ	*nikuzure*	a load falling off (a truck)	391
切り崩す	*kirikuzusu*	cut through, level (a mountain)	39

崩 崩 崩

1123	戈衤 十 4n 5e 2k	**SAI, saba(ku)** – pass judgment; **ta(tsu)** – cut out (cloth/leather)	
裁判	*saiban*	trial, hearing	1026
裁決	*saiketsu*	decision, ruling	356
独裁	*dokusai*	dictatorship	219
総裁	*sōsai*	president, general director	697
洋裁	*yōsai*	(Western-style) dressmaking	289

裁 裁 裁

1124	戈車 十 4n 7c 2k	**SAI, no(ru)** – be recorded, appear (in print); **no(seru)** – place on top of; load (luggage); publish, run (an ad)	
積載	*sekisai*	loading, carrying	656
満載	*mansai*	fully loaded	201
記載	*kisai*	statement, mention	371
連載	*rensai*	a serial	440

載 載 載

1125	戈木 十 4n 4a 2k	**SAI** – planting	
盆栽	*bonsai*	a bonsai, potted dwarf tree	1099

栽 栽 栽

1126	イ口 丷 2a 3d 2o	**ZOKU** – customs, manners; the world, laity; vulgar	
俗語	*zokugo*	colloquial language	67
俗名	*zokumyō*	secular name	82
民俗	*minzoku*	folk	177
風俗	*fūzoku*	manners, customs; public morals	29
通俗文学	*tsūzoku bungaku*	popular literature	150, 111, 109

俗 俗 俗

1127 欠 口 丷 (4j 3d 2o)

欲

YOKU – covetousness, desire; ***hos(suru)*** – desire, want; ***ho(shii)*** – want

食欲	*shokuyoku*	appetite	322
性欲	*seiyoku*	sexual desire, sex drive	98
欲望	*yokubō*	desire, appetite, craving	673
無欲	*muyoku*	free from avarice, unselfish	93

欲 欲 欲

1128 氵 口 丷 (3a 3d 2o)

浴

YOKU, a(biru) – be bathed in; ***a(biseru)*** – pour over, shower

入浴	*nyūyoku*	bathing, (hot) bath	52
浴室	*yokushitsu*	bathroom	166
海水浴場	*kaisuiyokujō*	(swimming) beach	117, 21, 154
日光浴	*nikkōyoku*	sunbathing	5, 138
浴衣	*yukata*	cotton kimono for summer	677

浴 浴 浴

1129 尸 艹 一 (3r 3k 1a)

展

TEN – expand

展示(会)	*tenji(kai)*	show, exhibition	615, 158
展望台	*tenbōdai*	observation platform	673, 492
親展	*shinten*	confidential	175
進展	*shinten*	development, evolution	437
発展途上国	*hatten tojōkoku*	developing country	96, 1072, 32, 40

展 展 展

1130 尸 艹 丷 (3r 3k 2o)

殿

DEN, TEN – hall, palace; mister; ***tono*** – lord; ***-dono*** – Mr.

宮殿	*kyūden*	palace	721
御殿	*goten*	palace	708
殿下	*denka*	His/Your Highness	31
湯殿	*yudono*	bathroom	632

殿 殿 殿

1131	糸 犭 一 6a 3g 1a2	***EN*** – relation, connection; marriage; fate; veranda; ***fuchi*** – edge, brink, rim, border		
縁				
絶縁	*zetsuen*	(electrical) insulation; break off relations	742	
因縁	*innen*	causality, connection, fate	554	
縁側	*engawa*	veranda, porch, balcony	609	
額縁	*gakubuchi*	(picture) frame	838	

1132	土 犭 阝 3b 3g 2d	***TSUI*** – fall		
墜				
墜落	*tsuiraku*	fall, (airplane) crash	839	
墜死	*tsuishi*	fatal fall, fall to one's death	85	
撃墜	*gekitsui*	shoot down (a plane)	1016	
失墜	*shittsui*	loss, fall	311	

1133	辶 犭 丷 2q 3g 2o	***SUI, to(geru)*** – accomplish, attain, carry through		
遂				
遂行	*suikō*	accomplish, execute, perform	68	
完遂	*kansui*	successful execution, completion	613	
(殺人)未遂	*(satsujin) misui*	attempted (murder)	576, 1, 306	
やり遂げる	*yaritogeru*	go through with, carry out		

1134	辶 犭 一 2q 3g 1a	***CHIKU*** – drive away, pursue, follow		
逐				
放逐	*hōchiku*	expulsion, banishment	512	
逐語訳	*chikugoyaku*	word-for-word/literal translation	67, 594	
逐次	*chikuji*	one after another, one by one	384	
逐一	*chikuichi*	one by one, in detail	2	
逐電	*chikuden, chikuten*	abscond, make a getaway	108	

1135	心 日 豸 4k 4c 3g	**KON, nengo(ro)** – intimacy, friendship		
	懇談	*kondan*	familiar talk, friendly chat	593
	懇意	*kon'i*	intimacy, friendship	132
	懇切	*konsetsu*	cordial; exhaustive, detailed	39
	懇願	*kongan*	entreaty, earnest appeal	581
	懇親会	*konshinkai*	social gathering	175, 158

懇 懇 懇

1136	土 日 豸 3b 4c 3g	**KON** – opening up farmland, cultivation		
	開墾	*kaikon*	clearing, reclamation (of land)	396
	開墾地	*kaikonchi*	developed/cultivated land	396, 118

墾 墾 墾

1137	夂 几 4i 2s	**SHO** – deal with, treat; sentence, condemn; behave, act		
	処分	*shobun*	disposal, disposition; punishment	38
	処置	*shochi*	disposition, measures, steps	426
	処理	*shori*	treat, manage, deal with	143
	対処	*taisho*	cope with, tackle	365
	処女	*shojo*	virgin	102

処 処 処

1138	扌 夂 几 3c 4i 2s	**KYO, KO** – be due to, based on		
	根拠	*konkyo*	basis, grounds	314
	拠点	*kyoten*	(military) position, base	169
	準拠	*junkyo*	be based on, conform to	778
	論拠	*ronkyo*	grounds/basis of an argument	293
	証拠	*shōko*	evidence	484

拠 拠 拠

1139 丷 王 口 2o 4f 3d

善

ZEN, yo(i) – good

善悪	*zen'aku*	good and evil; quality (whether good or bad)	304
善良	*zenryō*	good, honest, virtuous	321
善意	*zen'i*	good intentions; favorable sense	132
親善	*shinzen*	friendship	175
改善	*kaizen*	improvement, betterment	514

善 善 善

1140 糸 王 口 6a 4f 3d

繕

ZEN, tsukuro(u) – repair, mend

修繕	*shūzen*	repair	945
営繕	*eizen*	building and repairs	722

繕 繕 繕

1141 士 口 3p 3d

吉

KICHI, KITSU – good luck

吉報	*kippō*	good news, glad tidings	685
吉日	*kichijitsu*	lucky day	5
不吉	*fukitsu*	ill omen, portentous	94
石部金吉	*ishibe kinkichi*	man of strict morals	78, 86, 23
吉田	*Yoshida*	(surname)	35

吉 吉 吉

1142 言 士 口 7a 3p 3d

詰

KITSU, tsu(mu) – be pressed into, closely packed; **tsu(meru)** – cram, stuff; shorten; **tsu(maru)** – be stopped up, jammed; shrink; be cornered

詰問	*kitsumon*	cross-examination, tough questioning	162
詰め込む	*tsumekomu*	cram, stuff	776
気詰まり	*kizumari*	embarrassment, awkwardness	134

詰 詰 詰

1143	士 口 丷 3p 3d2 2o	**KI, yoroko(bu)** – be glad		
喜劇	*kigeki*	a comedy	797	
歓喜	*kanki*	joy, delight	1052	
狂喜	*kyōki*	wild joy, exultation	883	
一喜一憂	*ikki-ichiyū*	alternation of joy and sorrow	2, 1032	
大喜び	*ōyorokobi*	great joy	26	

喜 喜 喜

1144	木 土 口 4a 3b 3d	**JU** – tree, bush		
樹木	*jumoku*	tree	22	
果樹	*kaju*	fruit tree	487	
樹皮	*juhi*	bark (of a tree)	975	
樹脂	*jushi*	resin	1042	
樹立	*juritsu*	establish, found	121	

樹 樹 樹

1145	月 口 彡 4b 3d 3j	**BŌ, fuku(reru/ramu)** – swell, bulge, rise (dough), expand; sulk, pout		
膨大	*bōdai*	swelling; large, enormous	26	
青膨れ	*aobukure*	dropsical swelling	208	
膨れっ面	*fukurettsura*	sullen/sulky look	274	
下膨れ	*shimobukure*	full-cheeked, round-faced	31	

膨 膨 膨

1146	月 十 又 4b 2k 2h	**SHI** – limbs		
肢体	*shitai*	limbs; body and limbs	61	
下肢	*kashi*	lower limbs, legs	31	
上肢	*jōshi*	upper limbs, arms	32	
四肢	*shishi*	the limbs, members	6	

肢 肢 肢

1147	士 口 十 3p 3d 2k	***KO, tsuzumi*** – hand drum			
鼓		太鼓	*taiko*	drum	629
		鼓手	*koshu*	drummer	57
		鼓動	*kodō*	(heart) beat	231
		鼓舞	*kobu*	encouragement, inspiration	810

1148	又 彡 厂 2h 3j 2p	***HATSU, kami*** – hair (on the head)			
髪		散髪	*sanpatsu*	haircut, hairdressing	767
		洗髪	*senpatsu*	hair washing, a shampoo	692
		間一髪	*kan'ippatsu*	by a hairsbreadth	43, 2
		金髪	*kinpatsu*	blond	23
		白髪	*hakuhatsu, shiraga*	white/gray hair	205

1149	彡 土 口 3j 3b 3d	***CHŌ, ho(ru)*** – carve, engrave, chisel, sculpt			
彫		彫像	*chōzō*	carved statue	740
		彫金	*chōkin*	chasing, metal carving	23
		木彫	*mokuchō*	wood carving	22
		木彫り	*kibori*	wood carving	22
		浮き彫り	*ukibori*	relief	938

1150	⺍ 力 ノ 3n 2g 1c	***RETSU, oto(ru)*** – be inferior			
劣		劣等	*rettō*	inferiority	569
		劣等感	*rettōkan*	inferiority complex	569, 262
		優劣	*yūretsu*	superiority or inferiority, relative merit	1033
		劣勢	*ressei*	numerical inferiority	646
		劣性	*ressei*	inferior; recessive (gene)	98

1151	石 ⺌ ノ 5a 3n 1c	**SA, SHA, suna** – sand		
砂				
	砂利	*jari*	gravel	329
	土砂降り	*doshaburi*	pouring rain, downpour	24, 947
	土砂崩れ	*doshakuzure*	washout, landslide	24, 1122
	砂浜	*sunahama*	sandy beach	785
	砂時計	*sunadokei*	hourglass	42, 340
	砂 砂 砂			

1152	禾 ⺌ ノ 5d 3n 1c	**BYŌ** – second (of time/arc)		
秒				
	秒針	*byōshin*	second hand (of a clock)	341
	数秒	*sūbyō*	several seconds	225
	１分２０秒	*ippun nijūbyō*	1 minute 20 seconds	38
	秒速５メートル	*byōsoku gomētoru*	5 meters per second	502
	秒読み	*byōyomi*	countdown	244
	秒 秒 秒			

1153	扌 ⺌ ノ 3c 3n 1c	**SHŌ** – selection, summary, excerpt		
抄				
	抄録	*shōroku*	excerpt, abstract, summary	538
	抄本	*shōhon*	extract, abridged transcript	25
	抄訳	*shōyaku*	abridged translation	594
	詩抄	*shishō*	a selection of poems	570
	抄 抄 抄			

1154	女 ⺌ ノ 3e 3n 1c	**MYŌ** – strange, odd; a mystery; adroitness, knack		
妙				
	奥妙	*ōmyō*	secret, mystery	476
	妙案	*myōan*	good idea, ingenious plan	106
	妙技	*myōgi*	extraordinary skill	871
	妙手	*myōshu*	expert, master, virtuoso	57
	絶妙	*zetsumyō*	miraculous, superb, exquisite	742
	妙 妙 妙			

1155	木 一 丨 (4a 1a 1b)	**HAI, sakazuki** – wine cup (for sakè)	
杯	一杯	*ippai*	a glass (of); a drink; full	2
	二杯	*nihai*	2 glasses (of)	3
	祝杯	*shukuhai*	a toast	851
	銀杯	*ginpai*	silver cup	313
	デ杯(戦)	*Dehai(sen)*	Davis Cup (tournament)	301

1156	木 攵 (4a 4i)	**MAI** – (counter for thin, flat objects)	
枚	紙一枚	*kami ichimai*	1 sheet of paper	180, 2
	何枚	*nanmai*	how many (sheets/plates/stamps)	390
	枚挙	*maikyo*	enumerate, count, list	801
	枚数	*maisū*	number of sheets	225
	大枚	*taimai*	a big sum (of money)	26

1157	木 丨 (4a 1b)	**SATSU** – paper money, slip of paper; ***fuda*** – chit, card, label	
札	千円札	*sen'ensatsu*	1,000-yen bill/note	15, 13
	札束	*satsutaba*	bundle/roll of bills	501
	改札口	*kaisatsuguchi*	wicket, ticket gate	514, 54
	標/表札	*hyōsatsu*	nameplate	923, 272
	入札	*nyūsatsu*	a bid, tender	52

1158	一 卄 冂 ((1a) 3k 2r)	**SATSU** – (counter for books); **SAKU** – book	
冊	十二冊	*jūnisatsu*	12 books/volumes	12, 3
	別冊	*bessatsu*	separate volume	267
	分冊	*bunsatsu*	individual/separate volume	38
	冊子	*sasshi*	booklet, brochure, pamphlet	103
	短冊	*tanzaku*	strip of fancy paper (for a poem)	215

1159 亻 戸 艹 (2a 4m 3k)

偏

HEN, katayo(ru) – lean, incline; be one sided, partial

不偏(不党)	*fuhen(futō)*	nonpartisan	94, 495
偏向	*henkō*	propensity, leaning, deviation	199
偏見	*henken*	biased view, prejudice	63
偏食	*henshoku*	unbalanced diet	322
偏差	*hensa*	deviation, deflection, declination	658

偏 偏 偏

1160 辶 戸 艹 (2q 4m 3k)

遍

HEN – far, widespread, general

遍歴	*henreki*	travel, pilgrimage	480
遍路	*henro*	pilgrim	151
一遍	*ippen*	once, one time	2

遍 遍 遍

1161 艹 丷 一 (3k 2o 1a3)

瓶

BIN – bottle

花瓶	*kabin*	vase	255
瓶詰	*binzume*	bottled, in a glass jar	1142
ビール瓶	*bīrubin*	beer bottle	
鉄瓶	*tetsubin*	iron kettle	312
空き瓶	*akibin*	empty bottle	140

瓶 瓶 瓶

1162 亻 艹 丷 (2a 3k 2o)

併

HEI, awa(seru) – put together, unite, combine

合併	*gappei*	merger	159
併合	*heigō*	annexation, amalgamation, merger	159
併用	*heiyō*	use jointly/in combination	107
併発	*heihatsu*	(medical) complications	96
併記	*heiki*	write side by side/on the same page	371

併 併 併

1163	亻 艹 冂 2a2 3k 2r			
	RIN – principle, code			
	倫理	*rinri*	ethics, morals	143
	倫理学	*rinrigaku*	ethics, moral philosophy	143, 109
	人倫	*jinrin*	humanity, morality	1
	不倫	*furin*	immoral, illicit	94
	絶倫	*zetsurin*	peerless, unsurpassed	742

倫 倫 倫

1164	車 艹 冂 7c 3k 2r			
	RIN, wa – wheel, ring, circle; (counter for flowers)			
	車輪	*sharin*	wheel	133
	輪番	*rinban*	taking turns, in rotation	185
	五輪(大会)	*gorin (taikai)*	the Olympic Games	7, 26, 158
	競輪	*keirin*	bicycle race	852
	指輪	*yubiwa*	(finger) ring	1041

輪 輪 輪

1165	丷 一 丨 2o 1a2 1b2			
	HEI, nara(bu) – be lined up; ***nara(beru)*** – arrange, put side by side; ***nara(bi ni)*** – and; ***nami*** – ordinary, average			
	並行	*heikō*	parallel	68
	並列	*heiretsu*	stand in a row; parataxis	611
	並木	*namiki*	row of trees, roadside trees	22
	平年並み	*heinennami*	as in an average/normal year	202, 45

並 並 並

1166	丷 日 一 2o 4c 1a2			
	FU – general, universal			
	普通	*futsū*	usual, ordinary	150
	普(通)選(挙)	*fu(tsū) sen(kyo)*	general elections	150, 800, 801
	普遍的	*fuhenteki*	universal, ubiquitous	1160, 210
	普請	*fushin*	building, construction	661
	普段	*fudan*	usual, ordinary, everyday	362

普 普 普

1167	言 日 丷 7a 4c 2o

譜

FU – (sheet) music, notes, staff, score; a genealogy; record

楽譜	*gakufu*	(written) notes, the score	358
譜面	*fumen*	sheet music, score	274
暗譜	*anpu*	learning the notes by heart	348
年譜	*nenpu*	chronological record	45
系譜	*keifu*	genealogical chart, family tree	908

譜 譜 譜

1168	雫 一 丨 8d 1a3 1b2

霊

REI, RYŌ, tama – soul, spirit

霊肉	*reiniku*	body and soul/spirit	223
亡霊	*bōrei*	soul/spirit of a dead person	672
聖霊	*seirei*	the Holy Spirit	674
霊園	*reien*	cemetery park	447
万物の霊長	*banbutsu no reichō*	crown of creation, man	16, 79, 95

霊 霊 霊

1169	氵 日 一 3a 4c 1a

湿

SHITSU, shime(ru) – become damp; ***shime(su)*** – moisten

湿気	*shikke*	moisture, humidity	134
湿度	*shitsudo*	humidity	377
湿地	*shitchi*	damp ground, bog	118
湿布	*shippu*	wet compress, poultice	675

湿 湿 湿

1170	頁 日 丨 9a 4c 1b2

顕

KEN – clear, plain obvious

露顕	*roken*	discovery, disclosure, exposure	951
顕著	*kencho*	notable, striking, marked	859
顕花植物	*kenka shokubutsu*	flowering plant	255, 424, 79

顕 顕 顕

1171	貝 7b	口 3s	一 1a

貴

KI, tatto(i), tōto(i) – valuable, noble; ***tatto(bu), tōto(bu)*** – value, esteem, respect

貴重	*kichō*	valuable, precious	227
貴重品	*kichōhin*	valuables	227, 230
貴族	*kizoku*	nobleman, the nobility	221
富貴	*fūki*	riches and honors, wealth and rank	713

1172	辶 2q	貝 7b	口 3s

遺

I, [YUI] – leave behind, bequeath

遺伝	*iden*	heredity	434
遺体	*itai*	corpse, the remains	61
遺産	*isan*	an inheritance, estate	278
遺族	*izoku*	family of the deceased, survivors	221
遺言	*yuigon*	will, last wishes	66

1173	辶 2q	口 3s	卩 3d2

遣

KEN, tsuka(wasu) – send; give; ***tsuka(u)*** – use

派遣	*haken*	dispatch, send (a person)	912
小遣い(銭)	*kozukai(sen)*	pocket money	27, 648
気遣い	*kizukai*	worry, apprehension	134
心遣い	*kokorozukai*	solicitude, consideration	97

1174	辶 2q	卩 3d2	ノ 1c

追

TSUI, o(u) – drive away; pursue

追放	*tsuihō*	banishment, purge	512
追求	*tsuikyū*	pursue, follow up	724
追加	*tsuika*	addition, supplement	709
追い風	*oikaze*	favorable/tail wind	29
追い越す	*oikosu*	overtake, pass	1001

1175 辶 日 ノ
2q 4c 1c

迫

HAKU, sema(ru) – press (someone) for, urge; approach, draw near

切迫	*seppaku*	draw near, press, be imminent	39
迫力	*hakuryoku*	force, power, impressiveness	100
迫害	*hakugai*	persecution	518
窮迫	*kyūhaku*	straitened circumstances, poverty	897

迫 迫 迫

1176 亻 日 ノ
2a 4c 1c

伯

HAKU – eldest brother (cf. No. 1667); count, earl

画伯	*gahaku*	great artist, master painter	343
伯父	*oji*	uncle (elder brother of a parent)	113
伯母	*oba*	aunt (elder sister of a parent)	112

伯 伯 伯

1177 氵 日 ノ
3a 4c 1c

泊

HAKU, to(maru/meru) – (intr./tr.) put up (for the night), lodge

宿泊	*shukuhaku*	lodging	179
一泊	*ippaku*	overnight stay	2
泊り賃	*tomarichin*	hotel charges	751
泊り客	*tomarikyaku*	house guest; (hotel) guest	641

泊 泊 泊

1178 扌 日 ノ
3c 4c 1c

拍

HAKU, HYŌ – beat (in music)

拍手	*hakushu*	handclapping, applause	57
拍車	*hakusha*	a spur	133
拍子	*hyōshi*	time, tempo; chance, the moment	103
拍子木	*hyōshigi*	wooden clappers	103, 22
脈拍	*myakuhaku*	pulse	913

拍 拍 拍

1179 亠 巾 冖 2j 3f 2i

帝

TEI – emperor

帝国	*teikoku*	empire	40
帝国主義	*teikoku shugi*	imperialism	40, 155, 291
帝政	*teisei*	imperial rule	483
皇帝	*kōtei*	emperor	297
カール大帝	*Kāru Taitei*	Charlemagne	26

帝 帝 帝

1180 糸 巾 冖 6a 3f 2i

締

TEI, shi(meru) – tie, tighten; ***shi(maru)*** – be shut; tighten

条約の締結	*jōyaku no teiketsu*	conclusion of a treaty	654, 211, 485
取り締まり	*torishimari*	control, supervision	65
締め切り	*shimekiri*	closing (date), deadline	39
引き締める	*hikishimeru*	tighten, stiffen	216

締 締 締

1181 言 方 7a 4h

訪

HŌ, tazu(neru), otozu(reru) – visit

訪問	*hōmon*	visit	162
来訪	*raihō*	visit	69
訪日	*hōnichi*	visit to Japan	5
訪客	*hōkyaku*	visitor, guest	641
探訪	*tanbō*	making inquiries, inquiring into	535

訪 訪 訪

1182 女 方 3e 4h

妨

BŌ, samata(geru) – prevent, obstruct, hamper

妨害	*bōgai*	obstruction, disturbance, interference	518

妨 妨 妨

1183 亻 方 亠 2a 4h 2j

傍

BŌ, katawa(ra) – side

傍観	*bōkan*	look on, remain a spectator	604
傍聴	*bōchō*	hearing, attendance	1039
傍系	*bōkei*	collateral (descendant)	908
傍証	*bōshō*	supporting evidence, corroboration	484
傍受	*bōju*	intercept, monitor (a radio message)	260

傍 傍 傍

1184 亠 口 冖 2j 3d 2i

亭

TEI – restaurant, pavilion, arbor

亭主	*teishu*	host; innkeeper; husband	155
料亭	*ryōtei*	(Japanese) restaurant	319

亭 亭 亭

1185 亻 口 亠 2a 3d 2j

停

TEI – stop

停止	*teishi*	suspension, stopping	477
停滞	*teitai*	stagnation, accumulation	964
調停	*chōtei*	mediation, arbitration	342
停留所	*teiryūjo*	(bus/streetcar) stop	761, 153
各駅停車	*kakueki teisha*	a local (train)	642, 284, 133

停 停 停

1186 車 宀 口 7c 3m 3d

轄

KATSU – a wedge; control, administration

管轄	*kankatsu*	jurisdiction, competence	328
管轄官庁	*kankatsu kanchō*	the proper authorities	328, 326, 763
所轄	*shokatsu*	jurisdiction	153
統轄	*tōkatsu*	supervision, general control	830
直轄	*chokkatsu*	direct control/jurisdiction	423

轄 轄 轄

1187	車 十 一 7c 2k 1a		
軒	***KEN*** – (counter for buildings); ***noki*** – eaves		
一軒	*ikken*	1 house	2
軒数	*kensū*	number of houses	225
軒並	*nokinami*	row of houses	1165
軒先	*nokisaki*	edge of the eaves; front of the house	50

軒 軒 軒

1188	氵 十 一 3a 2k 1a		
汗	***KAN, ase*** – sweat		
発汗	*hakkan*	perspire, sweat	96
冷汗	*reikan, hiyaase*	a cold sweat	832
汗顔	*kangan*	sweating from shame	277

汗 汗 汗

1189	日 十 亻 4c 2k3 2a		
幹	***KAN*** – main part; ***miki*** – (tree) trunk		
幹部	*kanbu*	key officers, executives, management	86
幹事長	*kanjichō*	executive secretary, secretary-general	80, 95
根幹	*konkan*	basis, root, nucleus	314
語幹	*gokan*	stem of a word	67
新幹線	*Shinkansen*	New Trunk Line, bullet train	174, 299

幹 幹 幹

1190	日 十 一 4c 2k2 1a2		
乾	***KAN, kawa(ku/kasu)*** – (intr./tr.) dry, dry out		
乾季	*kanki*	the dry season	465
乾電池	*kandenchi*	dry cell, battery	108, 119
乾物	*kanbutsu*	dry provisions, groceries	79
乾杯	*kanpai*	a toast; Cheers!	1155

乾 乾 乾

1191	糸 日 巾 (6a 4c 3f)			
綿	**MEN, wata** – cotton			
	木綿	*momen*	cotton	22
	綿布	*menpu*	cotton (cloth)	675
	綿織物	*men'orimono*	cotton fabrics, cotton goods	680, 79
	海綿	*kaimen*	a sponge	117
	綿密	*menmitsu*	minute, close, meticulous	806

綿 綿 綿

1192	日 氵 ノ (4c 3a 1c)			
泉	**SEN, izumi** – spring, fountainhead, fountain			
	温泉	*onsen*	hot spring, spa	634
	冷泉	*reisen*	cold mineral spring	832
	泉水	*sensui*	garden pond, fountain	21
	源泉	*gensen*	fountainhead, source	580
	平泉	*Hiraizumi*	(town in Tohoku)	202

泉 泉 泉

1193	一 艹 一 ((1a2) 3k 1a)			
井	**SEI, [SHŌ], i** – a well			
	井泉	*seisen*	a well	1192
	油井	*yusei*	oil well	364
	天井	*tenjō*	ceiling	141
	井戸	*ido*	a well	152
	軽井沢	*Karuizawa*	(summer resort town NW of Tokyo)	547, 994

井 井 井

1194	囗 艹 一 (3s 3k 1a)			
囲	**I, kako(mu/u)** – surround, enclose; lay siege to			
	範囲	*han'i*	extent, scope, range	1092
	周囲	*shūi*	circumference, surroundings	91
	包囲	*hōi*	encirclement, siege	804
	取り囲む	*torikakomu*	surround, enclose; besiege	65

囲 囲 囲

1195 囚 口 亻 3s 2a

SHŪ – arrest, imprison, prisoner

囚人	*shūjin*	prisoner, convict	1
未決囚	*miketsushū*	unconvicted prisoner	306, 356
死刑囚	*shikeishū*	criminal sentenced to death	85, 887
女囚	*joshū*	female prisoner	102
免囚	*menshū*	released prisoner, ex-convict	733

囚 囚 囚

1196 耕 一 木 艹 (1a5) 4a 3k

KŌ, tagaya(su) – till, plow, cultivate

耕地	*kōchi*	arable land, cultivated land	118
耕作	*kōsaku*	cultivation, farming	360
農耕	*nōkō*	agriculture, farming	369

耕 耕 耕

1197 耗 一 木 丨 (1a5) 4a 1b

MŌ, [KŌ] – decrease

消耗	*shōmō*	consumption, wear and tear	845
損耗	*sonmō*	wear, wastage, loss	350
心神耗弱(者)	*shinshin kō/mō-jaku(sha)*	feebleminded (person)	97, 310, 218, 164

耗 耗 耗

1198 籍 ⺮ 木 日 6f 4a 4c

SEKI – (family) register

戸籍	*koseki*	census registration	152
本籍	*honseki*	one's domicile, legal residence	25
除籍	*joseki*	removal from the register	1065
国籍	*kokuseki*	nationality	40
書籍	*shoseki*	books	131

籍 籍 籍

1199 金 日 艹 8a 4c 3k

錯

SAKU – mix, be in disorder

錯覚	*sakkaku*	illusion	605
錯誤	*sakugo*	error	906
錯乱	*sakuran*	distraction, derangement	689
交錯	*kōsaku*	mixture; intricacy	114
倒錯	*tōsaku*	perversion	905

錯 錯 錯

1200 扌 日 艹 3c 4c 3k

措

SO – give up, discontinue, set aside

措置	*sochi*	measures, steps	426
報復措置	*hōfuku sochi*	retaliatory measures	685, 917, 426

措 措 措

1201 扌 王 一 3c 4f 1a

拝

HAI, oga(mu) – pray, venerate

参拝	*sanpai*	visit (a shrine/grave)	710
礼拝	*reihai*	worship, (church) services	620
拝見	*haiken*	see, have a look at	63
拝借	*haishaku*	borrow	766
拝み倒す	*ogamitaosu*	entreat (someone) into consent	905

拝 拝 拝

1202 木 門 日 4a2 8e 4c

欄

RAN – (newspaper) column; railing

家庭欄	*kateiran*	home-life section	165, 1112
投書欄	*tōshoran*	letters-to-the-editor column	1021, 131
欄外	*rangai*	margin (of a page)	83
空欄	*kūran*	blank column/space	140
欄干	*rankan*	railing, banister	584

欄 欄 欄

1203 氵 門 王 3a 8e 4f

潤

JUN, uruo(su) – moisten, wet, water; profit, enrich; ***uruo(u)*** – become wet; profit, become rich; ***uru(mu)*** – become wet/blurred/turbid/clouded

浸潤	*shinjun*	permeation, infiltration	1078
利潤	*rijun*	profits	329
潤飾/色	*junshoku*	embellishment	979, 204

潤 潤 潤

1204 氵 口 ⺌ 3a 3d 3n

涼

RYŌ, suzu(shii) – cool, refreshing; ***suzu(mu)*** – cool off, enjoy the evening cool

清涼飲料	*seiryō inryō*	carbonated beverage	660, 323, 319
涼味	*ryōmi*	the cool, coolness	307
涼風	*ryōfū*	cool breeze	29
夕涼み	*yūsuzumi*	the evening cool	81

涼 涼 涼

1205 冫 木 日 2b 4a 4c

凍

TŌ, kō(ru) – freeze (up); ***kogo(eru)*** – become frozen/numb

冷凍器	*reitōki*	refrigerator, freezer	832, 527
凍結	*tōketsu*	freeze (assets)	485
凍傷	*tōshō*	frostbite	633
凍死	*tōshi*	freeze to death	85
凍え死に	*kogoejini*	freeze to death	85

凍 凍 凍

1206 氵 丶 3a 1d

氷

HYŌ, kōri, hi – ice; ***kō(ru)*** – freeze (up)

氷山	*hyōzan*	iceberg	34
氷河	*hyōga*	glacier	389
流氷	*ryūhyō*	floating ice, ice floe	247
氷点(下)	*hyōten(ka)*	(below) the freezing point	169, 31
氷結	*hyōketsu*	freeze (over)	485

氷 氷 氷

1207 氵 丶 3a 1d

永

EI, naga(i) – long (time)

永住	*eijū*	permanent residence	156
永遠	*eien*	eternity	446
永眠	*eimin*	eternal sleep, death	849
永続	*eizoku*	permanence, perpetuity	243
永田町	*Nagatachō*	(area of Tokyo)	35, 182

永 永 永

1208 氵 丶 3a2 1d

泳

EI, oyo(gu) – swim

水泳	*suiei*	swimming	21
競泳	*kyōei*	swimming race	852
泳法	*eihō*	swimming style/stroke	123
遠泳	*en'ei*	long-distance swim	446
平泳ぎ	*hiraoyogi*	the breaststroke	202

泳 泳 泳

1209 言 氵 丶 7a 3a 1d

詠

EI, yo(mu) – compose, write (a poem)

詠歌	*eika*	composition of a poem; (Buddhist) chant	392
詠草	*eisō*	draft of a poem	249

詠 詠 詠

1210 𠂊 丶 2n 1d

久

KYŪ, [KU], hisa(shii) – long (time)

永久	*eikyū*	permanence, perpetuity, eternity	1207
長久	*chōkyū*	long continuance, eternity	95
持久	*jikyū*	endurance, persistence	451
久遠	*kuon*	eternity	446
久し振り	*hisashiburi*	(after) a long time	954

久 久 久

1211 刂 亠 亻 2f 2j 2a

刻

KOKU, kiza(mu) – cut fine, chop up; carve, engrave

彫刻	*chōkoku*	sculpture	1149
深刻	*shinkoku*	grave, serious	536
時刻	*jikoku*	time	42
一刻	*ikkoku*	moment; stubborn	2
夕刻	*yūkoku*	evening	81

刻 刻 刻

1212 木 亠 亻 4a 2j 2a

核

KAKU – core, nucleus

核心	*kakushin*	core, kernel	97
原子核	*genshikaku*	(atomic) nucleus	136, 103
核燃料	*kakunenryō*	nuclear fuel	652, 319
核兵器	*kakuheiki*	nuclear weapons	784, 527
結核	*kekkaku*	tuberculosis	485

核 核 核

1213 言 亠 亻 7a 2j 2a

該

GAI – (prefix) the said

当該官庁	*tōgai kanchō*	relevant authorities	77, 326, 763
当該人物	*tōgai jinbutsu*	the said person	77, 1, 79
該当	*gaitō*	pertain (to), come/fall under	77
該博な知識	*gaihaku na chishiki*	profound/vast learning	601, 214, 681

該 該 該

1214 言 彡 亻 7a 3j 2a

診

SHIN, mi(ru) – diagnose, examine

診察	*shinsatsu*	medical examination	619
検診	*kenshin*	medical examination	531
診断	*shindan*	diagnosis	1024
打診	*dashin*	percussion, tapping; sound out	1020
往診	*ōshin*	doctor's visit to a patient, house call	918

診 診 診

1215 王 彡 亻 4f 3j 2a

珍

CHIN, mezura(shii) – rare, unusual

珍品	*chinpin*	a rarity, curiosity	230
珍談	*chindan*	amusing story, anecdote	593
珍味	*chinmi*	a delicacy	307
珍重	*chinchō*	value highly, prize	227
珍客	*chinkyaku*	least-expected/welcome visitor	641

珍 珍 珍

1216 日 丨 4c 1b

旧

KYŪ – old, former

旧式	*kyūshiki*	old-type, old-fashioned	525
復旧	*fukkyū*	recovery, restoration	917
新旧	*shinkyū*	old and new	174
旧悪	*kyūaku*	one's past misdeed	304
旧約(聖書)	*Kyūyaku (Seisho)*	Old Testament	211, 674, 131

旧 旧 旧

1217 日 丷 丨 4c 2o 1b

児

JI, [NI] – small child, infant

児童	*jidō*	child, juvenile	410
育児園	*ikujien*	daycare nursery	246, 447
産児制限	*sanji seigen*	birth control	278, 427, 847
乳児	*nyūji*	(nursing) baby, infant	939
小児科医	*shōnikai*	pediatrician	27, 320, 220

児 児 児

1218 阝 日 ⺈ 2d 4c 2n

陥

KAN, ochii(ru) – fall, get, run (into); fall, be reduced; **otoshii(reru)** – ensnare, entice; capture

欠陥	*kekkan*	defect, shortcoming	383
陥落	*kanraku*	fall, capitulation	839
陥没	*kanbotsu*	depression, subsidence, cave-in	935
陥せい	*kansei*	pitfall, trap, plot	

陥 陥 陥

1219	心 4k	日 4c	十 2k

恵

KEI, E, megu(mu) – bestow a favor, bless

天恵	*tenkei*	gift of nature, natural advantage	141
恩恵	*onkei*	benefit, favor	555
互恵	*gokei*	mutual benefit, reciprocity	907
知恵	*chie*	wisdom, sense, brains, intelligence	214
知恵者	*chiesha*	wise/resourceful man	214, 164

恵 恵 恵

1220	禾 5d	日 4c	丷 3n

稲

TŌ, ine, [ina-] – rice plant

水稲	*suitō*	paddy rice	21
稲作	*inasaku*	rice crop	360
稲荷	*Inari*	god of harvests, fox deity	391
早稲	*wase*	(early-ripening variety of rice)	248
早稲田	*Waseda*	(area of Tokyo)	248, 35

稲 稲 稲

1221	禾 5d	日 4c	心 4k

穂

SUI, ho – ear, head (of grain)

稲穂	*inaho*	ear of rice	1220
穂先	*hosaki*	tip of an ear/spear/knife/brush	50
穂波	*honami*	waves of grain	666

穂 穂 穂

1222	艹 3k	禾 5d	囗 3s

菌

KIN – fungus, germ, bacteria

細菌	*saikin*	bacteria	695
保菌者	*hokinsha*	(germ) carrier	489, 164
殺菌	*sakkin*	sterilization	576
無菌	*mukin*	germ-free, sterilized	93
抗菌性	*kōkinsei*	antibacterial	824, 98

菌 菌 菌

1223 亠 田 ノ 2j 5f 1c2

畜

CHIKU – animal raising; domestic animals

家畜	*kachiku*	domestic animal, livestock	165
畜産	*chikusan*	stock raising	278
牧畜業	*bokuchikugyō*	stock farming, cattle	731, 279
畜舎	*chikusha*	cattle shed, barn	791
畜生	*chikushō*	beast, brute; Dammit!	44

畜 畜 畜

1224 艹 田 亠 3k 5f 2j

蓄

CHIKU, takuwa(eru) – store, save, put aside

貯蓄	*chochiku*	savings, saving	762
備蓄	*bichiku*	saving for emergencies, storing	768
蓄積	*chikuseki*	accumulation	656
蓄電池	*chikudenchi*	storage battery	108, 119

蓄 蓄 蓄

1225 亠 ノ 丶 2j 1c2 1d

玄

GEN – dark, mystery

玄関	*genkan*	entranceway	398
玄関番	*genkanban*	doorkeeper, doorman, porter	398, 185
玄米	*genmai*	unpolished/brown rice	224
玄人	*kurōto*	expert, professional, specialist	1

玄 玄 玄

1226 弓 亠 ノ 3h 2j 1c2

弦

GEN, tsuru – string; bowstring

弦楽器	*gengakki*	string instrument, the strings	358, 527
管弦楽(団)	*kangengaku(dan)*	orchestra	328, 358, 491
正弦曲線	*seigen kyokusen*	sine curve	275, 366, 299
上弦	*jōgen*	first quarter (of the moon)	32
下弦	*kagen*	last quarter (of the moon)	31

弦 弦 弦

1227	一 ノ 丶 1a 1c2 1d	***GEN, maboroshi*** – illusion, phantom, vision		
幻	幻覚	*genkaku*	hallucination	605
	幻影	*gen'ei*	vision, phantom, illusion	854
	幻想	*gensō*	fantasy, illusion	147
	夢幻	*mugen*	dreams and phantasms	811

幻 幻 幻

1228	山 ノ 丶 3o 1c4 1d2	***YŪ*** – quiet, deep		
幽	幽玄	*yūgen*	the profound, occult	1225
	幽霊	*yūrei*	ghost	1168
	幽閉	*yūhei*	confinement, imprisonment	397
	幽谷	*yūkoku*	deep ravine, narrow valley	653
	幽門	*yūmon*	pylorus	161

幽 幽 幽

1229	力 ノ 丶 2g 1c2 1d	***YŌ, osana(i)*** – very young; infantile, childish		
幼	幼児	*yōji*	baby, small child, tot	1217
	幼少	*yōshō*	infancy, childhood	144
	幼虫	*yōchū*	larva	873
	幼子	*osanago*	little child	103
	幼心	*osanagokoro*	child's mind/heart	97

幼 幼 幼

1230	禾 隹 5d 8c	***CHI*** – child		
稚	幼稚園	*yōchien*	kindergarten	1229, 447
	稚気	*chiki*	childlike state of mind	134
	稚児	*chigo*	child; child in a Buddhist procession	1217

稚 稚 稚

1231 糸 隹 6a 8c

維

I – tie, rope

維持	*iji*	maintenance, support	451
維持費	*ijihi*	upkeep expenses	451, 749
明治維新	*Meiji Ishin*	Meiji Restoration	18, 493, 174

維 維 維

1232 冫 隹 2b 8c

准

JUN – apply correspondingly, imitate, pattern after

批准	*hijun*	ratify	1029

准 准 准

1233 扌 隹 3c 8c

推

SUI, o(su) – infer, deduce; recommend, propose

推定	*suitei*	presumption, inference	355
推論	*suiron*	reasoning, inference	293
推理	*suiri*	reasoning, inference	143
類推	*ruisui*	(inference by) analogy	226
推進	*suishin*	propulsion, drive	437

推 推 推

1234 口 隹 3d 8c

唯

YUI, [I] – solely, only, merely

唯物論	*yuibutsuron*	materialism	79, 293
唯心論	*yuishinron*	spiritualism, idealism	97, 293
唯理論	*yuiriron*	rationalism	143, 293
唯美主義	*yuibi shugi*	estheticism	401, 155, 291
唯一	*yuiitsu*	the only, sole	2

唯 唯 唯

1235 ⺮ 亻 一 6f 2a 1a

笑

SHŌ, wara(u) – laugh, smile; ***e(mu)*** – smile

苦笑	*kushō*	wry smile, forced laugh	545
冷笑	*reishō*	scornful laugh, sneer	832
談笑	*danshō*	friendly talk, chat	593
大笑い	*ōwarai*	loud laughter, hearty laugh	26
笑顔	*egao*	smiling face	277

笑 笑 笑

1236 氵 立 3a 5b

泣

KYŪ, na(ku) – cry

感泣	*kankyū*	be moved to tears	262
号泣	*gōkyū*	wailing, lamentation	266
泣き声	*nakigoe*	tearful voice, sob, whimper	746
泣き落とす	*nakiotosu*	obtain (someone's) consent by tears	839
泣き虫	*nakimushi*	crybaby	873

泣 泣 泣

1237 戸 方 4m 4h

房

BŌ – a room; tassel; ***fusa*** – tassel, tuft, cluster

暖房	*danbō*	heating	635
独房	*dokubō*	solitary (prison) cell	219
官房長(官)	*kanbōchō(kan)*	chief secretary	326, 95
文房具	*bunbōgu*	stationery	111, 420
女房	*nyōbō*	(one's own) wife	102

房 房 房

1238 戸 亻 一 4m 2a 1a

戻

REI, modo(ru) – go/come back, return; ***modo(su)*** – give/send back, return, restore; throw up, vomit

取り戻す	*torimodosu*	regain	65
払い戻す	*haraimodosu*	pay back, refund	582
差し戻す	*sashimodosu*	send back (to a lower court)	658
逆戻り	*gyakumodori*	going backward, retrogression	444

戻 戻 戻

1239 氵 戸 亻 (3a 4m 2a)

涙

RUI, namida – teardrop

感涙	*kanrui*	tears of strong emotion	262
血涙	*ketsurui*	tears of blood, bitter tears	789
空涙	*soranamida*	false/crocodile tears	140
涙声	*namidagoe*	tearful voice	746
涙ぐましい	*namidagumashii*	touching, moving	

涙 涙 涙

1240 口 土 刂 (3d 3b 2f)

喫

KITSU – eat, drink, smoke

喫茶店	*kissaten*	teahouse, café	251, 168
喫煙	*kitsuen*	smoking	919
満喫	*mankitsu*	eat/drink one's fill, enjoy fully	201
喫する	*kissuru*	eat, drink, smoke	

喫 喫 喫

1241 氵 糸 土 (3a 6a 3b)

潔

KETSU – pure; ***isagiyo(i)*** – brave, manly, righteous, pure

清潔	*seiketsu*	clean, neat	660
純潔	*junketsu*	pure, chaste	965
潔白	*keppaku*	pure, upright, of integrity	205
高潔	*kōketsu*	noble, lofty, high-minded	190
不潔	*fuketsu*	impure, unclean, filthy	94

潔 潔 潔

1242 心 目 ノ (4k 5c 1c)

息

SOKU – son; breath; ***iki*** – breath

休息	*kyūsoku*	a rest, breather	60
消息	*shōsoku*	news, information	845
利息	*risoku*	interest (on a loan)	329
息切れ	*ikigire*	shortness of breath	39
息子	*musuko*	son	103

息 息 息

1243 心 日 口 4k 5c 3d

憩

KEI, iko(i) – rest; ***iko(u)*** – rest

休憩	*kyūkei*	rest, recess	60
休憩所	*kyūkeijo*	resting place, lobby	60, 153
休憩時間	*kyūkei jikan*	rest period, recess	60, 42, 43
小/少憩	*shōkei*	brief recess, a break	27, 144

1244 目 亻 一 5c 2a 1a

臭

SHŪ, kusa(i) – foul-smelling, smelling of

臭気	*shūki*	offensive odor, stink	134
悪臭	*akushū*	bad odor, stench	304
俗臭	*zokushū*	low taste, vulgarity	1126
古臭い	*furukusai*	old, outdated; trite, hackneyed	172
かび臭い	*kabikusai*	musty, moldy	

1245 广 亻 冂 3q 2a3 2r

腐

FU, kusa(ru/reru) – rot, go bad, spoil, turn sour; ***kusa(rasu)*** – spoil, rot, putrefy, corrode

豆腐	*tōfu*	tofu, bean curd	958
腐食	*fushoku*	corrosion	322
腐敗	*fuhai*	decomposition, decay; corruption	511
腐心	*fushin*	take pains, be intent on	97

1246 口 艹 囗 3d 3k 3s

嘆

TAN, nage(ku) – grieve, lament, bemoan; deplore, regret; ***nage(kawashii)*** – deplorable, regrettable

感嘆	*kantan*	admiration, exclamation	262
嘆願	*tangan*	entreaty, petition	581
嘆息	*tansoku*	sigh; lament	1242
悲嘆	*hitan*	grief, sorrow, lamentation	1034

1247	言 艹 口 7a 3k 3s	**KIN, tsutsushi(mu)** – be respectful		
謹	謹聴	*kinchō*	listen attentively	1039
	謹賀新年	*kinga shinnen*	Happy New Year.	756, 174, 45
	謹言	*kingen*	Sincerely/Respectfully yours,	66
	謹んで	*tsutsushinde*	respectfully, humbly	

1248	口 一 丨 3d 1a 1b	**HI, ina** – no		
否	否定	*hitei*	denial, negation	355
	否認	*hinin*	denial, repudiation, disavow	738
	否決	*hiketsu*	rejection, voting down	356
	賛否	*sanpi*	approval or disapproval, yes or no	745
	安否	*anpi*	how (someone) is getting on	105

1249	亻 口 一 2a 3d 1a2	**GAN, fuku(mu)** – hold in one's mouth; bear in mind; contain, include; **fuku(meru)** – include; give instructions		
含	含蓄	*ganchiku*	significance, implication	1224
	包含	*hōgan*	include, cover, imply	804
	含有	*gan'yū*	contain	265

1250	口 亻 一 3d 2a 1a2	**GIN** – sing, chant, recite		
吟	独吟	*dokugin*	(vocal) solo	219
	詩吟	*shigin*	recitation of Chinese poems	570
	吟詠	*gin'ei*	sing, recite; compose a poem	1209
	吟味	*ginmi*	close inquiry, scrutiny	307

1251 琴

王 亻 一 — 4f2 2a 1a2

KIN, koto – koto, Japanese zither

心の琴線	*kokoro no kinsen*	heartstrings	97, 299
木琴	*mokkin*	xylophone	22
風琴	*fūkin*	organ, harmonium	29
手風琴	*tefūkin*	accordion, concertina	57, 29
たて琴	*tategoto*	harp, lyre	

1252 叫

口 十 丨 — 3d 2k 1b

KYŌ, sake(bu) – shout, cry out

絶叫	*zekkyō*	scream, exclamation	742
叫び声	*sakebigoe*	a shout, cry, scream	746

1253 吐

口 土 — 3d 3b

TO, ha(ku) – spew, vomit, throw up; express, give vent to

吐血	*toketsu*	vomit blood	789
吐息	*toiki*	a sigh	1242
吐露	*toro*	express, voice, speak out	951
吐き気	*hakike*	nausea	134
吐き出す	*hakidasu*	vomit, disgorge, spew out	53

1254 呼

口 十 ノ — 3d 2k 1c2

KO, yo(bu) – call, send for, invite, name

点呼	*tenko*	roll call	169
呼応	*koō*	act in concert	827
呼び声	*yobigoe*	a call, cry, shout	746
呼び出す	*yobidasu*	page, call (on the telephone/a loudspeaker)	53
呼び戻す	*yobimodosu*	call back, recall	1238

1255	口 3d	欠 4j	
吹	***SUI, fu(ku)*** – blow		
	鼓吹	*kosui*	inspire, instill	1147
	吹雪	*fubuki*	snowstorm	949
	吹き込む	*fukikomu*	blow in; record (a song); inspire	776
	吹き飛ぶ	*fukitobu*	be blown away	530
	吹き出物	*fukidemono*	skin rash, spots, pimple	53, 79

吹 吹 吹

1256	口 3d	亻 2a	一 1a
吸	***KYŪ, su(u)*** – suck in, inhale; smoke		
	呼吸	*kokyū*	breathing	1254
	吸入	*kyūnyū*	inhale	52
	吸引	*kyūin*	absorb (by suction)	216
	吸収	*kyūshū*	absorb	757
	吸い取り紙	*suitorigami*	blotting paper	65, 180

吸 吸 吸

1257	亻 2a	一 1a	
及	***KYŪ, oyo(bu)*** – reach, amount to, extend to, match, equal; ***oyo(bosu)*** – exert; ***oyo(bi)*** – and, as well as		
	普及	*fukyū*	spread, come into wide use	1166
	及第点	*kyūdaiten*	passing mark/grade	404, 169
	言及	*genkyū*	refer to, mention	66
	言い及ぶ	*iioyobu*	refer to, touch upon	66

及 及 及

1258	扌 3c	亻 2a	一 1a
扱	***atsuka(u)*** – handle		
	取り扱う	*toriatsukau*	treat, deal with, handle	65
	取り扱い方	*toriatsukaikata*	how to handle	65, 70
	取(り)扱(い)注意	*toriatsukai chūi*	Handle with Care	65, 357, 132
	客扱い	*kyakuatsukai*	hospitality, service to customers	641

扱 扱 扱

1259 舌

口 3d　十 2k　ノ 1c

ZETSU, shita – tongue

舌戦	*zessen*	verbal warfare, war of words	301
弁舌	*benzetsu*	eloquence, tongue, speech	711
毒舌	*dokuzetsu*	venomous tongue, malicious remarks	522
二枚舌	*nimaijita*	forked tongue, duplicity	3, 1156
舌打ち	*shitauchi*	clicking one's tongue, tsk, tch	1020

舌 舌 舌

1260 括

扌 3c　口 3d　十 2k

KATSU – tie together, fasten

一括	*ikkatsu*	lump together, summarize	2
包括的	*hōkatsuteki*	comprehensive, general, sweeping	804, 210
総括	*sōkatsu*	generalization, summarization	697

括 括 括

1261 絹

糸 6a　月 4b　口 3d

KEN, kinu – silk

人絹	*jinken*	artificial silk, rayon	1
絹布	*kenpu*	silk fabric, silk	675
絹糸	*kenshi, kinuito*	silk thread	242
絹織物	*kinuorimono*	silk fabrics	680, 79
絹針	*kinubari*	needle for silk	341

絹 絹 絹

1262 肯

月 4b　卜 2m　一 1a

KŌ – agree to, consent

肯定	*kōtei*	affirmation, affirmative	355
首肯	*shukō*	assent, consent	148

肯 肯 肯

1263 力月 2g3 4b

脅

KYŌ, obiya(kasu), odo(kasu/su) – threaten

脅迫	*kyōhaku*	threat, intimidation	1175
脅迫状	*kyōhakujō*	threatening letter	1175, 626
脅し文句	*odoshimonku*	threatening words	111, 337

1264 戸月 4m 4b

肩

KEN, kata – shoulder

肩章	*kenshō*	epaulet, shoulder pips	857
比肩	*hiken*	rank (with), be comparable (to)	798
肩書き	*katagaki*	one's title, degree	131
肩代わり	*katagawari*	take-over, transfer (of business)	256
肩身が広い	*katami ga hiroi*	feel proud	59, 694

1265 月 ⺊ 一 4b 2m 1a

背

HAI, se – back; height; **sei** – height, stature; **somu(ku)** – act contrary (to); **somu(keru)** – avert, turn away

背景	*haikei*	background	853
背信	*haishin*	breach of faith, betrayal, infidelity	157
背中	*senaka*	the back	28
背広	*sebiro*	business suit	694

1266 月 冂 冖 4b 2r 2i

骨

KOTSU, hone – bone

骨格	*kokkaku*	skeleton, framework	643
頭骨	*tōkotsu*	skull	276
骨子	*kosshi*	essential part, main points	103
鉄骨	*tekkotsu*	steel frame	312
骨惜しみ	*honeoshimi*	avoid effort, spare oneself	765

1267 氵 月 冖 (3a 4b 2i)

滑

KATSU, sube(ru) – slide, glide; slip; ***name(raka)*** – smooth

滑走路	*kassōro*	runway	429, 151
潤滑油	*junkatsuyu*	lubricating oil	1203, 364
円滑	*enkatsu*	smooth, harmonious, amicable	13
滑り台	*suberidai*	(playground) slide	492

滑 滑 滑

1268 田 月 (5f 4b)

胃

I – stomach

胃病	*ibyō*	stomach disorder/trouble	380
胃酸	*isan*	stomach acid	516
胃弱	*ijaku*	weak digestion, indigestion, dyspepsia	218
胃下垂	*ikasui*	gastric ptosis	31, 1070
胃がん	*igan*	stomach cancer	

胃 胃 胃

1269 ⺊ 田 月 (2m 5f 4b)

膚

FU – the skin

皮膚	*hifu*	the skin	975
皮膚病	*hifubyō*	skin disease	975, 380
皮膚移植	*hifu ishoku*	skin graft/transplant	975, 1121, 424
完膚なきまで	*kanpu-naki made*	thoroughly, completely	613

膚 膚 膚

1270 月 日 一 (4b 4c 1a)

腸

CHŌ – intestines, entrails

胃腸	*ichō*	stomach and intestines	1268
大腸	*daichō*	large intestine, colon	26
腸閉そく	*chōheisoku*	intestinal obstruction, ileus	397
腸ねん転	*chōnenten*	twist in the intestines, volvulus	433
断腸の思い	*danchō no omoi*	heartrending grief	1024, 99

腸 腸 腸

1271	月 日 夂 4b 4c 4i	***FUKU, hara*** – belly; heart, mind		
腹	切腹	*seppuku*	hara-kiri	39
	立腹	*rippuku*	anger, offense	121
	空腹	*kūfuku*	empty belly, hunger	140
	腹巻き	*haramaki*	belly/stomach band	507
	太っ腹	*futoppara*	magnanimous; bold, daring	629

1272	月 十 一 4b 2k 1a	***KAN, kimo*** – liver; heart, spirit		
肝	肝硬変	*kankōhen*	cirrhosis of the liver	1009, 257
	肝油	*kan'yu*	cod-liver oil	364
	肝要	*kan'yō*	important, vital	419
	肝心	*kanjin*	main, vital, essential	97
	肝っ玉	*kimottama*	pluck, courage, grit	295

1273	月 日 一 4b 4c 1a	***TAN*** – gallbladder; courage		
胆	胆石	*tanseki*	gallstone	78
	大胆	*daitan*	bold, daring	26
	胆力	*tanryoku*	courage, mettle	100
	落胆	*rakutan*	discouragement, disappointment	839

1274	扌 日 一 3c 4c 1a	***TAN, katsu(gu)*** – carry on the shoulder; choose (someone); trick (someone); ***nina(u)*** – carry on the shoulder; bear, take on		
担	担当	*tantō*	being in charge, overseeing	77
	担任	*tannin*	charge, responsibility	334
	負担	*futan*	burden, load, liability	510
	担保	*tanpo*	a security, guarantee	489

1275 忄 日 一 (4k 4c 1a2)

恒

KŌ – always

恒久	*kōkyū*	permanence, perpetuity	1210
恒星	*kōsei*	fixed star, sidereal	730
恒心	*kōshin*	constancy, steadfastness	97
恒例	*kōrei*	established practice, custom	612
恒常	*kōjō*	constancy	497

恒 恒 恒

1276 土 日 一 (3b 4c 1a2)

垣

kaki – fence, hedge

石垣	*ishigaki*	stone wall	78
竹垣	*takegaki*	bamboo fence	129
生け垣	*ikegaki*	hedge	44
垣根	*kakine*	fence, hedge	314
垣間見る	*kaimamiru*	peek in, get a glimpse	43, 63

垣 垣 垣

1277 月 巾 亠 (4b 3f 2j)

肺

HAI – lung

肺病	*haibyō*	lung/pulmonary disease	380
肺結核	*haikekkaku*	pulmonary tuberculosis	485, 1212
肺がん	*haigan*	lung cancer	
肺活量	*haikatsuryō*	lung capacity	237, 411
肺肝	*haikan*	lungs and liver; one's innermost heart	1272

肺 肺 肺

1278 月 ⺍ 丨 (4b 3n 1b2)

脳

NŌ – brain

頭脳	*zunō*	brains, intelligence	276
脳下垂体	*nō kasuitai*	pituitary gland	31, 1070, 61
脳卒中	*nōsotchū*	cerebral hemorrhage	787, 28
洗脳	*sennō*	brainwashing	692
首脳会談	*shunō kaidan*	summit conference	148, 158, 593

脳 脳 脳

1279 心 ⺍ 丨 4k 3n 1b2

悩

NŌ, naya(mu) – be troubled, be distressed, suffer; **naya(masu)** – afflict, beset, worry

苦悩	*kunō*	affliction, distress, agony	545
悩殺	*nōsatsu*	enchant, captivate	576
伸び悩む	*nobinayamu*	continue stagnant, level off	1108
恋の悩み	*koi no nayami*	the torments of love	258

悩 悩 悩

1280 丨 ノ 丶 1b2 1c 1d

凶

KYŌ – evil, misfortune

凶作	*kyōsaku*	bad harvest	360
凶行	*kyōkō*	violence, crime, murder	68
凶悪	*kyōaku*	heinous, brutal	304
凶器	*kyōki*	murder/lethal weapon	527
吉凶	*kikkyō*	good or ill luck, fortune	1141

凶 凶 凶

1281 隹 亠 冂 8c 2j 2r

離

RI, hana(reru) – separate, leave; **hana(su)** – separate, keep apart

分離	*bunri*	separation, secession, segregation	38
離婚	*rikon*	divorce	567
離反	*rihan*	estrangement, alienation, breakaway	324
離陸	*ririku*	(airplane) takeoff	647
切り離す	*kirihanasu*	cut off, sever	39

離 離 離

1282 刂 ノ 丶 2f 1c 1d

刈

ka(ru) – cut (hair), clip, mow

刈り入れ	*kariire*	harvest, reaping	52
稲刈り	*inekari*	rice reaping/harvesting	1220
刈り取る	*karitoru*	mow, cut down	65
刈り込む	*karikomu*	cut, trim, prune	776
芝刈り機	*shibakariki*	lawn mower	250, 528

刈 刈 刈

1283	月 一 丨 4b 1a 1b2	***KYŌ, mune, [muna]*** – breast, chest	
胸像	*kyōzō*	(sculptured) bust	740
胸部	*kyōbu*	the chest	86
胸囲	*kyōi*	girth/circumference of the chest	1194
胸中	*kyōchū*	one's bosom, heart, feelings	28
度胸	*dokyō*	courage, daring, nerve	377

胸 胸 胸

1284	月 一 丨 4b 1a3 1b	***HŌ*** – sac, sheath; placenta	
細胞	*saibō, saihō*	cell	695
単細胞	*tansaibō*	1/single cell	300, 695
脳細胞	*nōsaibō*	brain cell	1278, 695
胞子	*hōshi*	spore	103
同胞	*dōhō*	brethren, countrymen	198

胞 胞 胞

1285	扌 一 丨 3c 1a3 1b	***HŌ, da(ku)*** – hug, hold in one's arms; ***ida(ku)*** – embrace, harbor (feelings); ***kaka(eru)*** – carry in one's arms; have (dependents); employ, hire	
抱負	*hōfu*	aspiration, ambition	510
介抱	*kaihō*	nursing, care	453
抱き合う	*dakiau*	embrace each other	159

抱 抱 抱

1286	艹 戈 匚 3k 4n 2t	***ZŌ, kura*** – storehouse, warehouse, repository	
冷蔵庫	*reizōko*	refrigerator	832, 825
蔵書	*zōsho*	collection of books, one's library	131
貯蔵	*chozō*	storage	762
蔵相	*zōshō*	minister of finance	146
大蔵省	*Ōkurashō*	Ministry of Finance	26, 145

蔵 蔵 蔵

1287	月 戈 艹 4b 4n 3k	***ZŌ*** – internal organs		
臓				
	内臓	*naizō*	internal organs, viscera	84
	臓器	*zōki*	internal organs, viscera	527
	心臓	*shinzō*	the heart	97
	肺臓	*haizō*	the lungs	1277
	肝臓	*kanzō*	the liver	1272

1288	貝 匚 又 7b 2t 2h	***KEN, kashiko(i)*** – wise, intelligent		
賢				
	賢明	*kenmei*	wise, intelligent	18
	先賢	*senken*	wise men of old, ancient sages	50
	賢人	*kenjin*	wise man, sage, the wise	1
	賢母	*kenbo*	wise mother	112
	悪賢い	*warugashikoi*	sly, wily, cunning	304

1289	土 匚 又 3b 2t 2h	***KEN, kata(i)*** – firm, hard, solid		
堅				
	堅実	*kenjitsu*	solid, sound, reliable	203
	堅固	*kengo*	strong, solid, steadfast	972
	中堅	*chūken*	mainstay, backbone, nucleus	28
	堅持	*kenji*	hold fast to, adhere to	451
	手堅い	*tegatai*	firm, solid, dependable	57

1290	糸 匚 又 6a 2t 2h	***KIN*** – hard, tight		
緊				
	緊張	*kinchō*	tension	1106
	緊迫	*kinpaku*	tension	1175
	緊急	*kinkyū*	emergency	303
	緊縮	*kinshuku*	contraction; austerity	1110
	緊密	*kinmitsu*	close, tight	806

1291 目 亻 匚 5c 2a 2t

覧

RAN – see, look at

展/博覧会	*ten/haku-rankai*	an exhibition	1129, 601, 158
遊覧船	*yūransen*	excursion ship, pleasure boat	1003, 376
観覧	*kanran*	viewing, inspection	604
一覧表	*ichiranhyō*	table, list	2, 272
回覧	*kairan*	read-and-pass-on circulation	90

1292 糸 夂 一 6a 4i 1a3

繁

HAN – fullness, luxury; frequency

繁栄	*han'ei*	prosperity	723
繁盛	*hanjō*	prosperity; success	719
繁華街	*hankagai*	thriving shopping area	1074, 186

1293 匚 一 2t 1a2

巨

KYO – large, gigantic

巨大	*kyodai*	huge, gigantic, enormous	26
巨人	*kyojin*	giant	1
巨漢	*kyokan*	very large man, big fellow	556
巨星	*kyosei*	giant star; great/prominent man	730
巨万	*kyoman*	millions, immense amount	16

1294 𧾷 匚 一 7d 2t 1a2

距

KYO – distance

距離	*kyori*	distance	1281
短/近距離	*tan/kin-kyori*	short distance	215, 445, 1281
長/遠距離	*chō/en-kyori*	long distance	95, 446, 1281
中距離競争	*chūkyori kyōsō*	medium-distance race	28, 1281, 852, 429

1295	扌 匚 一 3c 2t 1a2	***KYO, koba(mu)*** – refuse, decline		
拒	拒否	*kyohi*	denial, refusal; rejection, veto	1248
	拒否権	*kyohiken*	right of veto	1248, 335
	拒絶	*kyozetsu*	refusal, rejection, repudiation	742

1296	月 口 ノ 4b 3d 1c	***TAI*** – womb, uterus		
胎	胎盤	*taiban*	placenta, afterbirth	1098
	母胎	*botai*	mother's womb/uterus	112
	受胎	*jutai*	conception	260
	胎児	*taiji*	embryo, fetus	1217
	胎動	*taidō*	fetal movement, quickening	231

1297	心 口 ノ 4k 3d 1c	***TAI, nama(keru)*** – be idle, be lazy, neglect; ***okota(ru)*** – neglect, be remiss in, default on		
怠	怠業	*taigyō*	work stoppage, slowdown strike	279
	けん怠	*kentai*	fatigue, weariness	
	怠け者	*namakemono*	idler, lazybones	164

1298	月 女 囗 4b 3e 3s	***YŌ, koshi*** – pelvic region, loins, hips, small of back		
腰	腰部	*yōbu*	pelvic region, waist, hips, loins	86
	腰布	*koshinuno*	loincloth	675
	弱腰	*yowagoshi*	without backbone, faint-hearted	218
	物腰	*monogoshi*	one's manner, demeanor	79
	本腰	*hongoshi*	serious, in earnest	25

1299	月 宀 夗 (4b 3m 2n)
腕	**WAN, ude** – arm; ability, talent, skill

手腕	*shuwan*	ability, capability, skill	57
腕力	*wanryoku*	physical strength	100
腕前	*udemae*	ability, skill	47
腕輪	*udewa*	bracelet	1164
腕時計	*udedokei*	wristwatch	42, 340

腕 腕 腕

1300	月 口 冂 (4b 3d 2r)
胴	***DŌ*** – torso, trunk

胴体	*dōtai*	the body, torso; fuselage	61
胴上/揚げ	*dōage*	hoist (someone) shoulder-high	32, 631
胴回り	*dōmawari*	one's girth	90

胴 胴 胴

1301	氵 口 冂 (3a 3d 2r)
洞	***DŌ, hora*** – cave

洞察	*dōsatsu*	discernment, insight	619
空洞	*kūdō*	cave, cavity	140
洞穴	*dōketsu, horaana*	cave	899
洞くつ	*dōkutsu*	cave, grotto	
秋吉洞	*Akiyoshi-dō*	(largest cave in Japan)	462, 1141

洞 洞 洞

1302	戈 丨 丿 (4n 1b 1c2)
我	***GA, ware, wa*** – I, self; my, our

自我	*jiga*	self, ego	62
我利	*gari*	one's own interests, self-interest	329
無我	*muga*	self-effacement, selflessness	93
我勝ち	*waregachi*	each striving to be first	509
我が国	*wagakuni*	our country	40

我 我 我

1303 飠 戈 丨 8b 4n 1b

餓

GA – starve

餓死	*gashi*	starve to death	85

1304 飠 几 8b 2s

飢

KI, u(eru) – starve

飢餓	*kiga*	hunger, starvation	1303
飢きん	*kikin*	famine	
飢死に	*uejini*	starve to death	85

1305 木 几 4a 2s

机

KI, tsukue – desk

机上	*kijō*	desk-top, academic, theoretical, armchair	32
机上の空論	*kijō no kūron*	mere academic theorizing	32, 140, 293
事務机	*jimuzukue*	office desk	80, 235
書き物机	*kakimono-zukue*	writing desk	131, 79

1306 月 几 4b 2s

肌

hada – the skin; disposition, character, temperament

肌色	*hadairo*	flesh-colored	204
地肌	*jihada*	one's skin; surface of the ground	118
肌着	*hadagi*	underwear	657
肌触り	*hadazawari*	the touch, feel	874
肌寒い	*hadazamui*	chilly	457

1307	亻 口 尸 2a 3d 3r	***SŌ, kura*** – storehouse, warehouse, depository		
	倉庫	*sōko*	warehouse	825
	倉荷	*kurani*	warehouse goods	391

倉 倉 倉

1308	刂 口 尸 2f 3d 3r	***SŌ*** – creation		
	創造	*sōzō*	creation	691
	創作	*sōsaku*	(literary) creation	360
	創立	*sōritsu*	establishment, founding	121
	独創	*dokusō*	originality, creativity	219
	創価学会	*Sōka Gakkai*	(Buddhist sect)	421, 109, 158

創 創 創

1309	田 隹 亻 5f 8c 2a	***FUN, furu(u)*** – be enlivened, rouse up		
	興奮	*kōfun*	excitement	368
	奮発	*funpatsu*	exertion, strenuous effort; splurge	96
	奮起	*funki*	rouse oneself (to action), be inspired	373
	奮って	*furutte*	energetically, willingly	

奮 奮 奮

1310	隹 亻 十 8c 2a 2k	***DATSU, uba(u)*** – snatch away, take by force; captivate		
	争奪(戦)	*sōdatsu(sen)*	a competition, struggle	302, 301
	略奪	*ryakudatsu*	plunder, pillage, despoliation	841
	強奪	*gōdatsu*	seizure, robbery	217
	奪回/還	*dak-kai/kan*	recapture, retaking	90, 866
	奪い合う	*ubaiau*	scramble, struggle (for)	159

奪 奪 奪

1311 隹 又 (8c 2h) 隻

SEKI – (counter for ships); one (of a pair)

三隻	*sanseki*	3 ships	4
数隻(の船)	*sūseki (no fune)*	several (ships)	225, 376
隻眼	*sekigan*	one-eyed	848
一隻眼	*issekigan*	discerning eye	2, 848
隻手	*sekishu*	one-armed	57

1312 言 隹 艹 (7a 8c 3k) 護

GO – defend, protect

弁護士	*bengoshi*	lawyer, attorney	711, 572
保護	*hogo*	protection, preservation	489
援護	*engo*	support, backing, protection	1088
護衛	*goei*	guard, escort	815
護符	*gofu*	amulet, talisman	505

1313 犭 隹 艹 (3g 8c 3k) 獲

KAKU, e(ru) – obtain, acquire, gain

獲得	*kakutoku*	acquire, gain, win	374
捕獲	*hokaku*	catch; capture, seizure	890
漁獲	*gyokaku*	fishing, a catch of fish	699
乱獲	*rankaku*	excessive fishing/hunting	689
獲物	*emono*	game, a catch, trophy	79

1314 禾 隹 艹 (5d 8c 3k) 穫

KAKU – harvest

収穫	*shūkaku*	harvest, harvesting	757
収穫高	*shūkakudaka*	the yield, crop	757, 190
収穫期	*shūkakuki*	harvest time	757, 449

1315 心 口 丨
4k 3s2 1b

患

KAN, wazura(u) – be ill, suffer (from)

患者	*kanja*	a patient	164
急患	*kyūkan*	person suddenly taken ill	303
患部	*kanbu*	affected/diseased part	86
長患い	*nagawazurai*	long illness	95

1316 目 扌
5c 3c

看

KAN – see

看護婦	*kangofu*	nurse	1312, 316
看病	*kanbyō*	tending the sick, nursing	380
看守	*kanshu*	(prison) guard	490
看破	*kanpa*	see through, detect	665
看板	*kanban*	sign, signboard	1047

1317 亻 隹 山
2a 8c 3o

催

SAI, moyō(su) – hold, sponsor; feel

開催	*kaisai*	hold (a meeting)	396
主催	*shusai*	sponsorship, promotion	155
催眠	*saimin*	hypnosis	849
催涙ガス	*sairuigasu*	tear gas	1239
催し物	*moyōshimono*	(program of) entertainments	79

1318 疒 ト 一
5i 2m 1a2

症

SHŌ – illness, symptoms

病症	*byōshō*	nature of a disease	380
症状/候	*shōjō/kō*	symptom	626, 944
不眠症	*fuminshō*	insomnia	94, 849
自閉症	*jiheishō*	autism	62, 397
露出症	*roshutsushō*	exhibitionism	951, 53

1319 疒 几 又 (5i 2s 2h)

疫

EKI, [YAKU] – epidemic

疫病	*ekibyō*	epidemic, plague	380
悪疫	*akueki*	plague, pestilence, epidemic	304
防疫	*bōeki*	prevention of epidemics	513
検疫	*ken'eki*	quarantine	531
免疫	*men'eki*	immunity	733

1320 疒 冂 十 (5i 2r 2k)

痛

TSŪ, ita(mu) – feel painful, hurt; be damaged; **ita(meru)** – hurt, damage; cause pain; **ita(i)** – painful

苦痛	*kutsū*	pain	545
頭痛	*zutsū*	headache	276
痛飲	*tsūin*	drink heavily, carouse	323
痛手	*itade*	severe wound; hard blow	57

1321 疒 厂 又 (5i 2p 2h)

疲

HI, tsuka(reru) – get tired; **tsuka(rasu)** – (tr.) fatigue, tire

疲労	*hirō*	fatigue, weariness	233
気疲れ	*kizukare*	mental fatigue/exhaustion	134
疲れ果てる	*tsukarehateru*	be completely exhausted	487
(お)疲れ様	*(o)tsukaresama*	Thank you (for your tiring work).	403

1322 疒 日 丷 (5i 4c 3n)

療

RYŌ – heal, cure; treat medically

治療	*chiryō*	medical treatment, therapy	493
医療	*iryō*	medical treatment	220
診療	*shinryō*	diagnosis and treatment	1214
施療	*seryō*	free medical treatment	1004
療養所	*ryōyōsho, ryōyōjo*	sanatorium, nursing home	402, 153

1323 宀 日 丷 3m 4c 3n

寮

RYŌ – hostel, dormitory

学生寮	*gakuseiryō*	dormitory	109, 44
社員寮	*shainryō*	company dormitory	308, 163
独身寮	*dokushinryō*	dormitory for bachelors	219, 59
寮長	*ryōchō*	dormitory director	95
寮生	*ryōsei*	student living in a dormitory	44

寮 寮 寮

1324 亻 日 丷 2a2 4c 3n

僚

RYŌ – an official; companion

官僚	*kanryō*	bureaucrat	326
官僚主義	*kanryō shugi*	bureaucratism, bureaucracy	326, 155, 291
閣僚	*kakuryō*	cabinet member/minister	837
同僚	*dōryō*	colleague, coworker	198
僚友	*ryōyū*	fellow worker, colleague	264

僚 僚 僚

1325 一 丨 丶 1a 1b 1d

丈

JŌ – (unit of length, about 3 m); ***take*** – one's height

丈夫	*jōbu*	strong and healthy; strong, durable	315
偉丈夫	*ijōbu*	great man	1053, 315
気丈	*kijō*	stout-hearted, courageous	134
八丈島	*Hachijō-jima*	(island south of Tokyo)	10, 286
背丈	*setake*	one's height	1265

丈 丈 丈

1326 丬 士 丨 2b 3p 1b

壮

SŌ – manly, strong

壮大	*sōdai*	magnificent, grand, imposing	26
強壮	*kyōsō*	strong, robust, husky	217
壮健	*sōken*	healthy, hale and hearty	893
悲壮	*hisō*	tragic, touching, pathetic	1034
壮年	*sōnen*	prime of manhood/life	45

壮 壮 壮

1327	艹 土 冫 3k 3p 2b	***SŌ*** – villa, inn; solemn			
荘		別荘	*bessō*	country house, cottage, villa	267
		山荘	*sansō*	mountain villa	34
		荘重	*sōchō*	solemn, sublime, impressive	227
		荘厳	*sōgon*	sublime, grand, majestic	822

荘 荘 荘

1328	衤 土 冫 5e 3p 2b	***SŌ, SHŌ, yosō(u)*** – wear; feign, pretend, disguise oneself as			
装		服装	*fukusō*	style of dress, attire	683
		変装	*hensō*	disguise	257
		装置	*sōchi*	device, apparatus, equipment	426
		装飾	*sōshoku*	ornament, decoration	979
		武装	*busō*	arms, armament	1031

装 装 装

1329	衤 戈 亻 5e 4n 2a	***TAI, fukuro*** – sack, bag			
袋		手袋	*tebukuro*	glove	57
		足袋	*tabi*	Japanese socks (worn with kimono)	58
		紙袋	*kamibukuro*	paper sack/bag	180
		袋小路	*fukurokōji*	blind alley, cul-de-sac	27, 151
		胃袋	*ibukuro*	stomach	1268

袋 袋 袋

1330	衤 刂 ⺈ 5e 2f 2n	***RETSU, sa(keru/ku)*** – (intr./tr.) split, tear, rip			
裂		分裂	*bunretsu*	breakup, dissolution, division	38
		破裂	*haretsu*	burst, rupture, explode	665
		決裂	*ketsuretsu*	(negotiations) break down	356
		裂け目	*sakeme*	a rip, split, crack, fissure	55

裂 裂 裂

1331	火 刂 ⺈ 4d 2f 2n	

烈

RETSU – violent, intense

烈震	*resshin*	violent earthquake	953
熱烈	*netsuretsu*	ardent, fervent, vehement	645
壮烈	*sōretsu*	heroic, brave	1326
強烈	*kyōretsu*	intense, severe	217
痛烈	*tsūretsu*	severe, fierce, bitter	1320

烈 烈 烈

1332	⺍ 冫 亻 3n 2b 2a	

奨

SHŌ – urge, encourage

奨学金	*shōgakukin*	a scholarship	109, 23
奨学生	*shōgakusei*	student on a scholarship	109, 44
勧奨	*kanshō*	encouragement, promotion	1051
推奨	*suishō*	recommendation, commendation	1233

奨 奨 奨

1333	火 一 丨 4d 1a 1b	

灯

TŌ, hi – a light, lamp

電灯	*dentō*	electric light/lamp	108
灯火	*tōka*	a light, lamplight	20
街灯	*gaitō*	streetlight	186
船灯	*sentō*	ship light	376
灯台	*tōdai*	lighthouse	492

灯 灯 灯

1334	氵 口 丷 3a 3d 2o	

澄

CHŌ, su(mu) – become clear; ***su(masu)*** – make clear; perk (one's ears); look prim/ unconcerned/nonchalant

清澄	*seichō*	clear, limpid, lucid, serene	660
澄み切る	*sumikiru*	become perfectly clear	39
澄み渡る	*sumiwataru*	be crystal clear	378
澄まし顔	*sumashigao*	unconcerned look	277

澄 澄 澄

1335 災 火 ノ 4d 1c3

SAI, wazawa(i) – misfortune, disaster

災難	*sainan*	mishap, accident, calamity	557
災害	*saigai*	disaster, accident	518
火災	*kasai*	fire, blaze, conflagration	20
天災	*tensai*	natural disaster/calamity	141
震災	*shinsai*	earthquake disaster	953

1336 炎 火 4d2

EN, honō – flame

火炎瓶	*kaenbin*	firebomb, Molotov cocktail	20, 1161
炎症	*enshō*	inflammation	1318
肺炎	*haien*	pneumonia	1277
脳炎	*nōen*	brain inflammation, encephalitis	1278
中耳炎	*chūjien*	inflammation of the middle ear	28, 56

1337 淡 氵 火 3a 4d2

TAN, awa(i) – light, faint, pale; transitory

濃淡	*nōtan*	light and shade, shading	957
淡彩	*tansai*	light coloring	932
冷淡	*reitan*	indifferent, apathetic	832
淡水	*tansui*	fresh water	21
淡雪	*awayuki*	light snow	949

1338 滅 氵 戈 火 3a 4n 4d

METSU, horo(biru) – fall to ruin, perish, die out; ***horo(bosu)*** – ruin, destroy, overthrow, annihilate

破滅	*hametsu*	ruin, downfall, collapse	665
滅亡	*metsubō*	downfall, destruction	672
消滅	*shōmetsu*	extinction, disappearance	845
幻滅	*genmetsu*	disillusionment	1227

1339	戈 女 一 4n 3e 1a	*I* – authority, dignity, majesty; threat			
威		権威	*ken'i*	authority	335
		威勢	*isei*	power, influence; high spirits	646
		威厳	*igen*	dignity, stateliness	822
		威信	*ishin*	prestige, dignity	157
		脅威	*kyōi*	menace, threat, danger	1263

威 威 威

1340	力 厂 一 2g 2p2 1a	*REI* – encouragement; diligence; *hage(mu)* – be diligent; *hage(masu)* – encourage, urge on			
励		奨励	*shōrei*	encouragement, promotion	1332
		激励	*gekirei*	urging, encouragement	1017
		精励	*seirei*	diligence, industriousness	659
		励行	*reikō*	strict enforcement	68

励 励 励

1341	厂 一 丨 2p 1a 1b	*YAKU* – misfortune, disaster			
厄		厄介	*yakkai*	troublesome, burdensome; help, care	453
		厄介者	*yakkaimono*	a dependent; burden	453, 164
		厄日	*yakubi*	unlucky day; critical day	5
		厄年	*yakudoshi*	unlucky year; critical age	45
		厄払い	*yakubarai, yakuharai*	exorcism	582

厄 厄 厄

1342	厂 土 2p 3b	*ATSU* – pressure			
圧		圧力	*atsuryoku*	pressure	100
		圧迫	*appaku*	pressure, oppression	1175
		気圧	*kiatsu*	atmospheric pressure	134
		抑圧	*yokuatsu*	restraint, suppression	1057
		圧倒的	*attōteki*	overwhelming	905, 210

圧 圧 圧

1343	厂 火 2p 4d	***KAI, hai*** – ash			
灰		灰じん	*haijin*	ashes	
		石灰	*sekkai*	(chemical) lime	78
		灰皿	*haizara*	ashtray	1097
		火山灰	*kazanbai*	volcanic ash	20, 34
		灰色	*haiiro*	gray	204

1344	山 火 厂 3o 4d 2p	***TAN, sumi*** – charcoal			
炭		石炭	*sekitan*	coal	78
		木炭	*mokutan*	charcoal	22
		採炭	*saitan*	coal mining	933
		炭素	*tanso*	carbon	271
		炭酸	*tansan*	carbonic acid	516

1345	山 石 3o 5a	***GAN, iwa*** – rock			
岩		岩石	*ganseki*	rock	78
		火成岩	*kaseigan*	igneous rock	20, 261
		岩塩	*gan'en*	rock salt	1101
		岩屋	*iwaya*	cave, cavern	167
		岩登り	*iwanobori*	rock climbing	960

1346	氵 口 丨 3a 3s 1b	***CHŪ, oki*** – open sea			
沖		沖積世/期	*chūseki-sei/ki*	the alluvial epoch	656, 252, 449
		沖合	*okiai*	open sea, offshore	159

1347	亻 口 丨 (2a 3s 1b)	***CHŪ, naka*** – personal relations		
仲				
	仲裁	*chūsai*	arbitration	1123
	仲介	*chūkai*	mediation	453
	伯仲	*hakuchū*	be nearly equal, evenly matched	1176
	仲良く	*nakayoku*	on good terms, like good friends	321
	仲人	*nakōdo*	go-between, matchmaker	1

1348	心 口 丨 (4k 3s 1b)	***CHŪ*** – loyalty, faithfulness		
忠				
	忠実	*chūjitsu*	faithful, devoted, loyal	203
	忠義	*chūgi*	loyalty	291
	忠誠	*chūsei*	loyalty, allegiance	718
	忠告	*chūkoku*	advice, admonition	690
	忠臣蔵	*Chūshingura*	(the 47 Ronin story)	835, 1286

1349	糸 夂 辶 (6a 4i 2q)	***HŌ, nu(u)*** – sew		
縫				
	裁縫	*saihō*	sewing	1123
	縫合	*hōgō*	a suture, stitch	159
	天衣無縫	*ten'i-muhō*	of flawless beauty, perfect	141, 677, 93
	縫い目	*nuime*	seam, stitch	55
	仮縫い	*karinui*	temporary sewing, basting, fitting	1049

1350	山 夂 十 (3o 4i 2k)	***HŌ, mine*** – peak, summit		
峰				
	連峰	*renpō*	mountain range	440
	高峰	*kōhō*	lofty peak	190
	霊峰	*reihō*	sacred mountain	1168

1351 山 ⺊ 一 3o 2m2 1a2

峠

tōge – mountain pass

峠道	*tōgemichi*	road through a mountain pass	149
峠を越す	*tōge o kosu*	cross a pass	1001
十国峠	*Jikkoku Tōge*	(pass in Hakone)	12, 40

1352 山 亻 一 3o 2a 1a2

峡

KYŌ – gorge, ravine

山峡	*sankyō*	(mountain) gorge	34
峡谷	*kyōkoku*	gorge, ravine, canyon	653
海峡	*kaikyō*	strait, channel, narrows	117
峡湾	*kyōwan*	fjord	670

1353 犭 亻 一 3g 2a 1a2

狭

KYŌ, sema(i) – narrow, small (in area); ***seba(maru/meru)*** – (intr./tr.) narrow, contract

狭量	*kyōryō*	narrow-minded	411
偏狭	*henkyō*	narrow-minded, parochial	1159
狭心症	*kyōshinshō*	stricture of the heart, angina pectoris	97, 1318
狭苦しい	*semakurushii*	cramped	545

1354 扌 亻 一 3c 2a 1a2

挟

KYŌ, hasa(mu) – put between, interpose; ***hasa(maru)*** – get between, get caught/hemmed/sandwiched between

挟撃	*kyōgeki*	pincer attack	1016
挟み撃ち	*hasamiuchi*	pincer attack	1016
挟み込む	*hasamikomu*	put between, insert	776
挟み上げる	*hasamiageru*	pick up (with chopsticks)	32

1355 犭 十 冂 3g 2k2 2r

献

KEN, [KON] – present, offer

献金	*kenkin*	gift of money, contribution	23
献血	*kenketsu*	blood donation	789
献上	*kenjō*	presentation	32
文献	*bunken*	the literature, documentary records	111
献立	*kondate*	menu; arrangements, plan, program	121

1356 亻 犭 2a 3g

伏

FUKU, fu(su) – bend down, lie down/prostrate; ***fu(seru)*** – cast down (one's eyes), turn over; cover, put over; conceal

降伏	*kōfuku*	surrender, capitulation	947
伏兵	*fukuhei*	an ambush	784
潜伏	*senpuku*	hide; be dormant, latent	937
伏線	*fukusen*	foreshadowing	299

1357 厂 一 丨 2p 1a2 1b

丘

KYŪ, oka – hill

砂丘	*sakyū*	sand dune	1151

1358 山 厂 一 3o 2p 1a2

岳

GAKU, take – mountain, peak

山岳	*sangaku*	mountains	34
山岳部	*sangakubu*	mountaineering club	34, 86
岳父	*gakufu*	father of one's wife	113
谷川岳	*Tanigawa-dake*	(mountain about 150 km north of Tokyo)	653, 33

1359	匚 厂 一 2t 2p 1a	***SHŌ*** – workman, artisan			
匠		巨匠	*kyoshō*	(great) master	1293
		名匠	*meishō*	master craftsman	82
		師匠	*shishō*	master, teacher	409
		宗匠	*sōshō*	master, teacher	616
		意匠	*ishō*	a design	132

匠 匠 匠

1360	ロ 亻 一 3d 2a 1a2	***KI*** – strange, curious			
奇		好奇心	*kōkishin*	curiosity	104, 97
		奇妙	*kimyō*	strange, curious, odd	1154
		奇術	*kijutsu*	conjuring, sleight of hand	187
		奇病	*kibyō*	strange disease	380
		奇数	*kisū*	odd number	225

奇 奇 奇

1361	宀 ロ 亻 3m 3d 2a	***KI, yo(ru)*** – approach, draw near; meet; drop in; ***yo(seru)*** – bring near; push aside; gather together; send			
寄		寄付	*kifu*	contribution, donation	192
		寄宿舎	*kishukusha*	dormitory	179, 791
		寄生	*kisei*	parasitism	44
		立ち寄る	*tachiyoru*	drop in, stop (at)	121

寄 寄 寄

1362	山 ロ 亻 3o 3d 2a	***saki*** – cape, promontory, headland, point (of land)			
崎		長崎	*Nagasaki*	(city on western coast of Kyushu)	95
		宮崎	*Miyazaki*	(city on southern coast of Kyushu)	721

崎 崎 崎

1363 山 日 | 3o 4c 1b

岬

misaki – promontory, headland, point (of land)

宗谷岬	*Sōya-misaki*	(northern tip of Hokkaido)	616, 653
知床岬	*Shiretoko-misaki*	(eastern tip of Hokkaido)	214, 826
潮岬	*Shio-no-misaki*	(southern tip of Kii Peninsula)	468
足ずり岬	*Ashizuri-misaki*	(southern tip of Shikoku)	58

岬 岬 岬

1364 貝 罒 日 7b 5f 4c

贈

ZŌ, [SŌ], oku(ru) – give, present, bestow

贈与(証書)	*zōyo (shōsho)*	gift (certificate)	539, 484, 131
寄贈	*kizō, kisō*	presentation, donation, contribution	1361
贈答	*zōtō*	exchange of gifts	160
贈り物	*okurimono*	gift, present	79
贈り主	*okurinushi*	sender (of a gift)	155

贈 贈 贈

1365 心 罒 日 4k 5f 4c

憎

ZŌ, niku(mu) – hate; ***niku(i/rashii)*** – hateful, horrible, repulsive; ***niku(shimi)*** – hatred, animosity

愛憎	*aizō*	love and hate; partiality	259
憎悪	*zōo*	hatred	304
憎まれっ子	*nikumarekko*	bad/naughty boy	103
憎まれ口	*nikumareguchi*	offensive/malicious remarks	54

憎 憎 憎

1366 亻 罒 日 2a 5f 4c

僧

SŌ – Buddhist priest/monk

僧院	*sōin*	temple; monastery	614
僧正	*sōjō*	Buddhist high priest, bishop	275
高僧	*kōsō*	high/exemplary priest	190
僧服	*sōfuku*	priestly robe, monk's habit	683
小僧	*kozō*	young priest; apprentice; boy	27

僧 僧 僧

1367 尸 罒 日 (3r 5f 4c)

層

SŌ – layer, level

上層	*jōsō*	upper layer/classes/floors	32
多層	*tasō*	multilayer	229
層雲	*sōun*	stratus (cloud)	636
読者層	*dokushasō*	class/level of readers	244, 164
階層	*kaisō*	social stratum, class	588

層 層 層

1368 心 口 丷 (4k 3d 2o2)

悦

ETSU – joy

喜悦	*kietsu*	joy, delight	1143
悦楽	*etsuraku*	joy, pleasure, gaiety	358
法悦	*hōetsu*	religious exultation; ecstasy	123
満悦	*man'etsu*	delighted, very satisfied	201
悦に入る	*etsu ni iru*	be pleased (with)	52

悦 悦 悦

1369 門 口 丷 (8e 3d 2o2)

閲

ETSU – inspection, review

閲覧	*etsuran*	perusal, inspection, reading	1291
閲覧室	*etsuranshitsu*	reading room	1291, 166
校閲	*kōetsu*	revision (of a manuscript)	115
検閲	*ken'etsu*	censorship	531
閲歴	*etsureki*	one's career/personal history	480

閲 閲 閲

1370 月 口 丷 (4b 3d 2o2)

脱

DATSU – omit; escape; ***nu(gu)*** – take off (clothes); ***nu(geru)*** – come off, slip off (footwear/clothing)

脱衣所	*datsuisho, datsuijo*	changing/dressing room	677, 153
脱線	*dassen*	derailment; digression	299
離脱	*ridatsu*	secession, breakaway	1281
脱税	*datsuzei*	tax evasion	399

脱 脱 脱

1371	金 口 丷 8a 3d 2o2	*EI, surudo(i)* – sharp			
鋭		鋭利	*eiri*	sharp	329
		鋭気	*eiki*	spirit, mettle, energy	134
		精鋭	*seiei*	elite, choice	659
		新鋭	*shin'ei*	fresh, new	174
		鋭角	*eikaku*	acute angle	473
		鋭 鋭 鋭			

1372	十 口 丷 2k 3d 2o	*KOKU* – conquer			
克		克服	*kokufuku*	conquest, subjugation	683
		克己	*kokki*	self-denial, self-control	370
		克明	*kokumei*	faithful, conscientious	18
		克 克 克			

1373	心 亠 丨 4k 2j 1b	*BŌ, isoga(shii)* – busy			
忙		多忙	*tabō*	busy, hectic	229
		繁忙	*hanbō*	(very) busy	1292
		忙殺される	*bōsatsu sareru*	be busily occupied	576
		忙 忙 忙			

1374	亠 心 丨 2j 4k 1b	*BŌ, wasu(reru)* – forget			
忘		健忘(症)	*kenbō(shō)*	forgetfulness	893, 1318
		忘恩	*bōon*	ingratitude	555
		忘年会	*bōnenkai*	year-end party	45, 158
		忘れ物	*wasuremono*	article left behind	79
		度/胴忘れ	*do/dō-wasure*	forget for the moment	377, 1300
		忘 忘 忘			

1375 亠 目 丨 (2j 5c 1b)

盲

MŌ – blindness; ignorance

盲人	*mōjin*	blind person, the blind	1
盲目	*mōmoku*	blindness	55
色盲	*shikimō*	color blindness	204
文盲	*monmō*	illiteracy	111
盲腸	*mōchō*	appendix	1270

1376 亠 女 丨 (2j 3e 1b)

妄

MŌ, BŌ – without reason/authority

迷妄	*meimō*	illusion, fallacy	967
妄想	*mōsō*	wild fancy, foolish fantasy, delusion	147
妄信	*mōshin, bōshin*	blind belief, overcredulity	157
被害妄想	*higai mōsō*	delusions of persecution, paranoia	976, 518, 147

1377 艹 亠 丨 (3k 2j 1b4)

荒

KŌ, ara(i) – rough, wild, violent; ***a(reru)*** – get rough/stormy, run wild, go to ruin; ***a(rasu)*** – devastate, lay waste

荒廃	*kōhai*	desolation, devastation	961
荒野	*kōya*	wilderness, wasteland	236
荒れ狂う	*arekuruu*	rage, run amuck	883
荒れ仕事	*areshigoto*	heavy work, hard labor	333, 80

1378 心 艹 亠 (4k 3k 2j)

慌

KŌ, awa(teru) – get flustered, be in a flurry, panic; ***awa(tadashii)*** – bustling, flurried, confused

慌て者	*awatemono*	absentminded person, scatterbrain	164
大慌て	*ōawate*	great haste	26

1379 福 (礻 田 口 — 4e 5f 3d)

FUKU – fortune, blessing; wealth, welfare

幸福	*kōfuku*	happiness	684
祝福	*shukufuku*	blessing	851
福音	*fukuin*	the gospel; good news	347
福引き	*fukubiki*	lottery, raffle	216
七福神	*Shichifukujin*	the Seven Gods of Good Fortune	9, 310

1380 幅 (巾 田 口 — 3f 5f 3d)

FUKU, haba – width, breadth, range; influence

振幅	*shinpuku*	amplitude	954
大幅	*ōhaba*	broad; large, wholesale, substantial	26
幅の広い	*haba no hiroi*	wide, broad	694
横幅	*yokohaba*	breadth, width	781
幅が利く	*haba ga kiku*	be influential	329

1381 班 (王 刂 — 4f2 2f)

HAN – squad, group

首班	*shuhan*	head, chief	148
班長	*hanchō*	squad/group leader	95
救護班	*kyūgohan*	relief squad	725, 1312

1382 藩 (艹 米 田 — 3k 6b 5f)

HAN – feudal clan/lord

藩主	*hanshu*	lord of a feudal clan	155
藩学	*hangaku*	samurai school for clan children	109
廃藩置県	*haihan-chiken*	abolition of clans and establishment of prefectures	961, 426, 194

1383 宀 米 田 3m 6b 5f

審

SHIN – hearing, investigation, trial

審査	*shinsa*	examination, investigation	624
審議	*shingi*	deliberation, consideration	292
審問	*shinmon*	trial, hearing, inquiry	162
不審	*fushin*	doubt, suspicion	94
審判	*shinpan*	decision, judgment, refereeing	1026

審 審 審

1384 ⺊ 田 心 2m 5f 4k

慮

RYO – thought, consideration

考慮	*kōryo*	consideration, reflection	541
遠慮	*enryo*	reserve, restraint, hesitation	446
配慮	*hairyo*	consideration, solicitude	515
憂慮	*yūryo*	apprehension, concern	1032
焦慮	*shōryo*	impatience; worry	999

慮 慮 慮

1385 ⺊ 田 力 2m 5f 2g

虜

RYO – captive

捕虜	*horyo*	prisoner of war	890
捕虜収容所	*horyo shūyōjo*	POW camp	890, 757, 654, 153

虜 虜 虜

1386 力 田 一 2g 5f 1a

勇

YŪ, isa(mu) – be spirited, lively, encouraged

勇気	*yūki*	courage	134
武勇	*buyū*	bravery, valor	1031
勇士	*yūshi*	brave warrior, hero	572
勇退	*yūtai*	retire voluntarily	846
勇み足	*isamiashi*	overeagerness, rashness	58

勇 勇 勇

1387	隹 厂 ノ 8c 2p 1c	***YŪ*** – male; brave; great; ***osu, o*** – male			
雄		英雄	*eiyū*	hero	353
		雄弁	*yūben*	eloquence	711
		雄大	*yūdai*	grand, magnificent	26
		雄鳥	*ondori*	rooster, male bird	285
		両雄	*ryōyū*	2 great men (rivals)	200

1388	隹 ト 丨 8c 2m2 1b	***SHI, mesu, me*** – female			
雌		雌伏	*shifuku*	remain in obscurity, lie low	1356
		雌雄	*shiyū*	male and female; victory or defeat	1387
		雌犬	*mesuinu*	a bitch	280
		雌牛	*meushi*	(female) cow	281
		雌花	*mebana*	female flower	255

1389	糸 ト 丨 6a 2m2 1b	***SHI, murasaki*** – purple			
紫		紫外線	*shigaisen*	ultraviolet rays	83, 299
		紫煙	*shien*	tobacco smoke, blue cigarette smoke	919
		紫雲	*shiun*	auspicious purple clouds	636
		山紫水明	*sanshi-suimei*	beautiful scenery	34, 21, 18
		紫色	*murasakiiro*	purple	204

1390	ネ ト 一 4e 2m 1a	***SHI*** – happiness			
祉		福祉	*fukushi*	welfare, well-being	1379
		福祉国家	*fukushi kokka*	welfare state	1379, 40, 165
		社会福祉	*shakai fukushi*	social/public welfare	308, 158, 1379

1391	礻 口 丷 (5e 3d 2o)
裕	***YŪ*** – surplus

余裕	*yoyū*	room, margin, leeway; composure	1063
余裕しゃくしゃく	*yoyū-shakushaku*	calm and composed	1063
富裕	*fuyū*	wealth, affluence	713
裕福	*yūfuku*	wealth, affluence	1379

裕 裕 裕

1392	氵 宀 口 (3a 3m 3d)
溶	***YŌ, to(keru)*** – (intr.) melt, dissolve; ***to(kasu/ku)*** – (tr.) melt, dissolve

溶解	*yōkai*	(intr.) melt, dissolve	474
溶岩	*yōgan*	lava	1345
溶液	*yōeki*	solution	472
水溶性	*suiyōsei*	water-soluble	21, 98

溶 溶 溶

1393	木 厂 一 (4a 2p 1a)
析	***SEKI*** – divide, take apart, analyze

分析	*bunseki*	analysis	38
分析化学	*bunseki kagaku*	analytical chemistry	38, 254, 109
市場分析	*shijō bunseki*	market analysis	181, 154, 38
解析	*kaiseki*	analysis	474

析 析 析

1394	扌 厂 一 (3c 2p 1a)
折	***SETSU, o(reru)*** – (intr.) break; be folded; yield, compromise; ***o(ru)*** – (tr.) break; fold, bend; ***ori*** – occasion, opportunity

右折禁止	*usetsu kinshi*	No Right Turn	76, 482, 477
折半	*seppan*	divide into halves	88
曲折	*kyokusetsu*	twists and turns, complications	366
折り紙	*origami*	paper folding; paper for origami	180

折 折 折

1395	言 扌 厂 7a 3c 2p	**SEI, chika(u)** – swear, pledge, vow		
誓約	*seiyaku*	oath, vow, pledge	211	
宣誓	*sensei*	oath	625	
祈誓	*kisei*	oath, vow	621	
誓文	*seimon*	written oath	111	

誓 誓 誓

1396	辶 扌 厂 2q 3c 2p	**SEI, yu(ku)** – die		
逝去	*seikyo*	death	414	
急逝	*kyūsei*	sudden/untimely death	303	

逝 逝 逝

1397	口 扌 厂 3d 3c 2p	**TETSU** – wisdom		
哲学	*tetsugaku*	philosophy	109	
哲学者	*tetsugakusha*	philosopher	109, 164	
賢哲	*kentetsu*	wise man, sage	1288	
先哲	*sentetsu*	wise man of the past, sage of old	50	
哲人	*tetsujin*	wise man, philosopher	1	

哲 哲 哲

1398	口 戸 攵 3d 4m 4i	**KEI** – open; say		
啓発	*keihatsu*	enlightenment, edification	96	
啓示	*keiji*	revelation	615	
天啓	*tenkei*	divine revelation	141	
拝啓	*haikei*	Dear Sir:	1201	
啓もう	*keimō*	enlightenment, instruction		

啓 啓 啓

1399 日 車 厂

4c 7c 2p

暫

ZAN – (for) a while

暫時	*zanji*	(for) a short time	42
暫定	*zantei*	tentative, provisional	355

暫 暫 暫

1400 氵 車 厂

3a 7c 2p

漸

ZEN – gradually

漸次	*zenji*	gradually, step by step	384
漸進	*zenshin*	gradual progress	437
漸増	*zenzō*	increase gradually	712
漸減	*zengen*	decrease gradually, taper off	715

漸 漸 漸

1401 厂 一 丨

2p 1a 1b

斥

SEKI – retreat, recede; repel, reject

排斥	*haiseki*	rejection, exclusion, boycott	1036
排斥運動	*haiseki undō*	agitation for expulsion/exclusion	1036, 439, 231

斥 斥 斥

1402 言 厂 一

7a 2p 1a

訴

SO, utta(eru) – sue; complain of; appeal (to)

起訴	*kiso*	prosecution, indictment	373
提訴	*teiso*	bring before (the court), file (suit)	628
告訴	*kokuso*	complaint, accusation, charges	690
敗訴	*haiso*	losing a suit/case	511
勝訴	*shōso*	winning a suit/case	509

訴 訴 訴

1403	言 丷 ノ 7a 2o 1c			
訟	***SHŌ*** – accuse			
	訴訟	*soshō*	lawsuit, litigation	1402
	刑事訴訟	*keiji soshō*	criminal suit	887, 80, 1402
	民事訴訟	*minji soshō*	civil suit	177, 80, 1402
	離婚訴訟	*rikon soshō*	suit for divorce	1281, 567, 1402
	訴訟費用	*soshō hiyō*	costs of litigation	1402, 749, 107

1404	阝 車 2d 7c			
陣	***JIN*** – battle position, camp			
	陣営	*jin'ei*	camp, encampment	722
	陣地	*jinchi*	(military) position	118
	陣容	*jin'yō*	battle array, lineup	654
	退陣	*taijin*	decampment, withdrawal	846
	陣痛	*jintsū*	labor (pains)	1320

1405	阝 木 日 2d 4a 4c			
陳	***CHIN*** – state, explain; show; old			
	陳列	*chinretsu*	display, exhibit	611
	陳情	*chinjō*	petition, appeal	209
	陳述	*chinjutsu*	statement, declaration	968
	陳謝	*chinsha*	apology	901
	新陳代謝	*shinchin taisha*	metabolism; regeneration	174, 256, 901

1406	木 日 4a2 4c			
棟	***TŌ, mune, [muna]*** – ridge of a roof			
	上棟式	*jōtōshiki*	roof-laying ceremony	32, 525
	病棟	*byōtō*	(hospital) ward	380
	別棟	*betsumune*	separate building	267
	棟上げ式	*muneageshiki*	roof-laying ceremony	32, 525
	棟木	*munagi*	ridgepole, ridge beam	22

1407 壊

土 衤 罒 — 3b 5e 5g

KAI, kowa(reru) – get broken, break; ***kowa(su)*** – break, tear down, destroy, damage

壊滅	*kaimetsu*	destruction, annihilation	1338
破壊	*hakai*	destruction, wrecking	665
崩壊	*hōkai*	collapse, breakdown, cave-in	1122
壊血病	*kaiketsubyō*	scurvy	789, 380

1408 懐

心 衤 罒 — 4k 5e 5g

KAI – pocket; nostalgia; ***natsu(kashii)*** – dear, fond, longed-for; ***natsu(kashimu)*** – yearn for; ***natsu(ku)*** – take kindly (to); ***natsu(keru)*** – win over; tame; ***futokoro*** – breast (pocket)

懐中電灯	*kaichū dentō*	flashlight	28, 108, 1333
述懐	*jukkai*	(relating) one's thoughts and reminiscences	968
懐柔	*kaijū*	conciliation	774

1409 快

心 亻 一 — 4k 2a 1a2

KAI, kokoroyo(i) – pleasant, delightful

快適	*kaiteki*	comfortable, pleasant, agreeable	415
快活	*kaikatsu*	cheerful, lighthearted	237
全快	*zenkai*	complete recovery (from illness)	89
快晴	*kaisei*	fine weather, clear skies	662
快速電車	*kaisoku densha*	express train	502, 108, 133

1410 慢

心 罒 日 — 4k 5g 4c

MAN – be lazy, neglect

我慢	*gaman*	exercise patience, tolerate	1302
自慢	*jiman*	pride, boasting, vanity	62
怠慢	*taiman*	negligence, dereliction	1297
緩慢	*kanman*	slow, sluggish	1089
慢性	*mansei*	chronic	98

1411 氵 罒 日 3a 5g 4c

漫

MAN – aimless, random; involuntarily

漫画	*manga*	cartoon, comic book/strip	343
漫談	*mandan*	chat, idle talk	593
散漫	*sanman*	vague, loose, desultory	767
漫然	*manzen*	random, rambling, discursive	651
漫才	*manzai*	comic (stage) dialogue	551

漫 漫 漫

1412 宀 罒 心 3m 5g 4k

寧

NEI – peaceful, quiet; rather, preferably

丁寧	*teinei*	polite; careful, meticulous	184
安寧	*annei*	public peace/order	105

寧 寧 寧

1413 刂 丶 2f 1d

刃

JIN, ha – blade

白刃	*hakujin*	naked blade, drawn sword	205
刃先	*hasaki*	edge (of a blade)	50
刃物	*hamono*	edged tool, cutlery	79
もろ刃の剣	*moroha no tsurugi*	double-edged sword	879

刃 刃 刃

1414 心 刂 丶 4k 2f 1d

忍

NIN, shino(bu) – bear, endure; hide, lie hidden; avoid (being seen); ***shino(baseru)*** – hide, conceal

忍苦	*ninku*	endurance, stoicism	545
残忍	*zannin*	brutal, ruthless	650
忍者	*ninja*	(feudal) professional spy/assassin	164
忍び足	*shinobiashi*	stealthy steps	58

忍 忍 忍

1415	冂 十 一 2r 2k 1a

耐

TAI, ta(eru) – endure, bear, withstand; be fit, competent

忍耐	*nintai*	perseverance, patience	1414
耐熱	*tainetsu*	heatproof, heat-resistant	645
耐火	*taika*	fireproof, fire-resistant	20
耐久	*taikyū*	endurance; durability	1210
耐乏生活	*taibō seikatsu*	austerity	754, 44, 237

耐 耐 耐

1416	雨 冂 一 8d 2r 1a

需

JU – request, need, demand

需要(供給)	*juyō (kyōkyū)*	demand (and supply)	419, 197, 346
需給	*jukyū*	supply and demand	346
特需	*tokuju*	special procurement (in wartime)	282
軍需品	*gunjuhin*	war matériel	438, 230
必需品	*hitsujuhin*	necessary articles, necessities	520, 230

需 需 需

1417	亻 雨 冂 2a 8d 2r

儒

JU – Confucianism

儒教	*jukyō*	Confucianism	245
儒学	*jugaku*	Confucianism	109
儒学者	*jugakusha*	Confucian scholar	109, 164
儒家	*juka*	Confucian scholar, Confucianist	165

儒 儒 儒

1418	立 山 冂 5b 3o 2r

端

TAN – correct; end, tip; ***hashi*** – end, edge; ***hata*** – side, edge, nearby; ***ha*** – edge

極端	*kyokutan*	extreme, ultra-	336
異端	*itan*	heresy, heathenism	1061
道端	*michibata*	roadside, wayside	149
端折る	*hashoru*	tuck up; cut short, abridge	1394

端 端 端

1419 彳 攵 山 3i 4i 3o

微

BI – minute, slight

微妙	*bimyō*	delicate, subtle	1154
微笑	*bishō*	smile	1235
微熱	*binetsu*	a slight fever	645
微生物	*biseibutsu*	microorganism, microbe	44, 79
顕微鏡	*kenbikyō*	microscope	1170, 863

微 微 微

1420 彳 攵 王 3i 4i 4f

徵

CHŌ – collect; demand; sign, symptom

徴候	*chōkō*	sign, indication, symptom	944
象徴	*shōchō*	symbol	739
特徴	*tokuchō*	distinctive feature	282
徴兵	*chōhei*	conscription, military service; draftee	784
徴税	*chōzei*	tax collection	399

徵 徵 徵

1421 心 攵 王 4k 4i 4f

懲

CHŌ, ko(rasu/rashimeru) – chastise, punish, discipline; ***ko(riru)*** – learn by experience, be taught a lesson, be sick of

懲罰	*chōbatsu*	disciplinary measure, punishment	886
懲役	*chōeki*	penal servitude, imprisonment	375
勧善懲悪	*kanzen-chōaku*	good over evil, poetic justice	1051, 1139, 304

懲 懲 懲

1422 彳 攵 月 3i 4i 4b

徹

TETSU – pierce, go through

徹底的	*tetteiteki*	thorough	562, 210
貫徹	*kantetsu*	carry through, accomplish	914
徹夜	*tetsuya*	stay up all night	471
冷徹	*reitetsu*	coolheaded, levelheaded	832

徹 徹 徹

1423 扌 攵 月 3c 4i 4b

撤

TETSU – withdraw, remove

撤回	*tekkai*	withdraw, retract, rescind	90
撤去	*tekkyo*	withdraw, evacuate, remove	414
撤退	*tettai*	withdraw, pull out, retreat	846
撤兵	*teppei*	withdraw troops, disengage	784
撤廃	*teppai*	abolish, do away with, repeal	961

撤 撤 撤

1424 山 ネ 亠 3o 4e 3m

崇

SŪ – respect, revere; lofty, sublime

崇拝	*sūhai*	worship, adoration	1201
祖先崇拝	*sosen sūhai*	ancestor worship	622, 50, 1201
崇敬	*sūkei*	veneration, reverence	705
崇高	*sūkō*	lofty, sublime, noble	190

崇 崇 崇

1425 木 日 艹 4a 4c 3k

模

MO, BO – copy, imitate, model

模様	*moyō*	pattern, design; appearance; situation	403
模範	*mohan*	model, exemplar	1092
模型	*mokei*	(scale) model; a mold	888
模造	*mozō*	imitation	691
規模	*kibo*	scale, scope	607

模 模 模

1426 月 日 艹 4b 4c 3k

膜

MAKU – membrane

角膜	*kakumaku*	cornea	473
鼓膜	*komaku*	eardrum	1147
処女膜	*shojomaku*	hymen	1137, 102
腹膜炎	*fukumakuen*	peritonitis	1271, 1336
結膜炎	*ketsumakuen*	conjunctivitis, pinkeye	485, 1336

膜 膜 膜

1427 氵 日 艹 (3a 4c 3k)

漠

BAKU – vague, obscure; desert; wide

砂漠	*sabaku*	desert	1151
広漠	*kōbaku*	vast, boundless	694
漠然	*bakuzen*	vague, hazy, nebulous	651

1428 艹 日 丷 (3k 4c2 2o)

暮

BO, ku(reru) – grow dark, come to an end; ***ku(rasu)*** – live

歳暮	*seibo*	end of the year; year-end gift	479
野暮	*yabo*	uncouth, rustic, boorish	236
夕暮れ	*yūgure*	evening, twilight	81
一人暮らし	*hitorigurashi*	living alone	2, 1

1429 艹 日 土 (3k 4c 3b)

墓

BO, haka – a grave

墓地	*bochi*	cemetery	118
墓標	*bohyō*	grave marker/post	923
墓石	*boseki*	gravestone	78
墓穴	*boketsu*	grave (pit)	899
墓参り	*hakamairi*	visit to a grave	710

1430 艹 日 力 (3k 4c 2g)

募

BO, tsuno(ru) – appeal for, invite, raise; grow intense

募集	*boshū*	recruiting, solicitation	436
応募	*ōbo*	apply for, enlist, enroll	827
応募者	*ōbosha*	applicant, entrant	827, 164
募金	*bokin*	fund raising	23
公募	*kōbo*	offer for public subscription	126

1431 艹 日 心 3k 4c 4k

慕

BO, shita(u) – yearn for, love dearly; idolize

慕情	*bojō*	longing, love, affection	209
思慕	*shibo*	longing (for), deep attachment (to)	99
敬慕	*keibo*	love and respect	705
恋慕	*renbo*	love, affection	258
追慕	*tsuibo*	cherish (someone's) memory, sigh for	1174

慕 慕 慕

1432 艹 日 巾 3k 4c 3f

幕

MAKU – (stage) curtain; act (of a play); **BAKU** – shogunate

開幕	*kaimaku*	commencement of a performance	396
序幕	*jomaku*	opening act, prelude	770
除幕	*jomaku*	unveiling	1065
内幕	*uchimaku, naimaku*	behind-the-scenes story	84
幕府	*Bakufu*	Japan's feudal government, shogunate	504

幕 幕 幕

1433 氵 心 亻 3a 4k 2a

添

TEN, so(eru) – add (to), append; **so(u)** – accompany

添加	*tenka*	annex, append, affix	709
添付	*tenpu*	attach, append	192
添乗員	*tenjōin*	tour conductor	523, 163
付き添い	*tsukisoi*	attending (someone), escorting	192
力添え	*chikarazoe*	help, assistance	100

添 添 添

1434 艹 心 丷 3k 4k 2o

恭

KYŌ, uyauya(shii) – respectful, reverent, deferential

恭順	*kyōjun*	fealty, allegiance	769
恭敬	*kyōkei*	reverence, respect	705
恭賀新年	*kyōga shinnen*	Best wishes for a happy New Year.	756, 174, 45

恭 恭 恭

1435 氵 艹 丷 3a 3k 2o

洪

KŌ – flood, inundation; vast

洪水	*kōzui*	flood, inundation, deluge	21
洪積層	*kōsekisō*	diluvium, diluvial formation	656, 1367

洪 洪 洪

1436 口 丷 一 3d 2o 1a

呉

GO – Wu (dynasty of ancient China)

呉服	*gofuku*	drapery, dry goods	683
呉服屋	*gofukuya*	draper's shop, dry goods	683, 167
呉越	*Go-Etsu*	Wu and Yue/Yüeh (rival states of China)	1001

呉 呉 呉

1437 女 口 丷 3e 3d 2o

娯

GO – pleasure, enjoyment

娯楽	*goraku*	amusement, entertainment	358
娯楽番組	*goraku bangumi*	entertainment program	358, 185, 418

娯 娯 娯

1438 心 口 一 4k 3d 1a3

悟

GO, sato(ru) – perceive, understand, realize, be enlightened

覚悟	*kakugo*	readiness, preparedness, resoluteness	605
悟り	*satori*	comprehension, understanding; satori, spiritual awakening	

悟 悟 悟

1439	頁 一 丨 9a 1a 1b	***KŌ*** – item, clause, paragraph			
項		事項	*jikō*	matters, facts; items, particulars	80
		事項索引	*jikō sakuin*	subject index	80, 1059, 216
		要項	*yōkō*	essential points, gist	419
		条項	*jōkō*	provision, clause	564
		項目	*kōmoku*	heading, item	55

1440	頁 一 丨 9a 1a 1b	***CHŌ, itadaki*** – summit, top; ***itada(ku)*** – be capped with; receive			
頂		頂上	*chōjō*	summit, peak, top; climax	32
		山頂	*sanchō*	summit, mountain top	34
		頂点	*chōten*	zenith, peak, climax	169
		絶頂	*zetchō*	peak, height, climax	742

1441	亻 頁 ⺊ 2a 9a 2m	***KEI, katamu(ku/keru)*** – (intr./tr.) lean, incline, tilt			
傾		傾向	*keikō*	tendency, trend; inclination	199
		傾斜	*keisha*	inclination, slant, slope	1069
		左傾	*sakei*	leftward leanings, radicalization	75
		傾聴	*keichō*	listen	1039
		傾倒	*keitō*	devote oneself (to), be absorbed (in)	905

1442	氵 十 冂 3a 2k 2r	***HO, ura*** – bay, inlet; seashore			
浦		浦波	*uranami*	wave breaking on the beach, breaker	666
		津々浦々	*tsutsu-uraura*	throughout the land, the entire country	668
		浦島太郎	*Urashima Tarō*	(character in a folk tale)	286, 629, 980

1443 土 口 亻 3b 3d 2a

舗

HO – shop, store; pavement

店舗	*tenpo*	shop, store	168
老舗	*shinise, rōho*	long-established store	543
舗装	*hosō*	pave	1328
舗 (装) 道 (路)	*ho(sō)dō(ro)*	paved road/street	1328, 149, 151

舗 舗 舗

1444 扌 土 口 3c 3b 3d

捨

SHA, su(teru) – throw away; abandon, forsake

取捨	*shusha*	adoption or rejection, selection	65
喜捨	*kisha*	charity, almsgiving, donation	1143
捨て子	*sutego*	abandoned child, foundling	103
見捨てる	*misuteru*	abandon, desert, forsake	63
切り捨てる	*kirisuteru*	cut down; discard, omit	39

捨 捨 捨

1445 扌 口 亻 3c 3d 2a

拾

SHŪ, hiro(u) – pick up, find; ***JŪ*** – ten (in documents)

拾得物	*shūtokubutsu*	an acquisition	374, 79
収拾	*shūshū*	get under control, deal with	757
(金) 拾万円	*(kin)jūman'en*	100,000 yen	23, 16, 13
拾い物	*hiroimono*	something found lying on the ground, a find	79

拾 拾 拾

1446 氵 口 亠 3a 3d 2j

滴

TEKI, shizuku – a drop; ***shitata(ru)*** – drip, trickle

水滴	*suiteki*	drop of water	21
雨滴	*uteki*	raindrop	30
点滴	*tenteki*	falling drop of water/rain; (intravenous) drip	169
滴下	*tekika*	drip, trickle down	31

滴 滴 滴

1447 扌 口 亠 3c 3d 2j

摘

TEKI, tsu(mu) – pick, pluck, nip

摘発	*tekihatsu*	exposure, disclosure	96
摘出	*tekishutsu*	pluck out, extract; expose	53
指摘	*shiteki*	point out	1041
摘要	*tekiyō*	summary, synopsis	419
茶摘み	*chatsumi*	tea picking	251

摘 摘 摘

1448 糸 日 十 6a 4c 2k2

縛

BAKU, shiba(ru) – tie up, bind

束縛	*sokubaku*	restraint, constraint, shackles	501
捕縛	*hobaku*	capture, apprehension, arrest	890
縛り首	*shibarikubi*	(execution by) hanging	148
金縛り	*kanashibari*	be bound; be tied down with money	23

縛 縛 縛

1449 艹 日 氵 3k 4c 3a

薄

HAKU, usu(i) – thin (paper), weak (tea), light (color); ***usu(maru/ragu/reru)*** – thin out, fade; ***usu(meru)*** – dilute

浅薄	*senpaku*	shallow, superficial	649
薄情	*hakujō*	unfeeling, heartless, coldhearted	209
薄弱	*hakujaku*	feebleness	218
薄明	*hakumei*	twilight	18

薄 薄 薄

1450 ⺮ 日 氵 6f 4c 3a

簿

BO – record book, ledger, register

簿記	*boki*	bookkeeping	371
帳簿	*chōbo*	account book, ledger	1105
家計簿	*kakeibo*	housekeeping account book	165, 340
名簿	*meibo*	list of names, roster	82
会員名簿	*kaiin meibo*	list of members	158, 163, 82

簿 簿 簿

1451 攵 日 方 4i 4c 4h

敷

FU, shi(ku) – spread, lay, put down

敷設	*fusetsu*	laying, construction	577
屋敷	*yashiki*	mansion; residential lot	167
座敷	*zashiki*	a room, reception room	786
敷金	*shikikin*	a deposit, security	23
敷布	*shikifu*	(bed) sheet	675

敷 敷 敷

1452 糸 亠 丷 6a 2j 2o

絞

KŌ, shi(meru) – strangle, wring; ***shi(maru)*** – be wrung out, pressed together; ***shibo(ru)*** – wring, squeeze, press, milk

絞殺	*kōsatsu*	strangle to death; hang	576
絞首刑	*kōshukei*	(execution by) hanging	148, 887
お絞り	*oshibori*	wet towel (provided in restaurants)	

絞 絞 絞

1453 車 亠 丷 7c 2j 2o

較

KAKU – compare

比較	*hikaku*	comparison	798
比較的	*hikakuteki*	comparatively, relatively	798, 210
比較文学	*hikaku bungaku*	comparative literature	798, 111, 109
比較級	*hikakukyū*	the comparative (of an adjective)	798, 568

較 較 較

1454 糸 亠 ノ 6a 2j 1c

紋

MON – (family) crest; (textile) pattern

紋章	*monshō*	crest, coat of arms	857
菊の御紋	*kiku no gomon*	imperial chrysanthemum crest	475, 708
指紋	*shimon*	a fingerprint	1041
波紋	*hamon*	a ripple	666
紋切り形/型	*monkirigata*	conventional pattern	39, 395, 888

紋 紋 紋

1455 芽

艹 十 一 (3k 2k 1a)

GA, me – a sprout, bud

発芽	*hatsuga*	germinate, sprout, bud	96
麦芽	*bakuga*	malt	270
新芽	*shinme*	new bud, sprout, shoot	174
芽生え	*mebae*	bud, sprout, seedling	44
木の芽	*ki no me*	leaf bud; Japanese pepper bud	22

芽 芽 芽

1456 雅

隹 十 一 (8c 2k 1a)

GA – elegance, gracefulness

優雅	*yūga*	elegance, grace, refinement	1033
風雅	*fūga*	elegance, refinement, (good) taste	29
雅趣	*gashu*	elegance, tastefulness, artistry	1002
雅楽	*gagaku*	ancient Japanese court music	358

雅 雅 雅

1457 邪

阝 十 一 (2d 2k 1a)

JA – evil, wrong

邪推	*jasui*	groundless suspicion, mistrust	1233
邪道	*jadō*	evil course, vice; heresy	149
邪教	*jakyō*	heretical religion, heathenism	245
邪宗	*jashū*	heretical sect, heathenism	616
風邪	*kaze*	a cold	29

邪 邪 邪

1458 既

一 日 丨 (1a2 4c 1b)

KI, sude (ni) – already

既成(の)事実	*kisei (no) jijitsu*	accomplished fact	261, 80, 203
既製服	*kiseifuku*	ready-made clothes	428, 683
既婚	*kikon*	married	567
既報	*kihō*	previous report	685
既往症	*kiōshō*	previous illness; medical history	918, 1318

既 既 既

1459 木 日 一 4a 4c 1a2

概

GAI – general, approximate

概算	*gaisan*	rough estimate	747
概略	*gairyaku*	outline, summary	841
概括	*gaikatsu*	summary, generalization	1260
概況	*gaikyō*	general situation, outlook	850
概念	*gainen*	concept	579

概 概 概

1460 心 日 一 4k 4c 1a2

慨

GAI – regret, lament, deplore

慨嘆	*gaitan*	regret, lament, deplore	1246
感慨	*kangai*	deep emotion	262
感慨無量	*kangai-muryō*	filled with deep emotion	262, 93, 411

慨 慨 慨

1461 氵 土 厂 3a 3b2 2p

涯

GAI – shore; end, limit

生涯	*shōgai*	a life, one's lifetime	44
生涯教育	*shōgai kyōiku*	continuing education	44, 245, 246
一生涯	*isshōgai*	one's (whole) life (long)	2, 44
天涯	*tengai*	horizon; a distant land	141

涯 涯 涯

1462 亻 土 2a 3b2

佳

KA – good, beautiful

佳人	*kajin*	beautiful woman, a beauty	1
佳作	*kasaku*	a fine piece of work	360
風光絶佳	*fūkō-zekka*	scenic beauty	29, 138, 742
佳境	*kakyō*	interesting part, climax (of a story)	864

佳 佳 佳

1463	扌 十 3b2 2k
封	

FŪ – seal; ***HŌ*** – fief

同封	*dōfū*	enclose (with a letter)	198
封入	*fūnyū*	enclose (with a letter)	52
封書	*fūsho*	sealed letter/document	131
開封	*kaifū*	open (a letter)	396
封建制度	*hōken seido*	the feudal system	892, 427, 377

封 封 封

1464	扌 土 卜 3c 3b2 2m
掛	

ka(karu) – hang; cost, take; ***ka(keru)*** – hang up; put on top of; spend; multiply; ***kakari*** – expenses; tax; relation, connection

腰掛け	*koshikake*	seat, bench; stepping-stone	1298
掛け布団	*kakebuton*	quilt, bedspread	675, 491
掛け軸	*kakejiku*	hanging scroll	988
心掛け	*kokorogake*	intention; attitude; attention	97

掛 掛 掛

1465	土 卜 亻 3b 2m2 2a
赴	

FU, omomu(ku) – go, proceed; become

赴任	*funin*	proceed to one's new post	334
赴任地/先	*funin-chi/saki*	one's post, one's place of appointment	334, 118, 50

赴 赴 赴

1466	木 卜 4a 2m
朴	

BOKU – simple, plain

素朴	*soboku*	simple, unsophisticated	271
質朴	*shitsuboku*	simplehearted, unsophisticated	176
朴直	*bokuchoku*	simple and honest, ingenuous	423
朴とつ	*bokutotsu*	ruggedly honest, rudely simple	

朴 朴 朴

1467 艹 戈 丨 3k 4n 1b

茂

MO, shige(ru) – grow thick/rank

繁茂	*hanmo*	luxuriant growth	1292
生い茂る	*oishigeru*	grow luxuriantly	44

茂 茂 茂

1468 艹 田 3k 5f

苗

BYŌ, nae, [nawa] – seedling, sapling

苗木	*naegi*	sapling, seedling, young tree	22
苗床	*naedoko*	nursery, seedbed	826
苗代	*nawashiro*	bed for rice seedlings	256
苗字	*myōji*	family name, surname	110

苗 苗 苗

1469 扌 田 艹 3c 5f 3k

描

BYŌ, ega(ku) – draw, paint, sketch, depict, portray

描写	*byōsha*	depiction, portrayal, description	540
心理描写	*shinri byōsha*	psychological description	97, 143, 540
素描	*sobyō*	rough sketch	271
絵描き	*ekaki*	painter, artist	345

描 描 描

1470 犭 田 艹 3g 5f 3k

猫

BYŌ, neko – cat

愛猫	*aibyō*	pet cat	259
招き猫	*manekineko*	porcelain cat beckoning customers in stores	455
山猫	*yamaneko*	wildcat, lynx	34
山猫争議	*yamaneko sōgi*	wildcat strike	34, 302, 292
猫なで声	*nekonadegoe*	coaxing voice	746

猫 猫 猫

1471 ⺮ 日 丨 6f 4c 1b

笛

TEKI, fue – flute, whistle

警笛	*keiteki*	alarm whistle; (automobile) horn	706
汽笛	*kiteki*	steam whistle	135
霧笛	*muteki*	foghorn	950
口笛	*kuchibue*	a whistle	54
角笛	*tsunobue*	bugle; huntsman's horn	473

笛 笛 笛

1472 ⺮ 口 冂 6f 3d 2r

筒

TŌ, tsutsu – pipe, tube

封筒	*fūtō*	envelope	1463
水筒	*suitō*	canteen, flask	21
発煙筒	*hatsuentō*	smoke candle	96, 919
円筒	*entō*	cylinder	13
竹筒	*takezutsu*	bamboo tube	129

筒 筒 筒

1473 ⺮ 囗 口 6f 3s 3d

箇

KA – (single) object; (counter for inanimate objects)

箇所	*kasho*	place, part, passage (in a book)	153
箇条	*kajō*	article, provision, item	564
箇条書き	*kajōgaki*	an itemization	564, 131
一箇年	*ikkanen*	1 year	2, 45

箇 箇 箇

1474 ⺾ 土 又 3k 3b 2h

茎

KEI, kuki – stalk, stem

地下茎	*chikakei*	underground stem, rhizome	118, 31
球茎	*kyūkei*	(tulip) bulb	726
陰茎	*inkei*	penis	867
歯茎	*haguki*	gums	478

茎 茎 茎

1475	彳 3i	土 3b	又 2h

径

KEI – path; diameter

直径	*chokkei*	diameter	423
半径	*hankei*	radius	88
口径	*kōkei*	caliber	54
径路	*keiro*	course, route, process	151
直情径行	*chokujō keikō*	straightforwardness	423, 209, 68

径 径 径

1476	心 4k	土 3b	又 2h

怪

KAI, aya(shii) – dubious; suspicious-looking; strange, mysterious; poor, clumsy;
aya(shimu) – doubt, be sceptical; marvel at, be surprised

怪物	*kaibutsu*	monster, apparition; mystery man	79
奇怪	*kikai*	strange, mysterious; outrageous	1360

怪 怪 怪

1477	亠 2j	一 1a2	丨 1b2

斉

SEI – equal

一斉に	*issei ni*	all at once, all together	2
均斉	*kinsei*	symmetry, good balance	805

斉 斉 斉

1478	亠 2j	⺌ 3n	一 1a2

斎

SAI – religious purification; a room

書斎	*shosai*	a study, library	131
斎戒	*saikai*	purification	876
斎戒もく浴	*saikai mokuyoku*	ablution, purification	876, 1128

斎 斎 斎

1479 彳 目 十 3i 5c 2k

循

JUN – follow, circulate

循環	*junkan*	circulation	865
血液循環	*ketsueki junkan*	blood circulation	789, 472, 865
悪循環	*akujunkan*	vicious circle	304, 865

循 循 循

1480 子 厂 丨 2c 2p 1b

孤

KO – lone, alone

孤独	*kodoku*	solitary, lonely	219
孤立	*koritsu*	isolation	121
孤島	*kotō*	solitary/desert island	286
孤客	*kokaku*	solitary traveler	641
孤児(院)	*koji(in)*	orphan(age)	1217, 614

孤 孤 孤

1481 弓 厂 丨 3h 2p 1b

弧

KO – arc

弧状	*kojō*	arc-shaped	626
円弧	*enko*	circular arc	13
括弧	*kakko*	parentheses ( )	1260

弧 弧 弧

1482 彳 丷 ト 3i 2o 2m

従

JŪ, [JU], [SHŌ], shitaga(u) – obey, comply with, follow; ***shitaga(eru)*** – be attended by; conquer

服従	*fukujū*	obedience, submission	683
盲従	*mōjū*	blind obedience	1375
従来	*jūrai*	up to now, usual, conventional	69
従業員	*jūgyōin*	employee	279, 163

従 従 従

1483 糸 彳 丷
6a 3i 2o

縦

JŪ, tate – height, length; vertical

縦線	*jūsen*	vertical line	299
放縦	*hōjū*	self-indulgent, dissolute, licentious	512
縦横	*jūō, tateyoko*	length and breadth	781
縦断	*jūdan*	vertical section; traverse, travel across	1024

縦 縦 縦

1484 火 一 ノ
4d 1a3 1c

為

I – do

為政者	*iseisha*	statesman, administrator	483, 164
人為的	*jin'iteki*	artificial	1, 210
行為	*kōi*	act, deed, behavior, conduct	68
無為	*mui*	idleness, inaction	93
為替	*kawase*	money order; (foreign) exchange	744

為 為 為

1485 亻 火 一
2a 4d 1a3

偽

GI, itsuwa(ru) – lie, misrepresent, feign, deceive; ***nise*** – fake, sham, bogus, counterfeit

偽造	*gizō*	forgery	691
偽証	*gishō*	perjury	484
真偽	*shingi*	true or false, truth	422
偽物	*nisemono*	fake, imitation, counterfeit	79

偽 偽 偽

1486 亻 丨 ノ
2a2 1b 1c

似

JI, ni(ru) – be similar (to), be like, resemble

類似	*ruiji*	resemblance, similarity	226
相似	*sōji*	resemblance, similarity	146
似顔	*nigao*	likeness, portrait	277
空似	*sorani*	accidental resemblance	140
似合う	*niau*	be becoming, suit, go well (with)	159

似 似 似

1487 辛
立 5b 十 2k

SHIN, kara(i) – hot, spicy, salty; hard, trying

辛苦	*shinku*	hardships, labor, trouble	545
辛酸	*shinsan*	hardships, privations	516
辛勝	*shinshō*	win after a hard fight	509
辛抱	*shinbō*	patience, perseverance	1285
辛味	*karami*	pungent taste, spiciness	307

1488 宰
宀 3m 立 5b 十 2k

SAI – manage, rule

主宰	*shusai*	superintendence, presiding over	155
主宰者	*shusaisha*	president, chairman, leader	155, 164
宰相	*saishō*	prime minister, premier	146

1489 壁
土 3b 立 5b 尸 3r

HEKI, kabe – wall

障壁	*shōheki*	fence, wall, barrier, obstacle	858
防壁	*bōheki*	protective wall, bulwark	513
岩壁	*ganpeki*	rock wall/face	1345
壁画	*hekiga*	fresco, mural	343
壁紙	*kabegami*	wallpaper	180

1490 癖
疒 5i 立 5b 尸 3r

HEKI, kuse – personal habit, quirk, propensity

性癖	*seiheki*	disposition, proclivity	98
悪癖	*akuheki*	bad habit	304
潔癖	*keppeki*	love of cleanliness, fastidiousness	1241
盗癖	*tōheki*	kleptomania	1100
口癖	*kuchiguse*	habit of saying, favorite phrase	54

1491 ⻌ 立 尸 2q 5b 3r

避

HI, sa(keru) – avoid

回避	*kaihi*	evasion, avoidance	90
不可避	*fukahi*	unavoidable	94, 388
避難	*hinan*	refuge, evacuation	557
避妊	*hinin*	contraception	955
避雷針	*hiraishin*	lightning rod	952, 341

避 避 避

1492 艹 一 3k 1a2

甘

KAN, ama(i) – sweet; insufficiently salted; indulgent; overoptimistic; ***ama(eru)*** – coax, wheedle, act spoiled, presume upon (another's) love; ***ama(yakasu)*** – be indulgent

甘味料	*kanmiryō*	sweetener	307, 319
甘美	*kanbi*	sweet, dulcet	401
甘言	*kangen*	honeyed words, flattery	66

甘 甘 甘

1493 糸 艹 一 6a 3k 1a2

紺

KON – dark/navy blue

紺色	*kon'iro*	dark/navy blue	204
濃紺	*nōkon*	deep/dark/navy blue	957
紺屋	*kon'ya, kōya*	dyer, dyer's shop	167

紺 紺 紺

1494 木 艹 一 4a 3k 1a2

某

BŌ – a certain

某所	*bōsho*	a certain place	153
某氏	*bōshi*	a certain person	566
某国	*bōkoku*	a certain country	40
某日	*bōjitsu*	a certain day, one day	5
何某	*nanibō*	a certain person	390

某 某 某

1495 言 木 艹 7a 4a 3k

謀

BŌ, [MU], haka(ru) – plan, devise; deceive

陰謀	*inbō*	plot, intrigue, conspiracy	867
共謀	*kyōbō*	conspiracy, collusion	196
主謀者	*shubōsha*	ringleader, mastermind	155, 164
謀略	*bōryaku*	strategem, scheme	841
参謀	*sanbō*	(general) staff	710

謀 謀 謀

1496 女 木 艹 3e 4a 3k

媒

BAI – go-between

触媒	*shokubai*	catalyst	874
触媒作用	*shokubai sayō*	catalytic action	874, 360, 107
媒介	*baikai*	mediation; matchmaking	453
媒介物	*baikaibutsu*	a medium; carrier (of a disease)	453, 79
霊媒	*reibai*	(spiritualistic) medium	1168

媒 媒 媒

1497 扌 宀 ソ 3c 3m 2o

搾

SAKU, shibo(ru) – squeeze, press, extract, milk

圧搾	*assaku*	pressure, compression	1342
圧搾器	*assakuki*	press, compressor	1342, 527
搾乳	*sakunyū*	milk (a cow)	939
搾取	*sakushu*	exploitation	65
搾り取る	*shiboritoru*	press out, extract	65

搾 搾 搾

1498 言 ト 一 7a 2m 1a2

詐

SA – lie, deceive

詐称	*sashō*	misrepresent oneself	978
詐取	*sashu*	fraud, swindle	65

詐 詐 詐

1499 欠 艹 丷 4j 3k 2o

GI, azamu(ku) – deceive, dupe

詐欺	*sagi*	fraud	1498
詐欺師	*sagishi*	swindler	1498, 409

欺

1500 匚 丷 2t 2o

HITSU – compare; alone; **hiki** – (counter for animals)

匹敵	*hitteki*	be a match (for), comparable (to)	416
匹夫	*hippu*	man; man of humble position	315
犬一匹	*inu ippiki*	1 dog	280, 2

匹

1501 艹 丷 一 3k 2o 1a3

JIN, hanaha(da/dashii) – very much, extreme, great, enormous, intense

甚大	*jindai*	very great, immense, serious, heavy	26
激甚	*gekijin*	intense, violent, severe	1017
幸甚	*kōjin*	very glad, much obliged	684
甚六	*jinroku*	simpleton, blockhead	8

甚

1502 力 艹 丷 2g 3k 2o

KAN – perception, intuition, sixth sense

勘定	*kanjō*	counting, accounts, bill	355
割り勘	*warikan*	splitting the bill equally, Dutch treat	519
勘弁	*kanben*	pardon, forgive, overlook	711
勘違い	*kanchigai*	misunderstanding, mistaken idea	814
勘当	*kandō*	disown, disinherit	77

勘

1503 一 木 ノ 1a 4a 1c

朱

SHU – scarlet

朱色	*shuiro*	scarlet, cinnabar, vermilion	204
朱印	*shuin*	red seal	1043
朱肉	*shuniku*	red ink pad	223
朱筆を加える	*shuhitsu o kuwaeru*	correct, retouch	130, 709

朱 朱 朱

1504 王 木 一 4f 4a 1a

珠

SHU – pearl

真珠	*shinju*	pearl	422
珠玉	*shugyoku*	jewel, gem	295
珠算	*shuzan*	calculation on the abacus	747
数珠	*juzu*	rosary	225
真珠湾	*Shinju-wan*	Pearl Harbor	422, 670

珠 珠 珠

1505 一 木 ⺈ 1a 4a 2n

殊

SHU, koto (ni) – especially, in particular

特殊	*tokushu*	special, unique	282
特殊性	*tokushusei*	special characteristics, peculiarity	282, 98
殊勝	*shushō*	admirable, praiseworthy	509
殊の外	*koto no hoka*	exceedingly, exceptionally	83

殊 殊 殊

1506 目 十 ⺈ 5c 2k 2n

殖

SHOKU, fu(eru) – grow in number, increase; ***fu(yasu)*** – increase

増殖	*zōshoku*	increase, multiply, proliferate	712
生殖	*seishoku*	reproduction, procreation	44
繁殖	*hanshoku*	breeding, reproduction	1292
養殖	*yōshoku*	raising, culture, cultivation	402

殖 殖 殖

1507	⻌ 亻 一 2q 2a 1a2			
迭	***TETSU*** – alternation			
	更迭	*kōtetsu*	change (in personnel), reshuffle	1008

1508	禾 亻 一 5d 2a 1a2			
秩	***CHITSU*** – order, sequence			
	秩序	*chitsujo*	order, system, regularity	770
	安寧秩序	*annei-chitsujo*	peace and order	105, 1412, 770
	無秩序	*muchitsujo*	disorder, chaos, confusion	93, 770
	秩父	*Chichibu*	(resort area NW of Tokyo)	113

1509	亻 戈 2a 4n			
伐	***BATSU*** – attack; cut down			
	征伐	*seibatsu*	conquest, subjugation	1114
	討伐	*tōbatsu*	subjugation, suppression	1019
	殺伐	*satsubatsu*	bloody, savage, warlike, fierce	576
	伐採	*bassai*	timber felling, lumbering	933
	乱伐	*ranbatsu*	reckless deforestation, overcutting	689

1510	門 戈 亻 8e 4n 2a			
閥	***BATSU*** – clique, clan, faction			
	派閥	*habatsu*	clique, faction	912
	財閥	*zaibatsu*	financial combine	553
	軍閥	*gunbatsu*	military clique, the militarists	438
	藩閥	*hanbatsu*	clan, clique, faction	1382
	門閥	*monbatsu*	lineage; distinguished family	161

1511 門口丷 8e 3d 2o

TŌ, tataka(u) – fight, struggle

闘争	*tōsō*	struggle, conflict; strike	302
戦闘	*sentō*	battle, combat	301
奮闘	*funtō*	hard fighting, strenuous efforts	1309
春闘	*shuntō*	spring (labor) offensive	460
格闘	*kakutō*	hand-to-hand fighting, scuffle	643

闘 闘 闘

1512 頁木口 9a 4a 3s

RAI, tano(mu) – ask for, request; entrust (to); ***tano(moshii)*** – reliable, dependable; promising; ***tayo(ru)*** – rely, depend (on)

依頼	*irai*	request; entrust (to); reliance	678
信頼	*shinrai*	reliance, trust, confidence	157
頼信紙	*raishinshi*	telegram form	157, 180

頼 頼 頼

1513 氵頁木 3a 9a 4a

se – shallows; rapids

浅瀬	*asase*	shoal, shallows, sandbank; ford	649
早瀬	*hayase*	swift current, rapids	248
瀬戸際	*setogiwa*	crucial moment, crisis, brink (of war)	152, 618
瀬戸物	*setomono*	porcelain, china, earthenware	152, 79
瀬戸内海	*Setonaikai*	Inland Sea	152, 84, 117

瀬 瀬 瀬

1514 一木口 1a 4a 3s

SO, uto(mu) – shun, neglect, treat coldly; ***uto(i)*** – distant, estranged; know little (of)

疎遠	*soen*	estrangement, alienation	446
疎開	*sokai*	evacuation, removal	396
空疎	*kūso*	empty, unsubstantial	140
(意志の)疎通	*(ishi no) sotsū*	mutual understanding	132, 573, 150

疎 疎 疎

1515 石 木 ⺊ 5a 4a2 2m

礎

SO, ishizue – cornerstone, foundation (stone)

基礎	*kiso*	foundation, basis	450
基礎工事	*kiso kōji*	foundation work, groundwork	450, 139, 80
基礎知識	*kiso chishiki*	elementary knowledge	450, 214, 681
礎石	*soseki*	foundation (stone)	78
定礎式	*teisoshiki*	laying of the cornerstone	355, 525

礎 礎 礎

1516 ⺊ 亻 一 2m2 2a2 1a4

疑

GI, utaga(u) – be doubtful of, be suspicious of, distrust

疑問	*gimon*	question, doubt, problem	162
疑惑	*giwaku*	suspicion, distrust, misgivings	969
疑獄	*gigoku*	scandal	884
容疑者	*yōgisha*	a suspect	654, 164
質疑応答	*shitsugi-ōtō*	question and answer (session)	176, 827, 160

疑 疑 疑

1517 扌 ⺊ 亻 3c 2m2 2a2

擬

GI – imitate

擬人	*gijin*	personification	1
擬音	*gion*	an imitated sound; sound effects	347
模擬	*mogi*	imitation, simulated	1425
模擬試験	*mogi shiken*	mock/trial examination	1425, 526, 532

擬 擬 擬

1518 冫 ⺊ 亻 2b 2m2 2a2

凝

GYŌ, ko(ru) – grow stiff; be engrossed (in); be fastidious, elaborate (about); ***ko(rasu)*** – concentrate, strain

凝固	*gyōko*	solidification, coagulation, freezing	972
凝結	*gyōketsu*	coagulation, curdling, condensation	485
凝視	*gyōshi*	stare at, watch intently	606
凝り性	*korishō*	fastidiousness, perfectionism	98

凝 凝 凝

1519 扌 衤 宀
3c 4e 3m

擦

SATSU, su(reru) – rub, chafe; become worn; lose one's simplicity; **su(ru)** – rub, file

擦過傷	*sakkashō*	an abrasion, scratch	413, 633
靴擦れ	*kutsuzure*	shoe sore	1076
擦れ違う	*surechigau*	pass by each other	814
擦り傷	*surikizu*	an abrasion, scratch	633

擦 擦 擦

1520 扌 耳 日
3c 6e 4c

撮

SATSU – pick, pinch; summarize; **to(ru)** – take (a picture)

撮影	*satsuei*	photography, filming	854
撮影所	*satsueijo*	movie studio	854, 153
戸/野外撮影	*ko/ya-gai satsuei*	outdoor photography, outdoor shooting	152, 236, 83, 854
夜間撮影	*yakan satsuei*	night photography	471, 43, 854

撮 撮 撮

1521 十 田 ノ
2k 5f 1c2

卑

HI, iya(shimeru/shimu) – despise, look down on; **iya(shii)** – humble, lowly; base, ignoble, vulgar

男尊女卑	*danson-johi*	predominance of men over women	101, 704, 102
卑俗	*hizoku*	vulgar, coarse	1126
卑劣漢	*hiretsukan*	mean bastard, low-down skunk	1150, 556
卑語	*higo*	vulgar word/expression	67

卑 卑 卑

1522 石 田 十
5a 5f 2k

碑

HI – tombstone, monument

記念碑	*kinenhi*	monument, memorial	371, 579
墓碑	*bohi*	tombstone, gravestone	1429
石碑	*sekihi*	tombstone, (stone) monument	78
碑文	*hibun*	epitaph, inscription	111

碑 碑 碑

1523 田 丷 ノ 5f 2o 1c2

鬼

KI, oni – ogre, demon, devil; soul of a dead person

鬼神	*kijin, kishin, onigami*	fierce god; departed soul	310
餓鬼	*gaki*	hungry ghost; little brat	1303
鬼才	*kisai*	genius, man of remarkable talent	551
鬼ごっこ	*onigokko*	tag; blindman's buff	

鬼 鬼 鬼

1524 土 田 丷 3b 5f 2o

塊

KAI, katamari – lump, clod, clump

土塊	*dokai*	clod of dirt	24
金塊	*kinkai*	gold nugget/bar	23
肉塊	*nikkai*	piece of meat	223
塊根	*kaikon*	tuberous root	314
塊状	*kaijō*	massive	626

塊 塊 塊

1525 田 丷 一 5f 2o 1a2

魂

KON, tamashii – soul, spirit

霊魂	*reikon*	the soul	1168
商魂	*shōkon*	commercial spirit, salesmanship	412
魂胆	*kontan*	soul; ulterior motive	1273
負けじ魂	*makeji-damashii*	unyielding spirit	510
大和魂	*Yamato-damashii*	the Japanese spirit	26, 124

魂 魂 魂

1526 田 木 丷 5f 4a 2o

魅

MI – charm, enchant, fascinate

魅力	*miryoku*	charm, appeal, fascination	100
魅力的	*miryokuteki*	fascinating, captivating	100, 210
魅了	*miryō*	charm, captivate, hold spellbound	941
魅惑	*miwaku*	fascination, charm, lure	969

魅 魅 魅

1527 酉 田 丷 (7e 5f 2o)

醜

SHŪ, miniku(i) – ugly

醜聞	*shūbun*	scandal	64
醜悪	*shūaku*	ugly, abominable, scandalous	304
醜態	*shūtai*	unseemly sight; disgraceful behavior	387
醜女	*shūjo, shikome*	ugly woman	102
美醜	*bishū*	beauty or ugliness, appearance	401

醜 醜 醜

1528 广 田 木 (3q 5f 4a2)

魔

MA – demon, devil, evil spirit

悪魔	*akuma*	devil	304
魔術	*majutsu*	black magic, sorcery, witchcraft	187
魔法	*mahō*	magic	123
魔法瓶	*mahōbin*	thermos bottle	123, 1161
邪魔	*jama*	encumbrance, interruption, disturbance	1457

魔 魔 魔

1529 广 木 (3q 4a2)

麻

MA, asa – flax, hemp

大麻	*taima, ōasa*	hemp, marijuana	26
麻薬	*mayaku*	narcotics, drugs	359
麻ひ	*mahi*	paralysis	
小児麻ひ	*shōni mahi*	infantile paralysis, polio	27, 1217
麻糸	*asaito*	hempen yarn, linen thread	242

麻 麻 麻

1530 广 木 扌 (3q 4a2 3c)

摩

MA – rub, rub off, scape

摩擦	*masatsu*	friction	1519
冷水摩擦	*reisui masatsu*	rubdown with a wet towel	832, 21, 1519
あん摩	*anma*	massage, masseur, masseuse	

摩 摩 摩

1531 广 石 木 3q 5a 4a2

磨

MA, miga(ku) – polish, brush

研磨	*kenma*	grind, polish; study hard	896
磨滅	*mametsu*	wear, abrasion	1338
達磨	*daruma*	Bodhidharma; quadruple amputee; prostitute	448
歯磨き	*hamigaki*	toothpaste	478
磨き上げる	*migakiageru*	polish up	32

磨 磨 磨

1532 門 木 8e 4a

閑

KAN – leisure

閑静	*kansei*	quiet, peaceful	663
森閑	*shinkan*	stillness, quiet	128
安閑	*ankan*	idleness	105
閑散	*kansan*	leisure; (market) inactivity	767
農閑期	*nōkanki*	the slack season for farming	369, 449

閑 閑 閑

1533 ⺮ 門 日 6f 8e 4c

簡

KAN – simple, brief

簡単	*kantan*	simple, brief	300
簡略	*kanryaku*	simple, concise	841
簡潔	*kanketsu*	concise	1241
簡素	*kanso*	plain and simple	271
書簡	*shokan*	letter, correspondence	131

簡 簡 簡

1534 厂 木 日 2p 4a2 4c

暦

REKI, koyomi – calendar

西暦	*seireki*	the Western calendar, A.D.	72
旧暦	*kyūreki*	the old (lunar) calendar	1216
太陽暦	*taiyōreki*	the solar calendar	629, 630
還暦	*kanreki*	one's 60th birthday	866
花暦	*hanagoyomi*	floral calendar	255

暦 暦 暦

1535 艹 木 日 (3k 4a 4c) 菓

KA – cake; fruit

(お)菓子	*(o)kashi*	candy, confections, pastry	103
菓子屋	*kashiya*	candy store, confectionary shop	103, 167
和菓子	*wagashi*	Japanese-style confection	124, 103
茶菓	*chaka, saka*	tea and cake, refreshments	251
水菓子	*mizugashi*	fruit	21, 103

菓 菓 菓

1536 礻 木 日 (5e 4a 4c) 裸

RA, hadaka – naked

裸婦	*rafu*	nude woman	316
裸体画	*rataiga*	nude picture	61, 343
赤裸々	*sekirara*	naked; frank, outspoken	207
裸馬	*hadakauma*	unsaddled horse	283
裸一貫	*hadaka-ikkan*	with no property but one's own body	2, 914

裸 裸 裸

1537 礻 木 礻 (5e 4a2 4e) 襟

KIN, eri – neck; collar, lapel

胸襟	*kyōkin*	bosom, heart	1283
開襟シャツ	*kaikin shatsu*	open-necked shirt	396
襟巻き	*erimaki*	muffler, scarf	507
襟首	*erikubi*	nape, back/scruff of the neck	148
襟元	*erimoto*	the neck	137

襟 襟 襟

1538 ⺍ 木 日 (3n 4a 4c) 巣

SŌ, su – nest

卵巣	*ransō*	ovary	1058
炎症病巣	*enshō byōsō*	focus of an inflammation	1336, 1318, 380
古巣	*furusu*	old nest, one's old haunt	172
巣立ち	*sudachi*	leave the nest, become independent	121
空き巣(ねらい)	*akisu(nerai)*	sneak thief	140

巣 巣 巣

1539 弓 日 ⺍ (3h 4c 3n)

弾

DAN, tama – bullet; ***hazu(mu)*** – bounce; be stimulated; fork out, splurge on; ***hi(ku)*** – play (piano/guitar)

爆弾	*bakudan*	a bomb	1015
弾薬	*dan'yaku*	ammunition	359
弾丸	*dangan*	projectile, bullet, shell	644
弾力	*danryoku*	elasticity	100

弾 弾 弾

1540 ネ 日 ⺍ (4e 4c 3n)

禅

ZEN – Zen Buddhism

禅宗	*Zenshū*	the Zen sect	616
座禅	*zazen*	religious meditation (done while sitting)	786
禅僧	*zensō*	Zen priest	1366
禅寺	*zendera*	Zen temple	41
禅問答	*zen mondō*	Zen dialogue; incomprehensible dialogue	162, 160

禅 禅 禅

1541 一 亻 十 (1a4 2a 2k)

奉

HŌ, [BU], tatematsu(ru) – offer, present; revere

奉納	*hōnō*	dedication, offering	758
奉献	*hōken*	dedication, consecration	1355
信奉	*shinpō*	belief, faith	157
奉仕	*hōshi*	attendance; service	333
奉公	*hōkō*	public duty; domestic service	126

奉 奉 奉

1542 亻 十 一 (2a2 2k 1a4)

俸

HŌ – salary

俸給	*hōkyū*	salary, pay	346
年俸	*nenpō*	annual salary	45
号俸	*gōhō*	pay level, salary class	266
年功加俸	*nenkō kahō*	long-service pension/allowance	45, 818, 709
減俸	*genpō*	salary reduction, pay cut	715

俸 俸 俸

1543 木 亻 十 4a 2a 2k

棒

BŌ – stick, pole

鉄棒	*tetsubō*	iron bar; the horizontal bar (in gymnastics)	312
心棒	*shinbō*	axle, shaft	97
棒立ち	*bōdachi*	standing bolt upright	121
相棒	*aibō*	pal; accomplice	146
棒暗記	*bōanki*	rote memorization	348, 371

1544 一 亻 1a5 2a2

奏

SŌ, kana(deru) – play (a musical instrument)

演奏会	*ensōkai*	concert, recital	344, 158
前奏	*zensō*	prelude	47
独奏	*dokusō*	a solo (performance)	219
二重奏	*nijūsō*	duet	3, 227
伴奏	*bansō*	accompaniment	1027

1545 氵 亻 一 3a 2a 1a3

泰

TAI – calm, peace

泰然自若	*taizen jijaku*	imperturbability	651, 62, 544
安泰	*antai*	tranquility; security	105
泰平	*taihei*	peace, tranquility	202
泰西	*taisei*	Occident, the West	72
泰西名画	*taisei meiga*	a famous Western painting	72, 82, 343

1546 氵 木 亻 3a2 4a 2a

漆

SHITSU, urushi – lacquer

漆器	*shikki*	lacquerware	527
漆黒	*shikkoku*	jet-black, pitch-black	206
乾漆像	*kanshitsuzō*	dry-lacquered image (of Buddha)	1190, 740
漆くい	*shikkui*	mortar, plaster	
漆塗り	*urushinuri*	lacquered, japanned	1073

1547	丷 心 一 2o 4k 1a	***JI, itsuku(shimu)*** – love, treat with affection			
		慈善	*jizen*	charity, philanthropy	1139
		慈悲	*jihi*	mercy, benevolence, pity	1034
		慈恵	*jikei*	charity	1219
		慈愛	*jiai*	affection, kindness, love	259
		慈雨	*jiu*	beneficial/welcome rain	30

慈

1548	石 丷 一 5a 2o 1a	***JI*** – magnetism; porcelain			
		磁気	*jiki*	magnetism, magnetic	134
		磁石	*jishaku*	magnet	78
		電磁石	*denjishaku*	electromagnet	108, 78
		磁場	*jiba, jijō*	magnetic field	154
		磁器	*jiki*	porcelain	527

磁

1549	氵 丷 一 3a 2o 1a	***JI*** – more and more, luxuriant			
		滋養	*jiyō*	nourishment, nutrition	402
		滋養分	*jiyōbun*	nutritious element, nutriment	402, 38
		滋賀県	*Shiga-ken*	Shiga Prefecture	756, 194

滋

1550	一 十 ノ 1a3 2k 1c	***JU, kotobuki*** – congratulations; longevity			
		寿命	*jumyō*	lifespan, life	578
		天寿	*tenju*	one's natural span of life	141
		長寿	*chōju*	longevity	95
		喜寿	*kiju*	one's 77th birthday	1143
		寿司	*sushi*	raw fish and other delicacies with vinegared rice	842

寿

1551	金 十 一 8a 2k 1a3	***CHŪ, i(ru)*** – cast (metal)		
鋳	鋳造	*chūzō*	casting; minting, coinage	691
	鋳鉄	*chūtetsu*	cast iron	312
	改鋳	*kaichū*	recoinage; recasting	514
	鋳型	*igata*	a mold, cast	888
	鋳物	*imono*	an article of cast metal, a casting	79

1552	金 口 ⺈ 8a 3d 2n	***MEI*** – inscription, signature, name; precept, motto		
銘	銘記	*meiki*	bear in mind	371
	感銘	*kanmei*	deep impression	262
	銘柄	*meigara*	a brand (name)	985
	座右銘	*zayūmei*	motto	786, 76
	碑銘	*himei*	inscription; epitaph	1522

1553	戸 隹 4m 8c	***KO, yato(u)*** – employ; charter		
雇	終身雇用制	*shūshin koyōsei*	lifetime employment system	458, 59, 107, 427
	解雇	*kaiko*	dismiss, fire	474
	雇い人	*yatoinin*	employee; servant	1
	雇い主	*yatoinushi*	employer	155

1554	頁 隹 戸 9a 8c 4m	***KO, kaeri(miru)*** – look back; take into consideration		
顧	回顧	*kaiko*	recollection, retrospect	90
	回顧録	*kaikoroku*	reminiscences, memoirs	90, 538
	顧慮	*koryo*	regard, consideration	1384
	顧問	*komon*	adviser	162
	顧客	*kokaku, kokyaku*	customer	641

1555 戸 冫 一
4m 2b2 1a2

扇

SEN, ōgi – fan, folding fan

扇子	*sensu*	folding fan	103
扇風機	*senpūki*	electric fan	29, 528
扇形	*senkei, ōgigata*	fan shape, sector, segment	395
扇動	*sendō*	incitement, instigation, agitation	231
舞扇	*maiōgi*	dancer's fan	810

扇 扇 扇

1556 戸 ト 一
4m 2m 1a5

扉

HI, tobira – door; title page

開扉	*kaihi*	opening of the door	396
門扉	*monpi*	the doors of a gate	161

扉 扉 扉

1557 亻 𧾷
2a 7d

促

SOKU, unaga(su) – urge, prompt, spur on

促進	*sokushin*	promotion, acceleration	437
催促	*saisoku*	press, urge, demand	1317
促成	*sokusei*	artificially accelerate, force (growth)	261

促 促 促

1558 𧾷 冂 十
7d 2r 2k

踊

YŌ, odo(ru) – dance; ***odo(ri)*** – a dance, dancing

舞踊	*buyō*	a dance, dancing	810
盆踊り	*Bon odori*	Bon Festival dance	1099
踊り子	*odoriko*	dancer, dancing girl	103
踊り場	*odoriba*	dance hall/floor; (stairway) landing	154
踊り狂う	*odorikuruu*	dance ecstatically	883

踊 踊 踊

1559 踏

⻊ 日 氵 — 7d 4c 3a

TŌ, fu(mu) – step on; ***fu(maeru)*** – stand on, be based on

舞踏会	*butōkai*	ball, dance party	810, 158
雑踏	*zattō*	hustle and bustle, (traffic) congestion	575
踏査	*tōsa*	survey, field investigation	624
踏切	*fumikiri*	railroad crossing	39
足踏み	*ashibumi*	step, stamp, mark time	58

1560 躍

⻊ 隹 一 — 7d 8c 1a6

YAKU, odo(ru) – jump, leap, hop

飛躍	*hiyaku*	a leap; activity; rapid progress	530
活躍	*katsuyaku*	active, action	237
暗躍	*an'yaku*	behind-the-scenes maneuvering	348
躍進	*yakushin*	advance by leaps and bounds	437
躍動	*yakudō*	lively motion	231

1561 濯

氵 隹 一 — 3a 8c 1a6

TAKU – wash, rinse

洗濯	*sentaku*	washing, the wash, laundry	692
洗濯機	*sentakuki*	washing machine, washer	692, 528
洗濯物	*sentakumono*	the wash, laundry	692, 79

1562 兆

冫 丨 丿 — 2b 1b2 1c

CHŌ – sign, indication; trillion; ***kiza(shi)*** – sign, symptoms; ***kiza(su)*** – show signs; sprout, germinate

兆候	*chōkō*	sign, indication	944
前兆	*zenchō*	omen, portent, foreshadowing	47
吉兆	*kitchō*	good omen/sign	1141
億兆	*okuchō*	the multitude, the people	382

1563 跳 ⻊ 冫 丨 7d 2b 1b2

CHŌ, to(bu), ha(neru) – leap, spring up, jump, bounce

跳躍	*chōyaku*	spring, jump, leap	1560
跳び上がる	*tobiagaru*	jump up	32
跳ね上がる	*haneagaru*	jump up	32
走り高跳び	*hashiri-takatobi*	the (running) high jump	429, 190
飛び跳ねる	*tobihaneru*	jump up and down	530

跳 跳 跳

1564 挑 扌 冫 丨 3c 2b 1b2

CHŌ, ido(mu) – challenge

挑戦	*chōsen*	challenge	301
挑戦者	*chōsensha*	challenger	301, 164
挑発	*chōhatsu*	arouse, excite, provoke	96
挑発的	*chōhatsuteki*	provocative, suggestive	96, 210

挑 挑 挑

1565 眺 目 冫 丨 5c 2b 1b2

CHŌ, naga(meru) – look at, watch, gaze at

眺望	*chōbō*	a view (from a window)	673

眺 眺 眺

1566 逃 辶 冫 丨 2q 2b 1b2

TŌ, ni(geru) – run away, escape, flee; ***noga(reru)*** – escape; ***ni(gasu), noga(su)*** – let go, set free; let escape

逃走	*tōsō*	escape, flight, desertion	429
逃亡	*tōbō*	escape, flight, desertion	672
逃げ出す	*nigedasu*	break into a run, run off/away	53
見逃す	*minogasu*	overlook	63

逃 逃 逃

1567 木 氵 丨 4a 2b 1b2

桃

TŌ, momo – peach

桃源郷/境	*Tōgenkyō*	Shangri-la, paradise on earth	580, 855, 864
桃色	*momoiro*	pink	204
桃の節句	*Momo no Sekku*	Doll Festival (March 3)	464, 337
桃山時代	*Momoyama jidai*	Momoyama period (1573-1615)	34, 42, 256

1568 𧾷 戈 一 7d 4n 1a2

践

SEN – step, step up; realize, put into practice

実践	*jissen*	practice	203
実践的	*jissenteki*	practical	203, 210
実践理性批判	*Jissen Risei Hihan*	(Critique of Practical Reason—Kant)	203, 143, 98, 1029, 1026

1569 𧾷 亠 丨 7d 2j 1b2

跡

SEKI, ato – mark, traces, vestiges, remains, ruins

遺跡	*iseki*	remains, ruins, relics	1172
史跡	*shiseki*	historic site/relics	332
足跡	*ashiato, sokuseki*	footprint	58
傷跡	*kizuato*	a scar	633
跡継ぎ	*atotsugi*	successor, heir	1025

1570 攵 土 丨 4i 3b 1b2

赦

SHA – forgive

大赦	*taisha*	(general) amnesty	26
恩赦	*onsha*	an amnesty, general pardon	555
赦免	*shamen*	pardon, clemency	733
特赦	*tokusha*	an amnesty	282
容赦	*yōsha*	pardon, forgiveness, mercy	654

1571 糸 戈 土 6a 4n 3b

纖

SEN – fine, slender

纖維	*sen'i*	fiber, textiles	1231
纖維工業	*sen'i kōgyō*	textile industry	1231, 139, 279
合成纖維	*gōsei sen'i*	synthetic fiber	159, 261, 1231
化纖	*kasen*	synthetic fiber	254
纖細	*sensai*	delicate, fine, subtle	695

纖 纖 纖

1572 ⺊ 厂 一 2m 2p 1a

虚

KYO, [KO] – empty

虚無主義	*kyomu shugi*	nihilism	93, 155, 291
虚栄(心)	*kyoei(shin)*	vanity	723, 97
虚弱	*kyojaku*	weak, feeble, frail	218
虚偽	*kyogi*	false, untrue	1485
虚空	*kokū*	empty space, the air	140

虚 虚 虚

1573 戈 ⺊ 厂 4n 2m 2p

戯

GI, tawamu(reru) – play, sport; jest; flirt

遊戯	*yūgi*	amusement	1003
戯曲	*gikyoku*	drama, play	366
前戯	*zengi*	(sexual) foreplay	47
戯画	*giga*	a caricature	343
悪戯	*akugi, itazura*	mischief, prank; lewdness	304

戯 戯 戯

1574 ⺊ 厂 匚 2m 2p 2t

虐

GYAKU, shiita(geru) – oppress, tyrannize

虐待	*gyakutai*	treat cruelly, mistreat	452
暴虐	*bōgyaku*	tyrannical, cruel	1014
虐殺	*gyakusatsu*	massacre, slaughter, butchery	576
残虐	*zangyaku*	cruel, brutal, inhuman	650
自虐的	*jigyakuteki*	self-torturing	62, 210

虐 虐 虐

1575 衤 立 月 5e 5b 4b

襲

SHŪ, oso(u) – attack, assail; succeed to, inherit

来襲	*raishū*	attack, assault, invasion	69
空襲	*kūshū*	air raid	140
夜襲	*yashū*	night attack	471
世襲	*seshū*	hereditary	252
因襲	*inshū*	long-established custom, convention	554

襲 襲 襲

1576 衤 王 丷 4e 4f 2o

祥

SHŌ – happiness; good omen

不祥事	*fushōji*	scandal	94, 80
発祥	*hasshō*	origin	96
発祥地	*hasshōchi*	birthplace, cradle	96, 118
吉祥	*kisshō*	good omen	1141
吉祥天	*Kichijōten, Kisshōten*	(Buddhist goddess)	1141, 141

祥 祥 祥

1577 言 王 丷 7a 4f 2o

詳

SHŌ, kuwa(shii) – detailed, full; familiar with (something)

詳細	*shōsai*	details, particulars	695
不詳	*fushō*	unknown, unidentified	94
未詳	*mishō*	unknown, unidentified	306
詳報	*shōhō*	full/detailed report	685
詳述	*shōjutsu*	detailed explanation, full account	968

詳 詳 詳

1578 火 日 土 4d 4c 3b

默

MOKU, dama(ru) – become silent, say nothing

沈黙	*chinmoku*	silence	936
黙認	*mokunin*	tacit approval	738
黙殺	*mokusatsu*	take no notice of, ignore	576
黙秘権	*mokuhiken*	right against self-incrimination	807, 335

默 默 默

1579 犭 皿 子 3g 5h 2c

猛

MŌ – strong, fierce

猛烈	*mōretsu*	fierce, violent, strong	1331
猛打	*mōda*	hard hit, heavy blow	1020
猛暑	*mōsho*	fierce heat	638
猛犬	*mōken*	vicious dog	280
猛者	*mosa*	man of courage, stalwart veteran	164

猛 猛 猛

1580 犭 ⺍ 几 3g 3n 2s

猟

RYŌ – hunting

猟師	*ryōshi*	hunter	409
密猟者	*mitsuryōsha*	poacher	806, 164
猟犬	*ryōken*	hunting dog	280
猟銃	*ryōjū*	hunting gun, shotgun	829
禁猟	*kinryō*	prohibition on hunting	482

猟 猟 猟

1581 犭 宀 寸 3g 3m 2k

狩

SHU, ka(ri) – hunting; ***ka(ru)*** – hunt

狩猟(期)	*shuryō(ki)*	hunting (season)	1580, 449
狩り小屋	*karigoya*	hunting cabin	27, 167
狩人	*karyūdo*	hunter	1
潮干狩り	*shiohigari*	shell gathering (at low tide)	468, 584
みかん狩り	*mikangari*	picking mandarin oranges	

狩 狩 狩

1582 犭 田 ⺍ 3g 5f 3n

獣

JŪ, kemono – animal, beast

野獣	*yajū*	wild animal	236
猛獣	*mōjū*	vicious animal, ferocious beast	1579
怪獣	*kaijū*	monster	1476
鳥獣保護区域	*chōjū hogo kuiki*	wildlife sanctuary	285, 489, 1312, 183, 970
獣医	*jūi*	veterinarian	220

獣 獣 獣

1583 猶

犭 3g　酉 7e　丷 2o

YŪ – delay; still, still more

猶予	*yūyo*	postponement, deferment	393
猶予なく	*yūyonaku*	without delay, promptly	393
執行猶予	*shikkō yūyo*	suspended sentence, probation	686, 68, 393

猶 猶 猶

1584 猿

犭 3g　土 3b　口 3d

EN, saru – monkey

野猿	*yaen*	wild monkey	236
類人猿	*ruijin'en*	anthropoid ape	226, 1
猿知恵	*sarujie*	cleverness in managing petty matters	214, 1219
犬猿の仲	*ken'en no naka*	hating each other, like cats and dogs	280, 1347

猿 猿 猿

1585 衡

彳 3i　田 5f　⺈ 2n

KŌ – scales, weigh

均衡	*kinkō*	balance, equilibrium	805
平衡	*heikō*	balance, equilibrium	202
平衡感覚	*heikō kankaku*	sense of equilibrium	202, 262, 605
度量衡	*doryōkō*	weights and measures	377, 411

衡 衡 衡

1586 換

扌 3c　⺈ 2n　冂 2r

KAN, ka(eru) – substitute; ***ka(waru)*** – be replaced

交換	*kōkan*	exchange, substitution	114
転換	*tenkan*	conversion, switchover; diversion	433
変換	*henkan*	change, conversion	257
換算(率)	*kansan(ritsu)*	conversion, exchange (rate)	747, 788
乗り換える	*norikaeru*	transfer, change (trains)	523

換 換 換

1587 口 ⺈ 冂 3d 2n 2r

喚

KAN – call

召喚	*shōkan*	summons, subpoena	995
(証人)喚問	*(shōnin) kanmon*	summons (of a witness)	484, 1, 162
喚起	*kanki*	evoke, awaken, call forth	373
叫喚	*kyōkan*	shout, outcry, scream	1252
あ鼻叫喚	*abi-kyōkan*	(2 Buddhist hells); bedlam	813, 1252

喚 喚 喚

1588 虫 口 冂 6d 3d 2r

融

YŪ – dissolve, melt

融合	*yūgō*	fusion	159
融通	*yūzū*	accommodation, loan; versatility	150
金融	*kin'yū*	money, finance	23
金融機関	*kin'yū kikan*	financial institution	23, 528, 398
融資	*yūshi*	financing, loan	750

融 融 融

1589 阝 口 冂 2d 3d 2r

隔

KAKU, heda(teru) – separate, interpose; estrange; ***heda(taru)*** – be distant, apart; become estranged

間隔	*kankaku*	space, spacing, interval	43
隔離	*kakuri*	isolation, quarantine	1281
遠隔	*enkaku*	distant, remote, outlying	446
横隔膜	*ōkakumaku*	the diaphragm	781, 1426

隔 隔 隔

1590 口 王 3d 4f

呈

TEI – offer, present, exhibit

進呈	*shintei*	give, present	437
贈呈	*zōtei*	present, donate	1364
献呈本	*kenteibon*	presentation copy	1355, 25
謹呈	*kintei*	With the compliments of the author	1247
露呈	*rotei*	exposure, disclosure	951

呈 呈 呈

1591	日 ト 亻 4c 2m 2a	**ZE** – right, correct, just			
		是非	*zehi*	right and wrong; by all means	498
		是正	*zesei*	correct, rectify	275
		是認	*zenin*	approval, sanction	738
		是々非々	*zeze-hihi*	being fair and unbiased	498

是 是 是

1592	土 日 ト 3b 4c 2m	***TEI, tsutsumi*** – bank, embankment, dike			
		堤防	*teibō*	embankment, dike, levee	513
		防波堤	*bōhatei*	breakwater	513, 666

堤 堤 堤

1593	又 2h	***mata*** – again; also, moreover			
		又聞き	*matagiki*	hearsay, secondhand information	64
		又貸し	*matagashi*	sublease	748
		又々	*matamata*	once again	
		又は	*mata wa*	or, either ... or ...	

又 又 又

1594	又 2h2	***SŌ, futa*** – pair, both			
		双方	*sōhō*	both parties/sides	70
		双生児	*sōseiji*	twins	44, 1217
		双眼鏡	*sōgankyō*	binoculars	848, 863
		双肩	*sōken*	one's shoulders	1264
		双子	*futago*	twins	103

双 双 双

1595 力 女 又 2g 3e 2h

努

DO, tsuto(meru) – exert oneself, make efforts, strive

努力	*doryoku*	effort, endeavor	100
努力家	*doryokuka*	hard worker	100, 165

努 努 努

1596 心 女 又 4k 3e 2h

怒

DO, oko(ru), ika(ru) – get angry

怒気	*doki*	(fit of) anger	134
激怒	*gekido*	wild rage, wrath, fury	1017
怒髪天を突く	*dohatsu ten o tsuku*	be infuriated	1148, 141, 898
怒号	*dogō*	angry roar	266
喜怒	*kido*	joy and anger, emotion	1143

怒 怒 怒

1597 心 攵 亻 4k 4i 2a

悠

YŪ – distant; leisure

悠然	*yūzen*	calm, perfect composure	651
悠長	*yūchō*	leisurely, slow, easygoing	95
悠々	*yūyū*	calm, composed, leisurely	
悠揚	*yūyō*	composed, calm, serene	631
悠久	*yūkyū*	eternity, perpetuity	1210

悠 悠 悠

1598 心 月 刂 4k 4b 2f

愉

YU – joy, pleasure

愉快	*yukai*	pleasant, merry, cheerful	1409
不愉快	*fuyukai*	unpleasant, disagreeable	94, 1409
愉楽	*yuraku*	pleasure, joy	358

愉 愉 愉

1599	言 7a	月 4b	刂 2f

諭

YU, sato(su) – admonish, remonstrate, warn, counsel

教諭	*kyōyu*	teacher, instructor	245
説諭	*setsuyu*	admonition, reproof, caution	400
諭旨	*yushi*	official suggestion (to a subordinate)	1040

諭 諭 諭

1600	疒 5i	月 4b	心 4k

癒

YU – heal, cure

癒着	*yuchaku*	heal up, adhere, knit together	657
治癒	*chiyu*	healing, cure, recovery	493
平癒	*heiyu*	recovery	202

癒 癒 癒

1601	心 4k	禾 5d	火 4d

愁

SHŪ, ure(i) – grief, sorrow, distress; anxiety, cares; ***ure(eru)*** – grieve, be distressed; fear, be apprehensive

郷愁	*kyōshū*	homesickness, nostalgia	855
旅愁	*ryoshū*	loneliness on a journey	222
憂愁	*yūshū*	melancholy, grief, gloom	1032
ご愁傷様	*goshūshō-sama*	My heartfelt sympathy.	633, 403

愁 愁 愁

1602	心 4k	几 2s	一 1a

恐

KYŌ, oso(reru) – fear, be afraid of; ***oso(roshii)*** – terrible, frightful, awful

恐縮	*kyōshuku*	be very grateful; be sorry	1110
恐慌	*kyōkō*	panic	1378
恐妻家	*kyōsaika*	henpecked husband	671, 165
空恐ろしい	*soraosoroshii*	have a vague fear	140

恐 恐 恐

1603 ⺮ 木 几 (6f 4a 2s)

築

CHIKU, kizu(ku) – build, erect

建築	*kenchiku*	architecture, construction	892
建築家	*kenchikuka*	architect	892, 165
新築	*shinchiku*	new construction	174
改築	*kaichiku*	rebuilding, reconstruction	514
築山	*tsukiyama*	mound, artificial hill	34

築 築 築

1604 金 广 ノ (8a 3q 1c)

鉱

KŌ – ore

鉱石	*kōseki*	ore, mineral, crystal	78
鉱物	*kōbutsu*	mineral	79
鉄鉱	*tekkō*	iron ore	312
鉱山	*kōzan*	a mine	34
鉱業	*kōgyō*	mining	279

鉱 鉱 鉱

1605 金 口 冂 (8a 3d 2r)

銅

DŌ – copper

銅山	*dōzan*	copper mine	34
銅版画	*dōhanga*	copper print	1046, 343
銅像	*dōzō*	bronze statue	740
青銅	*seidō*	bronze	208
銅メダル	*dōmedaru*	bronze medal	

銅 銅 銅

1606 金 口 丷 (8a 3d 2o)

鉛

EN, namari – lead

鉛筆	*enpitsu*	pencil	130
黒鉛	*kokuen*	graphite	206
鉛版	*enban*	stereotype, printing plate	1046
鉛毒	*endoku*	lead poisoning	522
鉛色	*namariiro*	lead color/gray	204

鉛 鉛 鉛

1607	氵 口 丷 (3a 3d 2o)	***EN, so(u)*** – stand along (a street), run parallel (to)		
	沿岸	*engan*	coast, shore	586
	沿海	*enkai*	coastal waters, coast	117
	沿線	*ensen*	along the (train) line	299
	沿革	*enkaku*	history, development	1075
	川沿い	*kawazoi*	along the river	33

沿

1608	金 山 冂 (8a 3o 2r)	***KŌ, hagane*** – steel		
	鋼鉄	*kōtetsu*	steel	312
	特殊鋼	*tokushukō*	special steel	282, 1505
	鋼板	*kōhan, kōban*	steel plate	1047
	製鋼所	*seikōjo*	steel plant	428, 153
	製鋼業	*seikōgyō*	steel industry	428, 279

鋼

1609	糸 山 冂 (6a 3o 2r)	***KŌ, tsuna*** – rope, cord		
	綱領	*kōryō*	plan, program, platform	834
	綱紀	*kōki*	official discipline, public order	372
	手綱	*tazuna*	bridle, reins	57
	綱渡り	*tsunawatari*	tightrope walking	378
	横綱	*yokozuna*	sumo grand champion	781

綱

1610	刂 山 冂 (2f 3o 2r)	***GŌ*** – strength, hardness		
	外柔内剛	*gaijū-naigō*	gentle-looking but sturdy	83, 774, 84
	剛健	*gōken*	strong and sturdy, virile	893
	剛勇	*gōyū*	valor, bravery	1386
	金剛石	*kongōseki*	diamond	23, 78

剛

1611	刂 月 ⺌ 2f 4b 3n

削

SAKU, kezu(ru) – whittle down, sharpen (a pencil); delete; curtail

削除	*sakujo*	deletion, elimination	1065
削減	*sakugen*	reduction, cutback	715
添削	*tensaku*	correction (of a composition)	1433
鉛筆削り	*enpitsukezuri*	pencil sharpener	1606, 130

削 削 削

1612	糸 冂 丷 6a 2r 2o

網

MŌ, ami – net

漁網	*gyomō*	fishing net	699
交通網	*kōtsūmō*	traffic network	114, 150
支店網	*shitenmō*	network of branch offices	318, 168
金網	*kanaami*	wire mesh/netting	23
網袋	*amibukuro*	net (shopping) bag	1329

網 網 網

1613	土 亠 几 3b 2j 2s

坑

KŌ – pit, hole

炭坑	*tankō*	coalpit, coal mine	1344
坑夫	*kōfu*	coal miner	315
坑道	*kōdō*	(mine) shaft, level, gallery	149
坑内事故	*kōnai jiko*	mine accident	84, 80, 173
廃坑	*haikō*	abandoned mine	961

坑 坑 坑

1614	冖 几 2i 2s

冗

JŌ – redundant, superfluous

冗談	*jōdan*	a joke	593
冗語	*jōgo*	redundancy	67
冗員	*jōin*	superfluous member/personnel, overstaffing	163
冗長	*jōchō*	redundant, verbose	95
冗漫	*jōman*	wordy, verbose, rambling	1411

冗 冗 冗

1615 冖 十 丷 2i 2k 2o

冠

KAN, kanmuri – crown

王冠	*ōkan*	(royal) crown; bottle cap	294
金冠	*kinkan*	gold crown	23
栄冠	*eikan*	crown (of victory), laurels	723
弱冠	*jakkan*	20 years of age; youth	218
草冠	*kusakanmuri*	Grapheme No. 3k [艹]	249

冠 冠 冠

1616 一 口 丨 1a2 3s 1b2

亜

A – rank next, come after, sub-; Asia

亜熱帯	*anettai*	subtropical zones, subtropics	645, 963
亜鉛	*aen*	zinc	1606
亜麻	*ama*	flax	1529
亜流	*aryū*	follower, epigone	247
東亜	*Tōa*	East Asia	71

亜 亜 亜

1617 礻 尸 寸 4e 3r 2k

尉

I – officer

尉官	*ikan*	officer below the rank of major	326
大尉	*taii*	captain	26
中尉	*chūi*	lieutenant	28
少尉	*shōi*	second lieutenant	144
准尉	*jun'i*	warrant officer	1232

尉 尉 尉

1618 心 礻 尸 4k 4e 3r

慰

I, nagusa(meru) – comfort, console, cheer up; amuse, divert; ***nagusa(mu)*** – be diverted; banter; make a plaything of

慰問	*imon*	consolation, sympathy	162
慰安	*ian*	comfort, recreation, amusement	105
慰霊祭	*ireisai*	a memorial service	1168, 617
慰謝料	*isharyō*	consolation money, solatium	901, 319

慰 慰 慰

1619	亻 一 2a 1a2

仁

JIN, [NI] – virtue, benevolence, humanity, charity

仁義	*jingi*	humanity and justice	291
仁愛	*jin'ai*	benevolence, charity, philanthropy	259
仁術	*jinjutsu*	benevolent act; the healing art	187
仁徳	*jintoku*	benevolence, goodness	1038
仁王(門)	*Niō(mon)*	Deva (gate)	294, 161

仁 仁 仁

1620	尸 ⺊ 3r 2m

尼

NI, ama – nun

尼僧	*nisō*	nun	1366
尼寺	*amadera*	convent	41

尼 尼 尼

1621	氵 尸 ⺊ 3a 3r 2m

泥

DEI, doro – mud

泥炭	*deitan*	peat	1344
雲泥の差	*undei no sa*	enormous difference	636, 658
泥沼	*doronuma*	bog, quagmire	996
泥棒	*dorobō*	thief, robber, burglar, burglary	1543

泥 泥 泥

1622	氵 日 ⺊ 3a 4c 2m

渇

KATSU, kawa(ku) – be thirsty

飢渇	*kikatsu*	hunger and thirst	1304
渇望	*katsubō*	craving, longing, thirst	673
枯渇	*kokatsu*	run dry, become depleted	974
渇水	*kassui*	water shortage	21
渇きを覚える	*kawaki o oboeru*	feel thirsty	605

渇 渇 渇

1623 衤 日 ⺊ 5e 4c 2m

褐

KATSU – woolen/quilted clothing

褐色	*kasshoku*	brown	204
茶褐色	*chakasshoku*	brown, chestnut brown	251, 204
赤褐色	*akakasshoku*	reddish brown	207, 204
黒褐色	*kokkasshoku*	dark/blackish brown	206, 204

褐 褐 褐

1624 扌 日 ⺊ 3c 4c 2m

掲

KEI, kaka(geru) – put up (a sign), hoist (a flag); publish, print

掲揚	*keiyō*	hoist, raise, fly (a flag)	631
掲示	*keiji*	notice, bulletin	615
掲示板	*keijiban*	bulletin board	615, 1047
掲載	*keisai*	publish, print, carry, mention	1124
前掲	*zenkei*	shown above, aforementioned	47

掲 掲 掲

1625 氵 虫 罒 3a 6d 5g

濁

DAKU, nigo(ru) – become muddy/turbid; **nigo(su)** – make turbid

混濁	*kondaku*	turbidity, muddiness	799
清濁	*seidaku*	purity and impurity, good and evil	660
濁流	*dakuryū*	muddy river, turbid waters	247
濁音	*dakuon*	voiced sound; cardiac dullness	347

濁 濁 濁

1626 氵 火 ⺊ 3a 4d 2m

潟

kata – beach, lagoon, inlet

干潟	*higata*	dry beach, beach at ebb tide	584
新潟県	*Niigata-ken*	Niigata Prefecture	174, 194

潟 潟 潟

1627 一 丨 ノ 1a2 1b2 1c

KŌ, taku(mi) – skill, dexterity, ingenuity

技巧	*gikō*	art, craftsmanship, technical skill	871
巧妙	*kōmyō*	skilled, clever, ingenious	1154
巧者	*kōsha*	skilled, adroit, clever	164
精巧	*seikō*	elaborate, exquisite, sophisticated	659
老巧	*rōkō*	experienced, seasoned, veteran	543

巧 巧 巧

1628 木 一 丨 4a 1a 1b

KYŪ, ku(chiru) – rot, decay

不朽	*fukyū*	immortal, undying	94
不朽の名作	*fukyū no meisaku*	immortal masterpiece	94, 82, 360
腐朽	*fukyū*	deteriorate, rot away, molder	1245
老朽	*rōkyū*	senescence, advanced age	543
朽ち葉	*kuchiba*	decayed/dead leaves	253

朽 朽 朽

1629 言 亻 一 7a 2a 1a3

KO, hoko(ru) – boast of, be proud of

誇張	*kochō*	exaggeration, overstatement	1106
誇大妄想(狂)	*kodai mōsō(kyō)*	delusions of grandeur, megalomania	26, 1376, 147, 883
誇示	*koji*	display, flaunt	615
勝ち誇る	*kachihokoru*	exult in one's triumph	509

誇 誇 誇

1630 广 冂 ⺊ 3q 2r2 2m2

REI, uruwa(shii) – beautiful, pretty

美麗	*birei*	beautiful, pretty	401
華麗	*karei*	glory, splendor, magnificence	1074
麗人	*reijin*	beautiful woman	1
端麗	*tanrei*	grace, elegance, beauty	1418
美辞麗句	*biji-reiku*	speech full of rhetorical flourishes	401, 688, 337

麗 麗 麗

1631 艹 火 广 (3k 4d 3q) 薦

SEN, susu(meru) – recommend; advise; offer, present

推薦	*suisen*	recommendation	1233
推薦状	*suisenjō*	letter of recommendation	1233, 626
他薦	*tasen*	recommendation (by another)	120
自薦	*jisen*	self-recommendation	62

薦 薦 薦

1632 广 夂 心 (3q 4i 4k) 慶

KEI – rejoice, be happy over; congratulate

慶賀	*keiga*	congratulation	756
慶祝	*keishuku*	congratulation; celebration	851
慶事	*keiji*	happy event, matter for congratulation	80
慶応	*Keiō*	(Japanese era, 1865-68)	827
国慶節	*Kokkeisetsu*	Anniversary of Founding of P.R. China	40, 464

慶 慶 慶

1633 月 口 艹 (4b 3s2 3k) 覇

HA – supremacy, domination, hegemony

覇権	*haken*	hegemony	355
覇者	*hasha*	supreme ruler; champion, titleholder	164
制覇	*seiha*	conquest, domination; championship	427
覇気	*haki*	ambition, aspirations	134
連覇	*renpa*	successive championships	440

覇 覇 覇

1634 日 夂 彳 (4c 4i 3i) 覆

FUKU, ō(u) – cover; conceal; ***kutsugae(ru)*** – be overturned; ***kutsugae(su)*** – overturn, overthrow

覆面	*fukumen*	mask	274
転覆	*tenpuku*	overturn, topple	433
覆水盆に返らず	*fukusui bon ni kaerazu*	What's done is done.	21, 1099, 442

覆 覆 覆

1635	尸 日 夂 3r 4c 4i	
履	**RI, ha(ku)** – put on, wear (shoes/pants)	
履歴書	*rirekisho* curriculum vitae	480, 131
履行	*rikō* perform, fulfill, implement	68
草履	*zōri* (toe-strap) sandals	249
履き物	*hakimono* footwear	79
履き古し	*hakifurushi* worn-out shoes/socks	172

履 履 履

1636	言 一 丨 7a 1a 1b	
託	**TAKU** – entrust (to), leave in the care (of)	
委託	*itaku* trust, charge, commission	466
信託	*shintaku* trust	157
託児所	*takujisho* day nursery	1217, 153
託宣	*takusen* oracle, revelation from God	625
結託	*kettaku* conspiracy, collusion	485

託 託 託

1637	尸 虫 冂 3r 6d 2r	
属	**ZOKU** – belong (to)	
所属	*shozoku* belong, be assigned (to)	153
付属	*fuzoku* attached, affiliated, incidental	192
金属	*kinzoku* metal	23
専属	*senzoku* belong exclusively (to)	600
従属	*jūzoku* subordination, dependence	1482

属 属 属

1638	口 虫 尸 3d 6d 3r	
嘱	**SHOKU** – request, entrust, commission	
嘱託	*shokutaku* part-time worker	1636
委嘱	*ishoku* commission, charge, request	466
嘱望	*shokubō* expect much of	673

嘱 嘱 嘱

1639 亻 日 冂 2a 4c 2r

偶

GŪ – (married) couple; even number; doll; chance, accidental

偶然	*gūzen*	chance, accident	651
偶発	*gūhatsu*	chance occurrence	96
偶像	*gūzō*	image, statue, idol	740
配偶者	*haigūsha*	spouse	515, 164
偶数	*gūsū*	even number	225

偶 偶 偶

1640 阝 日 冂 2d 4c 2r

隅

GŪ, sumi – corner, nook

一隅	*ichigū*	corner, nook	2
片隅	*katasumi*	corner, nook	1045
四隅	*yosumi*	the 4 corners	6
隅々	*sumizumi*	every nook and cranny, all over	
隅田川	*Sumida-gawa*	Sumida River	35, 33

隅 隅 隅

1641 辶 日 冂 2q 4c 2r

遇

GŪ – treat, deal with; entertain, receive; meet

待遇	*taigū*	treatment; service; pay	452
優遇	*yūgū*	cordial reception, hospitality	1033
冷遇	*reigū*	cold reception, inhospitality	832
境遇	*kyōgū*	one's circumstances	864
奇遇	*kigū*	chance meeting	1360

遇 遇 遇

1642 心 日 冂 4k 4c 2r

愚

GU, oro(ka) – foolish, stupid

愚劣	*guretsu*	stupidity, foolishness, nonsense	1150
愚鈍	*gudon*	stupid, dim-witted	966
愚問	*gumon*	stupid question	162
愚連隊	*gurentai*	gang of hoodlums	440, 795

愚 愚 愚

1643	辶 日 艹 2q 4c2 3k	***SŌ, a(u)*** – meet, see, come across, encounter		
	遭難	*sōnan*	disaster, accident, mishap	557
	遭難者	*sōnansha*	victim	557, 164
	遭難信号	*sōnan shingō*	distress signal, SOS	557, 157, 266
	遭遇	*sōgū*	encounter	1641
	災難に遭う	*sainan ni au*	meet with disaster	1335, 557

1644	木 日 艹 4a 4c2 3k	***SŌ*** – tub, tank, vat		
	水槽	*suisō*	water tank, cistern	21
	浴槽	*yokusō*	bathtub	1128

1645	日 4c3	***SHŌ*** – clear; crystal		
	結晶	*kesshō*	crystal, crystallization	485
	愛の結晶	*ai no kesshō*	fruit of love, child	259, 485
	晶化	*shōka*	crystallization	254
	水晶	*suishō*	(rock) crystal, quartz	21
	紫水晶	*murasaki zuishō*	amethyst	1389, 21

1646	口 日 3d 4c2	***SHŌ, tona(eru)*** – chant; cry; advocate, espouse		
	合唱(団)	*gasshō(dan)*	chorus	159, 491
	独唱	*dokushō*	vocal solo	219
	唱歌	*shōka*	singing	392
	主/首唱	*shushō*	advocacy, promotion	155, 148
	提唱	*teishō*	advocate	628

1647 言 ⺍ 山 7a 3n 3o

謡

YŌ – song; Noh chanting; ***uta(u)*** – sing

民謡	*min'yō*	folk song	177
童謡	*dōyō*	children's song	410
歌謡	*kayō*	song	392
歌謡曲	*kayōkyoku*	popular song	392, 366
謡曲	*yōkyoku*	Noh song	366

謡 謡 謡

1648 扌 ⺍ 山 3c 3n 3o

揺

YŌ, yu(reru/ragu/rugu) – shake, sway, vibrate, roll, pitch, joggle; ***yu(ru/suru/suburu/saburu)*** – shake, rock, joggle

動揺	*dōyō*	shaking; unrest, tumult	231
揺(す)り起こす	*yu(su)riokosu*	awaken by shaking	373
揺り返し	*yurikaeshi*	aftershock	442

揺 揺 揺

1649 山 一 ノ 3o 1a2 1c

缶

KAN – can

缶詰	*kanzume*	canned goods	1142
製缶工場	*seikan kōjō*	cannery, canning factory	428, 139, 154
缶切り	*kankiri*	can opener	39
空き缶	*akikan*	empty can	140

缶 缶 缶

1650 阝 山 一 2d 3o 1a3

陶

TŌ – porcelain, pottery

陶器	*tōki*	china, ceramics, pottery	527
陶磁器	*tōjiki*	ceramics, china and porcelain	1548, 527
陶芸	*tōgei*	ceramic art	435
陶工	*tōkō*	potter	139

陶 陶 陶

1651	扌 日 十 3c 4c 2k	***SŌ, sa(su)*** – insert		
	挿入	*sōnyū*	insertion	52
	挿話	*sōwa*	episode, little story	238
	挿し木	*sashiki*	a cutting	22
	挿し絵	*sashie*	an illustration	345

挿 挿 挿

1652	扌 車 冖 3c 7c 2i	***KI*** – shake, brandish; direct, command; scatter		
	指揮	*shiki*	command, direct, conduct	1041
	指揮者	*shikisha*	(orchestra) conductor	1041, 164
	指揮官	*shikikan*	commander	1041, 326
	発揮	*hakki*	exhibit, display, manifest	96
	揮発	*kihatsu*	volatilization	96

揮 揮 揮

1653	車 ⺌ 冖 7c 3n 2i	***KI, kagaya(ku)*** – shine, gleam, sparkle, be brilliant		
	光輝	*kōki*	brilliance, brightness; glory	138
	輝度	*kido*	(degree of) brightness	377
	光り輝く	*hikarikagayaku*	shine, beam, glisten	138
	輝かしい	*kagayakashii*	bright, brilliant	

輝 輝 輝

1654	糸 木 口 6a 4a 3d3	***ku(ru)*** – reel, wind; spin (thread); turn (pages); consult (a reference book), look up; count		
	繰り返す	*kurikaesu*	repeat	442
	繰り言	*kurigoto*	same old story, complaint	66
	繰り延べ	*kurinobe*	postponement, deferment	1115
	繰り上げる	*kuriageru*	advance, move up (a date)	32

繰 繰 繰

1655 扌 木 口 3c 4a 3d3

操

SŌ, ayatsu(ru) – manipulate, operate; ***misao*** – chastity; constancy, fidelity, honor

操縦	*sōjū*	control, operate, manipulate	1483
(遠隔)操作	*(enkaku) sōsa*	(remote) control	446, 1589, 360
体操	*taisō*	gymnastics, exercises	61
節操	*sessō*	fidelity, integrity; chastity	464

操 操 操

1656 火 木 口 4d 4a 3d3

燥

SŌ – dry

乾燥	*kansō*	dry (up/out)	1190
乾燥器	*kansōki*	(clothes) dryer	1190, 527
無味乾燥	*mumi-kansō*	dry, uninteresting	93, 307, 1190
焦燥	*shōsō*	impatience, nervous restlessness	999

燥 燥 燥

1657 艹 木 口 3k 4a 3d3

藻

SŌ, mo – water plant

藻類	*sōrui*	water plants	226
海藻	*kaisō*	saltwater plant, seaweed	117
藻草	*mogusa*	water plant	249

藻 藻 藻

1658 日 艹 十 4c 3k 2k

暁

GYŌ, akatsuki – dawn, daybreak

暁天	*gyōten*	dawn, daybreak	141
暁星	*gyōsei*	morning stars; Venus	730
今暁	*kongyō*	early this morning	51
通暁	*tsūgyō*	thorough knowledge, mastery	150
暁には	*akatsuki niwa*	in the event, in case (of)	

暁 暁 暁

1659 艹 十 亻 3k 2k 2a

奔

HON – run

奔走	*honsō*	running about, efforts	429
奔放	*honpō*	wild, extravagant, uninhibited	512
狂奔	*kyōhon*	rush madly about	883
奔馬	*honba*	galloping/runaway horse	283
出奔	*shuppon*	abscond; elope	53

奔 奔 奔

1660 口 貝 艹 3d 7b 3k

噴

FUN, fu(ku) – emit, spout, spew forth

噴火	*funka*	(volcanic) eruption	20
噴水	*funsui*	jet of water; fountain	21
噴出	*funshutsu*	eruption, gushing, spouting	53
噴射	*funsha*	jet, spray, injection	900
噴霧器	*funmuki*	sprayer, vaporizer	950, 527

噴 噴 噴

1661 心 貝 艹 4k 7b 3k

憤

FUN, ikidō(ru) – resent, be enraged, be indignant

憤慨	*fungai*	indignation, resentment	1460
公憤	*kōfun*	public/righteous indignation	126
義憤	*gifun*	righteous indignation	291
憤然と	*funzen to*	indignantly	651
発憤	*happun*	be stimulated, roused	96

憤 憤 憤

1662 土 貝 艹 3b 7b 3k

墳

FUN – burial mound, tomb

墳墓	*funbo*	grave, tomb	1429
古墳	*kofun*	ancient burial mound, old tomb	172
前方後円墳	*zenpō-kōen fun*	ancient burial mound (square at the head and rounded at the foot)	47, 70, 48, 13

墳 墳 墳

1663 皿 匚 一 5h 2t 1a4

監

KAN – keep watch over

監視	*kanshi*	keeping watch, supervision, surveillance	606
監査	*kansa*	inspection; auditing	624
総監	*sōkan*	inspector/superintendent general	697
監禁	*kankin*	imprison, confine	482
監獄	*kangoku*	prison	884

監 監 監

1664 金 皿 匚 8a 5h 2t

鑑

KAN – model, pattern, example; mirror

鑑定	*kantei*	appraisal, expert opinion	355
鑑賞	*kanshō*	admiration, enjoyment	500
鑑別	*kanbetsu*	discrimination, differentiation	267
年鑑	*nenkan*	yearbook, almanac	45
印鑑	*inkan*	one's seal, seal impression	1043

鑑 鑑 鑑

1665 舟 皿 匚 6c 5h 2t

艦

KAN – warship

軍艦	*gunkan*	warship	438
戦艦	*senkan*	battleship	301
航空母艦	*kōkū bokan*	aircraft carrier	823, 140, 112
潜水艦	*sensuikan*	submarine	937, 21
艦隊	*kantai*	fleet, squadron	795

艦 艦 艦

1666 舟 壬 廴 6c 3p 2q

艇

TEI – small boat

艦艇	*kantei*	naval vessels	1665
舟艇	*shūtei*	boat, craft	1094
巡視艇	*junshitei*	patrol boat	777, 606
艇庫	*teiko*	boathouse	825
艇身	*teishin*	a boat length	59

艇 艇 艇

1667 又 2h ⺌ 3n ⺊ 2m

叔

SHUKU – younger sibling of a parent (cf. No. 1176)

叔母	*oba, shukubo*	aunt	112
叔父	*oji, shukufu*	uncle	113

叔 叔 叔

1668 氵 3a ⺌ 3n 又 2h

淑

SHUKU – graceful; polite; pure

淑女	*shukujo*	lady, gentlewoman	102
淑徳	*shukutoku*	feminine virtues	1038
私淑	*shishuku*	look up to as one's model	125

淑 淑 淑

1669 宀 3m ⺌ 3n 又 2h

寂

JAKU, [SEKI], sabi(shii) – lonely; ***sabi(reru)*** – decline in prosperity; ***sabi*** – elegant simplicity

静寂	*seijaku*	stillness, silence	663
閑寂	*kanjaku*	quietness, tranquility	1532
寂然	*sekizen, jakunen*	lonesome, desolate	651
寂りょう	*sekiryō*	loneliness, desolation	

寂 寂 寂

1670 目 5c ⺌ 3n 又 2h

督

TOKU – lead, command; superintend, supervise

監督	*kantoku*	supervision, direction; (movie) director	1663
督励	*tokurei*	encourage, urge	1340
督促	*tokusoku*	urge, press, dun	1557
総督	*sōtoku*	governor-general	697
家督相続	*katoku sōzoku*	succession to a house, heirship	165, 146, 243

督 督 督

1671 亠 口 豕 2j 3d 3g

豪

GŌ – strength, power; splendor, magnificence

豪華	*gōka*	splendor, gorgeousness, pomp	1074
豪壮	*gōsō*	magnificent, grand	1326
富豪	*fugō*	man of great wealth, multimillionaire	713
豪族	*gōzoku*	powerful/influential family	221
豪雨	*gōu*	heavy rainfall, torrential downpour	30

豪 豪 豪

1672 亠 口 子 2j 3d 2c

享

KYŌ – enjoy; receive

享楽	*kyōraku*	enjoyment	358
享楽主義	*kyōraku shugi*	epicureanism, hedonism	358, 155, 291
享受	*kyōju*	enjoy, have, be given	260
享有	*kyōyū*	enjoyment, possession	265
享年75歳	*kyōnen nanajūgosai*	dead at the age of 75	45, 479

享 享 享

1673 阝 口 亠 2d 3d 2j

郭

KAKU – enclosure, quarters; red-light district

輪郭	*rinkaku*	contours, outline	1164
外郭	*gaikaku*	outer wall (of a castle); perimeter	83
外郭団体	*gaikaku dantai*	auxiliary organization	83, 491, 61
城郭	*jōkaku*	castle, fortress; castle walls	720
郭公	*kakkō*	(Japanese) cuckoo	126

郭 郭 郭

1674 土 口 亠 3b 3d 2j

塾

JUKU – private school

私塾	*shijuku*	private class at a teacher's home	125
学習塾	*gakushūjuku*	(private) cram school	109, 591
塾生	*jukusei*	student of a *juku*	44

塾 塾 塾

1675	亠 ⺆ 丨 2j 3d 1b	***AI, awa(re)*** – sorrowful, piteous; ***awa(remu)*** – pity, sympathize			
哀		哀愁	*aishū*	sadness, sorrow, grief	1601
		悲哀	*hiai*	sorrow, grief, misery	1034
		哀話	*aiwa*	sad story, pathetic tale	238
		哀歌	*aika*	doleful song, elegy, lament	392
		喜怒哀楽	*kido-airaku*	joy and pathos, emotions	1143, 1596, 358

哀 哀 哀

1676	亠 口 一 2j 3s 1a	***SUI, otoro(eru)*** – grow weak, decline, wane			
衰		老衰	*rōsui*	feebleness of old age, senility	543
		衰弱	*suijaku*	weakening, debility	218
		衰微	*suibi*	decline, wane	1419
		衰亡	*suibō*	decline and fall, ruin, downfall	672
		盛衰	*seisui*	rise and fall, vicissitudes	719

衰 衰 衰

1677	一 口 十 (1a) 3s 2k	***CHŪ*** – heart, mind, inside			
衷		衷心	*chūshin*	one's inmost heart/feelings	97
		衷情	*chūjō*	one's inmost feelings	209
		苦衷	*kuchū*	anguish, predicament	545
		和洋折衷	*wayō setchū*	blending of Japanese and Western styles	124, 289, 1394

衷 衷 衷

1678	⺆ 十 一 3d2 2k 1a	***SŌ, mo*** – mourning			
喪		喪失	*sōshitsu*	loss	311
		喪服	*mofuku*	mourning clothes	683
		喪章	*moshō*	mourning badge/band	857
		喪主	*moshu*	chief mourner	155
		喪中	*mochū*	period of mourning	28

喪 喪 喪

1679 卜 日 十 2m 4c 2k

卓

TAKU – table, desk; high

食卓	*shokutaku*	dining table	322
卓球	*takkyū*	table tennis, ping-pong	726
電卓	*dentaku*	(desk-top) calculator	108
卓上	*takujō*	table-top, desk-top	32
卓越	*takuetsu*	be superior, excel, surpass	1001

卓 卓 卓

1680 心 日 卜 4k 4c 2m

悼

TŌ, ita(mu) – grieve over, mourn, lament

追悼	*tsuitō*	mourning	1174
追悼会/式	*tsuitō-kai/shiki*	memorial services	1174, 158, 525
哀悼	*aitō*	condolence, mourning, grief	1675
悼辞	*tōji*	message of condolence, funeral address	688

悼 悼 悼

1681 卜 貝 2m 7b

貞

TEI – chastity, constancy, righteousness

貞淑	*teishuku*	chastity, feminine modesty	1668
貞節	*teisetsu*	fidelity, chastity	464
貞操	*teisō*	chastity, female honor, virginity	1655
貞潔	*teiketsu*	chaste and pure	1241
不貞	*futei*	unchastity, infidelity	94

貞 貞 貞

1682 禾 日 5d 4c

香

KŌ, [KYŌ], kao(ri), ka – fragrance, aroma; **kao(ru)** – smell sweet

香気	*kōki*	fragrance, aroma, sweet smell	134
香料	*kōryō*	spices; perfume	319
線香	*senkō*	stick of incense	299
色香	*iroka*	color and scent; (feminine) beauty	204

香 香 香

1683	禾 5d	一 1a	ノ 1c

秀

SHŪ, hii(deru) – excel, surpass

優秀	*yūshū*	excellent, superior	1033
秀逸	*shūitsu*	superb, masterly	734
秀麗	*shūrei*	graceful, beautiful, handsome	1630
秀才	*shūsai*	talented man, bright boy/girl	551
けい秀画家	*keishū gaka*	accomplished woman painter	343, 165

秀 秀 秀

1684	言 7a	禾 5d	一 1a

誘

YŪ, saso(u) – invite; induce; lure, entice

誘惑	*yūwaku*	temptation, seduction	969
勧誘	*kan'yū*	invitation, canvassing, solicitation	1051
誘因	*yūin*	enticement, inducement	554
誘発	*yūhatsu*	induce, give rise to	96
誘い水	*sasoimizu*	pump priming	21

誘 誘 誘

1685	辶 2q	禾 5d	一 1a

透

TŌ, su(ku) – be transparent; leave a gap; ***su(kasu)*** – look through; leave a space; ***su(keru)*** – shine through

透明	*tōmei*	transparent	18
透視	*tōshi*	seeing through; fluoroscopy; clairvoyance	606
浸透	*shintō*	permeation, osmosis, infiltration	1078
透き通る	*sukitōru*	be transparent	150

透 透 透

1686	扌 3c	隹 8c	一 1a

携

KEI, tazusa(eru) – carry (in one's hand), have with one; ***tazusa(waru)*** – participate (in)

携帯	*keitai*	carrying, bring with; portable	963
必携	*hikkei*	handbook, manual; indispensable	520
提携	*teikei*	cooperation, tie-up	628
連携	*renkei*	cooperation, league, concert	440

携 携 携

1687 言 艹 丷
7a 3k 2o

謙

KEN – modesty, humility

謙虚	*kenkyo*	modest, humble	1572
謙譲	*kenjō*	modest, humble	1013
謙譲の美徳	*kenjō no bitoku*	the virtue of modesty	1013, 401, 1038
恭謙	*kyōken*	modesty, humility, deference	1434
謙そん	*kenson*	modesty, humility	

謙 謙 謙

1688 女 艹 丷
3e 3k 2o

嫌

KEN, [GEN], kira(u) – dislike, hate

嫌悪	*ken'o*	hatred, dislike, loathing	304
嫌疑	*kengi*	suspicion	1516
機嫌	*kigen*	mood, humor	528
大嫌い	*daikirai*	hate, strong aversion	26
毛嫌い	*kegirai*	antipathy, prejudice	287

嫌 嫌 嫌

1689 广 艹 丷
3q 3k 2o

廉

REN – pure; honest; low price

清廉	*seiren*	integrity, uprightness	660
清廉潔白	*seiren-keppaku*	spotless integrity	660, 1241, 205
廉売	*renbai*	bargain sale	239
廉価	*renka*	low price	421

廉 廉 廉

1690 耳 心
6e 4k

恥

CHI, haji – shame, disgrace; **ha(jiru)** – feel shame; **ha(jirau)** – be shy; **ha(zukashii)** – shy, ashamed

無恥	*muchi*	shameless, brazen	93
破廉恥	*harenchi*	shameless, disgraceful	665, 1689
恥毛	*chimō*	pubic hair	287
恥知らず	*hajishirazu*	shameless person	214

恥 恥 恥

1691	攵耳一 4i 6e 1a
敢	***KAN*** – daring, bold

勇敢	*yūkan*	brave, daring, courageous	1386
果敢	*kakan*	resolute, determined, bold, daring	487
敢然	*kanzen*	bold, fearless	651
敢闘	*kantō*	fight courageously	1511
敢行	*kankō*	take decisive action, dare; carry out	68

敢 敢 敢

1692	扌耳氵 3c 6e 2b
摂	***SETSU*** – act in place of; take

摂取	*sesshu*	take in, ingest	65
摂生	*sessei*	taking care of one's health	44
摂政	*sesshō*	regency, regent	483
摂理	*setsuri*	providence	143
摂氏２０度	*sesshi nijūdo*	20 degrees centigrade	566, 377

摂 摂 摂

1693	氵⺊氵 3a 2m 2b
渋	***JŪ, shibu(i)*** – astringent, puckery; glum; quiet and tasteful; ***shibu*** – astringent juice (of unripe persimmons); ***shibu(ru)*** – hesitate, be reluctant

渋滞	*jūtai*	delay, retardation	964
渋面	*jūmen, shibuzura*	sour face, scowl	274
渋味	*shibumi*	puckery taste; severe elegance	307

渋 渋 渋

1694	田土氵 5f 3b 2b
塁	***RUI*** – parapet, rampart; base (in baseball)

堅塁	*kenrui*	fortress, stronghold	1289
敵塁	*tekirui*	enemy's fortress/position	416
塁審	*ruishin*	base umpire	1383
本塁打	*honruida*	home run	25, 1020
満塁	*manrui*	bases loaded	201

塁 塁 塁

1695	一 米 丨 1a3 6b 1b2			
粛	***SHUKU*** – quietly, softly, solemnly			
	静粛	*seishuku*	stillness, quiet, hush	663
	厳粛	*genshuku*	solemnity, austerity, gravity	822
	自粛	*jishuku*	self-discipline, self-control	62
	粛清	*shukusei*	(political) purge	660
	粛党	*shukutō*	purge disloyal elements from a party	495

1696	广 冂 十 3q 2r 2k			
庸	***YŌ*** – mediocre, ordinary			
	中庸	*chūyō*	middle path, golden mean	28
	凡庸	*bon'yō*	mediocre, run-of-the-mill	1102
	登庸	*tōyō*	appointment, promotion	960

1697	广 口 十 3q 3d 2k			
唐	***TŌ*** – Tang, T'ang (Chinese dynasty); ***Kara*** – China, Cathay			
	唐突	*tōtotsu*	abrupt	898
	毛唐(人)	*ketō(jin)*	hairy barbarian, foreigner	287, 1
	遣唐使	*kentōshi*	Japanese envoy to Tang China	1173, 331
	唐様	*karayō*	Chinese style	403

1698	米 广 口 6b 3q 3d			
糖	***TŌ*** – sugar			
	砂糖	*satō*	sugar	1151
	製糖	*seitō*	sugar manufacturing	428
	糖分	*tōbun*	sugar content	38
	糖質	*tōshitsu*	sugariness, saccharinity	176
	血糖	*kettō*	blood sugar	789

1699 米 广 土 6b 3q 3b

粧

SHŌ – adorn (one's person)

化粧	*keshō*	makeup	254
化粧品	*keshōhin*	cosmetics	254, 230
化粧室	*keshōshitsu*	dressing room; lavatory	254, 166
化粧箱	*keshōbako*	a vanity, dressing case	254, 1091
薄化粧	*usugeshō*	light makeup	1449, 254

粧 粧 粧

1700 米 立 6b 5b

粒

RYŪ, tsubu – a grain

粒状	*ryūjō*	granular, granulated	626
粒子	*ryūshi*	(atomic) particle; grain (in film)	103
素粒子	*soryūshi*	elementary/subatomic particle	271, 103
米粒	*kometsubu*	grain of rice	224
雨粒	*amatsubu*	raindrop	30

粒 粒 粒

1701 米 丷 刂 6b 2o 2f

粉

FUN, kona, ko – flour, powder

粉末	*funmatsu*	powder	305
製粉所	*seifunjo*	flour mill	428, 153
粉飾	*funshoku*	makeup; embellishment	979
粉ミルク	*konamiruku*	powdered milk	
メリケン粉	*merikenko*	wheat flour	

粉 粉 粉

1702 糸 丷 刂 6a 2o 2f

紛

FUN, magi(reru) – be mistaken (for), be hardly distinguishable; get mixed, disappear (among); be diverted; ***magi(rasu/rawasu)*** – divert, distract; conceal; evade; ***magi(rawashii)*** – ambiguous, liable to be confused

紛争	*funsō*	dispute, strife	302
紛失	*funshitsu*	loss, be missing	311

紛 紛 紛

1703 糸 十 丨 6a 2k 1b

糾

KYŪ – twist (rope); ask, inquire into

糾弾	*kyūdan*	impeach, censure	1539
糾明	*kyūmei*	study, inquiry, investigation	18
糾問	*kyūmon*	close examination, grilling	162
紛糾	*funkyū*	complication, entanglement	1702
糾合	*kyūgō*	rally, muster	159

糾 糾 糾

1704 米 日 土 6b 4c2 3b

糧

RYŌ, [RŌ], kate – food, provisions

食糧	*shokuryō*	food, foodstuffs	322
糧食	*ryōshoku*	provisions, food supplies	322
兵糧	*hyōrō*	(military) provisions	784
日々の糧	*hibi no kate*	one's daily bread	5
心の糧	*kokoro no kate*	food for thought	97

糧 糧 糧

1705 土 日 火 3b2 4c 4d

墨

BOKU, sumi – India ink, ink stick

水墨画	*suibokuga*	India-ink painting	21, 343
白墨	*hakuboku*	chalk	205
墨守	*bokushu*	adherence (to tradition)	490
墨絵	*sumie*	India-ink drawing	345
入れ墨	*irezumi*	tattooing; a tattoo	52

墨 墨 墨

1706 ⺊ 口 2m 3d

占

SEN, shi(meru) – occupy, hold; **urana(u)** – tell fortunes

占有	*sen'yū*	occupancy, possession	265
占領	*senryō*	occupation, capture	834
独占	*dokusen*	monopoly	219
買い占め	*kaishime*	cornering (the market)	241
星占い	*hoshiuranai*	astrology; horoscope	730

占 占 占

1707 米 口 卜 6b 3d 2m

粘

NEN, neba(ru) – be sticky; stick to it, persevere

粘着(力)	*nenchaku(ryoku)*	adhesion, viscosity	657, 100
粘土	*nendo*	clay	24
粘液	*nen'eki*	mucus	472
粘膜	*nenmaku*	mucous membrane	1426
粘り強い	*nebarizuyoi*	tenacious, persistent	217

粘 粘 粘

1708 米 十 一 6b 2k 1a

粋

SUI – purity, essence; elite, choice; elegant, fashinable, chic; considerateness

純粋	*junsui*	pure, genuine	965
粋人	*suijin*	man of refined tastes, man about town	1
精粋	*seisui*	pure, selfless	659
粋狂	*suikyō*	whimsical, capricious	883

粋 粋 粋

1709 酉 十 一 7e 2k 1a

酔

SUI, yo(u) – get drunk, be intoxicated; feel sick

麻酔	*masui*	anesthesia; narcosis	1529
泥酔	*deisui*	get dead drunk	1621
心酔	*shinsui*	be fascinated (with), ardently admire	97
酔っ払い	*yopparai*	a drunk	582
船酔い	*funayoi*	seasickness	376

酔 酔 酔

1710 石 十 一 5a 2k 1a

砕

SAI, kuda(keru) – break, be smashed; condescend, get familiar; ***kuda(ku)*** – break, smash, pulverize

粉砕	*funsai*	pulverize, shatter, crush	701
砕石	*saiseki*	rubble, broken stone	78
紛骨砕身	*funkotsu-saishin*	make one's utmost efforts	1701, 1266, 59
玉砕	*gyokusai*	death for honor	295

砕 砕 砕

1711 酉 土 口
7e 3b 3d

酷

KOKU – severe, harsh, cruel

残酷	*zankoku*	cruel	650
冷酷	*reikoku*	heartless, cruel	832
酷評	*kokuhyō*	sharp/harsh criticism	1028
酷使	*kokushi*	work (someone) hard	331
酷暑	*kokusho*	intense heat, swelter	638

酷 酷 酷

1712 扌 厂 又
3c 2p 2h

披

HI – open

披露	*hirō*	announcement	951
結婚披露宴	*kekkon hirōen*	wedding reception	485, 567, 951, 640
披見	*hiken*	open and read (a letter)	63

披 披 披

1713 扌 厂 又
3c 2p 2h

抜

BATSU, nu(ku) – pull out; remove; leave out; outdistance, surpass; ***nu(keru)*** – come/fall out; be omitted; be gone; escape; ***nu(karu)*** – make a blunder; ***nu(kasu)*** – omit, skip over

抜群	*batsugun*	preeminent, outstanding	794
選抜	*senbatsu*	selection, picking out	800
骨抜き	*honenuki*	unboned; emasculated, toothless	1266

抜 抜 抜

1714 扌 尸 土
3c 3r 3b

握

AKU, nigi(ru) – grasp, grip, take hold of

握手	*akushu*	shake hands	57
掌握	*shōaku*	hold, seize, grasp	499
一握り	*hitonigiri*	handful	2
握り飯	*nigirimeshi*	rice ball	325
握り締める	*nigirishimeru*	grasp tightly, clench	1180

握 握 握

1715 扌 隹 亠 3c 8c 2j

擁

YŌ – embrace

抱擁	*hōyō*	embrace	1285
擁護	*yōgo*	protect, defend	1312
擁立	*yōritsu*	support, back	121

1716 宀 土 丷 3m 3b 2o

窒

CHITSU – plug up, obstruct; nitrogen

窒息	*chissoku*	suffocation, asphyxiation	1242
窒息死	*chissokushi*	death from suffocation	1242, 85
窒素	*chisso*	nitrogen	271

1717 宀 丷 刂 3m 2o 2f

窃

SETSU – steal

窃盗	*settō*	theft, thief	1100
窃盗罪	*settōzai*	theft, larceny	1100, 885
窃盗犯	*settōhan*	thief	1100, 882
窃取	*sesshu*	steal	65
ひょう窃	*hyōsetsu*	plagiarism	

1718 扌 宀 丷 3c 3m 2o

控

KŌ, hika(eru) – hold back, refrain from; note down; wait

控除	*kōjo*	deduct, subtract	1065
控訴	*kōso*	(intermediate) appeal (to a higher court)	1402
手控え	*tebikae*	note, memo; holding off/back	57
控え室	*hikaeshitsu*	anteroom, lobby	166
控え目	*hikaeme*	moderate, reserved	55

1719 貝 一 丨 7b 1a2 1b

貢

KŌ, [KU], mitsu(gu) – pay tribute; support (financially)

貢献	*kōken*	contribution, services	1355
年貢	*nengu*	annual tribute	45
貢ぎ(物)	*mitsugi(mono)*	tribute	79

貢 貢 貢

1720 扌 土 一 3c 3b 1a

拷

GŌ – beat, torture

拷問	*gōmon*	torture	162
拷問具	*gōmongu*	instrument of torture	162, 420

拷 拷 拷

1721 扌 亻 一 3c 2a 1a2

扶

FU – help

扶養	*fuyō*	support (a family)	402
扶養義務	*fuyō gimu*	duty of supporting (someone)	402, 291, 235
扶養料	*fuyōryō*	sustenance allowance, alimony	402, 319
扶助	*fujo*	aid, support, relief	623
扶持	*fuchi*	rice ration allotted to a samurai	451

扶 扶 扶

1722 扌 舟 几 3c 6c 2s

搬

HAN – carry, transport

運搬	*unpan*	transport, conveyance, delivery	439
搬送	*hansō*	convey, carry	441
搬入	*hannyū*	carry/send in	52
搬出	*hanshutsu*	carry/take out	53

搬 搬 搬

1723	月 一 丨 4b 1a2 1b2	***HI, koe, ko(yashi)*** – manure, dung, night soil; ***ko(yasu)*** – fertilize; ***ko(eru)*** – grow fat; grow fertile; have fastidious taste		
肥				
	肥料	*hiryō*	manure, fertilizer	319
	肥満	*himan*	corpulence, fatness, obesity	201
	肥大	*hidai*	fleshiness, corpulence	26

肥 肥 肥

1724	扌 一 丨 3c 1a2 1b2	***HA*** – take, grasp; bundle		
把				
	把握	*haaku*	grasp, comprehend	1714
	把持	*haji*	hold on to, grasp	451
	一把	*ichiwa*	1 bundle	2
	三把	*sanba*	3 bundles	4
	十把	*jippa*	10 bundles	12

把 把 把

1725	心 彡 亻 4k 3j 2a	***SAN, ZAN, miji(me)*** – piteous, wretched, miserable		
惨				
	悲惨	*hisan*	misery, distress, tragedy	1034
	惨事	*sanji*	disaster, tragic accident	80
	惨状	*sanjō*	miserable state, disastrous scene	626
	惨敗	*sanpai, zanpai*	crushing defeat	511
	惨死	*zanshi*	tragic/violent death	85

惨 惨 惨

1726	尸 丶 3r 1d3	***JIN, tsu(kusu)*** – exhaust, use up; render (service), make efforts; ***tsu(kiru)*** – be exhausted, be used up, run out, end; ***tsu(kasu)*** – exhaust, use up, run out of		
尽				
	尽力	*jinryoku*	efforts, exertions; assistance	100
	無尽蔵	*mujinzō*	inexhaustible supply	93, 1286
	論じ尽くす	*ronjitsukusu*	discuss fully/exhaustively	293

尽 尽 尽

1727 欠ネ士 4j 4e 3p

款

KAN – article, section; goodwill, friendship

借款	*shakkan*	(international) loan	766
長期借款	*chōki shakkan*	long-term loan	95, 449, 766
定款	*teikan*	articles of association/incorporation	355
約款	*yakkan*	agreement, provision, clause	211
落款	*rakkan*	signature (and seal)	839

1728 士冖几 3p 2i 2s2

殻

KAKU, kara – husk, hull, shell

地殻	*chikaku*	the earth's crust	118
地殻変動	*chikaku hendō*	movement of the earth's crust	118, 257, 231
貝殻	*kaigara*	seashell	240
卵の殻	*tamago no kara*	eggshell	1058

1729 士禾冖 3p 5d 2i

穀

KOKU – grain, cereals

穀物	*kokumotsu*	grain	79
穀類	*kokurui*	grains	226
五穀	*gokoku*	the 5 grains (rice, wheat and barley, 2 millets, beans)	7
穀倉	*kokusō*	granary, grain elevator	1307
脱穀機	*dakkokuki*	threshing machine, thresher	1370, 528

1730 士冖ト 3p 2i 2m

壱

ICHI – one (in documents)

金壱万円	*kin ichiman'en*	10,000 yen	23, 16, 13

1731	亻 木 ⺍ 2a 4a 2n	**KETSU** – excel			
傑		傑出	*kesshutsu*	excel, be eminent	53
		傑作	*kessaku*	masterpiece	360
		傑物	*ketsubutsu*	great man, outstanding figure	79
		豪傑	*gōketsu*	hero, great man	1671
		豪傑笑い	*gōketsu warai*	broad/hearty laugh	1671, 1235

傑 傑 傑

1732	目 ⺍ 冖 5c 3n 2i	**SHUN, matata(ku)** – wink, blink, twinkle			
瞬		瞬間	*shunkan*	instant, moment	43
		瞬時	*shunji*	moment, instant	42
		一瞬	*isshun*	instant; for an instant	2
		瞬刻	*shunkoku*	instant, moment	1211

瞬 瞬 瞬

1733	心 一 ノ 4k 1a3 1c3	**KAI, ku(iru)** – regret, rue; **ku(yamu)** – regret, rue; lament, mourn over; offer condolences; **kuya(shii)** – vexatious, vexing			
悔		後悔	*kōkai*	regret	48
		悔悟	*kaigo*	repentance, remorse	1438
		悔やみ(状)	*kuyami(jō)*	(letter of) condolence	626

悔 悔 悔

1734	木 一 ノ 4a 1a3 1c3	**BAI, ume** – ume, Japanese plum/apricot (tree)			
梅		梅雨	*baiu, tsuyu*	the rainy season	30
		紅梅	*kōbai*	ume with red/pink blossoms	820
		梅見	*umemi*	ume-blossom viewing	63
		梅酒	*umeshu*	ume brandy	517
		梅干し	*umeboshi*	pickled ume	584

梅 梅 梅

1735	夂 一 ノ 4i 1a3 1c3	**BIN** – agile, alert			
敏		敏速	*binsoku*	promptness, alacrity	502
		敏感	*binkan*	sensitive	262
		鋭敏	*eibin*	sharp, keen, acute	1371
		機敏	*kibin*	smart, astute, alert	528
		敏腕	*binwan*	able, capable	1299

敏 敏 敏

1736	亻 一 ノ 2a 1a3 1c3	***BU, anado(ru)*** – despise			
侮		軽侮	*keibu*	scorn, contempt	547
		侮言	*bugen*	an insult	66
		侮べつ	*bubetsu*	scorn, contempt	

侮 侮 侮

1737	厂 口 一 2p 3d 1a2	***SHIN, kuchibiru*** – lip			
唇		口唇	*kōshin*	lips	54
		紅唇	*kōshin*	red lips	820
		唇音	*shin'on*	a labial (sound)	347
		上唇	*uwa-kuchibiru, jōshin*	upper lip	32
		下唇	*shita-kuchibiru, kashin*	lower lip	31

唇 唇 唇

1738	厂 十 一 2p 2k 1a2	***JOKU, hazukashi(meru)*** – humiliate, disgrace			
辱		侮辱	*bujoku*	insult	1736
		恥辱	*chijoku*	disgrace, dishonor	1690
		汚辱	*ojoku*	disgrace, dishonor	693
		雪辱	*setsujoku*	vindication; revenge	949

辱 辱 辱

1739	貝 月 厂 7b 4b 2p

賄

WAI, makana(u) – provide board; supply, furnish; pay, finance

贈賄	*zōwai*	giving a bribe, bribery	1364
収賄	*shūwai*	accepting a bribe, bribery	757
賄ろ	*wairo*	a bribe	
賄い付き	*makanaitsuki*	with meals	192

賄 賄 賄

1740	月 辶 厂 4b2 2q 2p

髄

ZUI – marrow

骨髄	*kotsuzui*	bone marrow	1266
せき髄	*sekizui*	spinal cord	
脳髄	*nōzui*	brain	1278
真/神/心 髄	*shinzui*	essence, quintessence, soul	422, 310, 97
精髄	*seizui*	essence, quintessence, soul	659

髄 髄 髄

1741	阝 月 辶 2d 4b 2q

随

ZUI – follow

追随	*tsuizui*	follow (someone)	1174
随意	*zuii*	voluntary, optional	132
随筆	*zuihitsu*	essay, miscellaneous writings	130
付随現象	*fuzui genshō*	concomitant phenomenon	192, 298, 739
随一	*zuiichi*	most, greatest, first	2

随 随 随

1742	土 月 阝 3b 4b 2d

堕

DA – fall

堕落	*daraku*	depravity, corruption	839
堕胎	*datai*	abortion	1296

堕 堕 堕

1743 心 月 厂 4k 4b 2p

惰

DA – lazy, inactive

怠惰	*taida*	laziness, idleness, sloth	1297
惰性	*dasei*	inertia; force of habit	98
惰気	*daki*	inactivity, dullness	134
惰眠	*damin*	idle slumber, lethargy	849

惰 惰 惰

1744 亻 厂 一 2a 2p 1a2

佐

SA – help

補佐	*hosa*	aid; assistant, adviser	889
少佐	*shōsa*	major; lieutenant commander (in the navy)	144
大佐	*taisa*	colonel; captain (in the navy)	26
佐官	*sakan*	field officer	326
土佐	*Tosa*	(city and region in Shikoku)	24

佐 佐 佐

1745 女 月 ⺊ 3e 4b 2m

婿

SEI, muko – son-in-law; bridegroom

花婿	*hanamuko*	bridegroom	255
婿養子	*mukoyōshi*	son-in-law taken into the family	402, 103
婿選び	*mukoerabi*	looking for a husband for one's daughter	800

婿 婿 婿

1746 女 土 一 3e 3b 1a

姓

SEI, SHŌ – surname, family name

姓名	*seimei*	(one's full) name	82
同姓	*dōsei*	same surname; namesakes	198
改姓	*kaisei*	change one's surname	514
旧姓	*kyūsei*	one's former/maiden name	1216
百姓	*hyakushō*	farmer	14

姓 姓 姓

1747	女 口 3e 3d	***JO, NYO*** – equal, like, as, as if			
		突如	*totsujo*	suddenly, unexpectedly	898
		躍如	*yakujo*	vivid, lifelike	1560
		欠如	*ketsujo*	lack, deficiency	383
		如実	*nyojitsu*	true to life, realistic	203
		如何	*ikaga*	how	390

如 如 如

1748	女 口 亻 3e 3s 2a	***IN*** – marriage			
		婚姻	*kon'in*	marriage, matrimony	567
		婚姻法	*kon'inhō*	the Marriage Law	567, 123
		姻族	*inzoku*	relatives by marriage	221

姻 姻 姻

1749	女 宀 豕 3e 3m 3g	***KA*** – marry (a man); blame; ***totsu(gu)*** – get married; ***yome*** – bride, young wife, daughter-in-law			
		転嫁	*tenka*	remarriage; impute (blame)	433
		花嫁	*hanayome*	bride	255
		嫁入り	*yomeiri*	marriage, wedding (of a woman)	52

嫁 嫁 嫁

1750	禾 宀 豕 5d 3m 3g	***KA, kase(gu)*** – work, earn (a living)			
		稼働	*kadō*	operation, work	232
		稼業	*kagyō*	one's trade/occupation	279
		出稼ぎ	*dekasegi*	work away from home	53
		時間稼ぎ	*jikankasegi*	playing/stalling for time	42, 43
		稼ぎ手	*kasegite*	breadwinner; hard worker	57

稼 稼 稼

1751	土 冖 犭
	3b 2i 3g

塚

tsuka – mound, hillock

貝塚	*kaizuka*	heap of shells	240
あり塚	*arizuka*	anthill	
一里塚	*ichirizuka*	milepost, milestone	2, 142

塚 塚 塚

1752	女 日 丨
	3e 4c 1b

娘

musume – daughter; girl

孫娘	*magomusume*	granddaughter	910
娘婿	*musumemuko*	son-in-law	1745
娘盛り	*musumezakari*	(a girl in) the prime of youth	719
娘心	*musumegokoro*	girlish mind/innocence	97
田舎娘	*inakamusume*	country girl	35, 791

娘 娘 娘

1753	氵 日 丨
	3a 4c 1b

浪

RŌ – waves; wander

波浪	*harō*	waves, high seas	666
浮浪	*furō*	vagrancy, vagabondage	938
流浪	*rurō*	vagrancy, wandering	247
浪人	*rōnin*	lordless samurai; unaffiliated person	1
浪費	*rōhi*	waste, squander	749

浪 浪 浪

1754	月 日 丨
	4b 4c 1b

朗

RŌ, hoga(raka) – clear, bright, cheerful

明朗	*meirō*	bright, clear, cheerful	18
朗々	*rōrō*	clear, sonorous	
朗詠	*rōei*	recite (a Japanese/Chinese poem)	1209
朗読	*rōdoku*	read aloud, recite	244
朗報	*rōhō*	good news, glad tidings	685

朗 朗 朗

1755 心 日 ノ 4k 4c 1c

KON, ura(mu) – bear ill will/a grudge against, feel resentment/reproachful; ***ura(meshii)*** – reproachful, rueful, have a grudge, feel bitter (against)

遺恨	*ikon*	grudge, rancor, malice, enmity	1172
悔恨	*kaikon*	remorse, contrition	1733
痛恨	*tsūkon*	great sorrow, bitter regret	1320

恨

1756 女 一 丨 3e 1a2 1b

HI – (married) princess

王妃	*ōhi*	queen, empress	294
皇太子妃	*kōtaishihi*	the crown princess	297, 629, 103
妃殿下	*hidenka*	Her Imperial Highness	1130, 31

妃

1757 女 匚 一 3e 2t 1a2

hime – princess

姫君	*himegimi*	princess	793
舞姫	*maihime*	dancing girl, dancer	810
歌姫	*utahime*	songstress	392
姫路	*Himeji*	(city with a famous castle, about 100 km west of Osaka)	151

姫

1758 立 日 丨 5b 4c 1b

RYŪ, tatsu – dragon

飛竜	*hiryū*	flying dragon	530
竜宮	*ryūgū*	Palace of the Dragon King	721
恐竜	*kyōryū*	dinosaur	1602
竜骨	*ryūkotsu*	keel	1266
竜巻	*tatsumaki*	tornado	507

竜

1759	氵 立 日 (3a 5b 4c)		
滝	***taki*** – waterfall		
滝口	*takiguchi*	top/crest of a waterfall	54
滝つぼ	*takitsubo*	bottom/basin of a waterfall	
滝登り	*takinobori*	(salmon) climbing a waterfall	960
華厳の滝	*Kegon no Taki*	(waterfall near Nikko)	1074, 822

滝 滝 滝

1760	糸 日 丨 (6a 4c2 1b)		
縄	***JŌ, nawa*** – rope		
縄文	*jōmon*	(ancient Japanese) straw-rope pattern	111
自縄自縛に陥る	*jijō-jibaku ni ochiiru*	fall in one's own trap	62, 1448, 1218
縄張	*nawabari*	rope off; one's domain	1106
縄跳び	*nawatobi*	skipping/jumping rope	1563

縄 縄 縄

1761	亻 口 一 (2a 3d 1a2)		
伺	***SHI, ukaga(u)*** – visit, call at; ask, inquire		
伺候	*shikō*	wait upon, attend; make a courtesy call	944
奉伺	*hōshi*	attend, serve	1541
暑中伺い	*shochū ukagai*	hot-season greeting	638, 28
進退伺い	*shintai ukagai*	informal resignation	437, 846

伺 伺 伺

1762	食 口 一 (8b 3d 1a2)		
飼	***SHI, ka(u)*** – raise, keep (animals)		
飼育	*shiiku*	raising, breeding	246
飼料	*shiryō*	feed, fodder	319
飼い主	*kainushi*	(pet) owner, master	155
羊飼い	*hitsujikai*	shepherd	288
飼い犬	*kaiinu*	pet dog	280

飼 飼 飼

1763 飠 一 丨 8b 1a3 1b

飽

HŌ, a(kiru) – get (sick and) tired of; ***a(kasu)*** – cloy, satiate, surfeit; tire, bore, make (someone) fed up

飽食	*hōshoku*	gluttony, engorgement	322
飽和	*hōwa*	saturation	124
見飽きる	*miakiru*	get tired of seeing	63
…に飽かして	*… ni akashite*	regardless of …	

1764 石 一 丨 5a 1a3 1b

砲

HŌ – gun, cannon

大砲	*taihō*	cannon	26
鉄砲	*teppō*	gun	312
砲撃	*hōgeki*	shelling, bombardment	1016
砲兵	*hōhei*	artillery, artilleryman, gunner	784
(十字)砲火	*(jūji) hōka*	(cross) fire	12, 110, 20

1765 氵 一 丨 3a 1a3 1b

泡

HŌ, awa – bubble, foam, froth, suds

気泡	*kihō*	(air) bubble	134
水泡	*suihō*	foam, bubble	21
発泡	*happō*	foaming	96
泡立つ	*awadatsu*	bubble foam, lather up	121
泡を食う	*awa o kuu*	be flurried, lose one's head	322

1766 广 火 艹 3q 4d 3k

庶

SHO – all; illegitimate child

庶務	*shomu*	general affairs	235
庶務課	*shomuka*	general affairs section	235, 488
庶民	*shomin*	the (common) people	177
庶民的	*shominteki*	popular, common, democratic	177, 210
庶子	*shoshi*	illegitimate child	103

1767	辶 火 艹 2q 4d 3k	**SHA, saegi(ru)** – interrupt, obstruct, block			
遮		遮断	*shadan*	interception, isolation, cutoff	1024
		遮断機	*shadanki*	railroad-crossing gate	1024, 528
		遮断器	*shadanki*	circuit breaker	1024, 527

遮 遮 遮

1768	石 隹 火 5a 8c 4d	**SHŌ** – sunken rock			
礁		暗礁	*anshō*	sunken rock, unseen reef, snag	348
		岩礁	*ganshō*	(shore) reef	1345
		環礁	*kanshō*	atoll	865
		さんご礁	*sangoshō*	coral reef	
		離礁	*rishō*	(a ship) off the rocks, refloat	1281

礁 礁 礁

1769	言 欠 口 7a 4j 3d	**SHI, haka(ru)** – consult, confer, solicit advice			
諮		諮問	*shimon*	question, inquiry	162
		諮問機関	*shimon kikan*	advisory body	162, 528, 398

諮 諮 諮

1770	言 艹 口 7a 3k 3d	**DAKU** – consent, agree to			
諾		承諾	*shōdaku*	consent, agreement	942
		許諾	*kyodaku*	consent, approval, permission	737
		受諾	*judaku*	acceptance (of an offer)	260
		内諾	*naidaku*	informal consent	84
		諾否	*dakuhi*	acceptance or refusal, definite reply	1248

諾 諾 諾

1771 匸 艹 口 (2t 3k 3d) 匿

TOKU – shelter, hide

匿名	*tokumei*	anonymity; pseudonym	82
隠匿	*intoku*	conceal, stash away, cover up	868
隠匿者	*intokusha*	hoarder, concealer	868, 164
隠匿物資	*intoku busshi*	secret cache of goods	868, 79, 750

匿 匿 匿

1772 彳 車 一 (3i 7c 1a3) 衝

SHŌ – collision

衝撃	*shōgeki*	shock	1016
(正面)衝突	*(shōmen) shōtotsu*	(head-on) collision	275, 274, 898
緩衝地帯	*kanshō chitai*	buffer zone	1089, 118, 963
折衝	*sesshō*	negotiations	1394
衝動(行為)	*shōdō (kōi)*	(acting on) impulse	231, 68, 1484

衝 衝 衝

1773 火 車 力 (4d 7c 2g) 勲

KUN – merit

勲功	*kunkō*	distinguished sevice, merits	818
勲章	*kunshō*	order, decoration, medal	857
勲一等	*kun ittō*	First Order of Merit	2, 569
殊勲	*shukun*	distinguished service, meritorious deeds	1505
偉勲	*ikun*	brilliant exploit, great achievement	1053

勲 勲 勲

1774 艹 車 火 (3k 7c 4d) 薫

KUN, kao(ru) – be fragrant, smell good

薫香	*kunkō*	incense; fragrance	1682
薫風	*kunpū*	balmy breeze	29
薫陶	*kuntō*	discipline, training; education	1650
風薫る五月	*kaze kaoru gogatsu*	the balmy month of May	29, 7, 17

薫 薫 薫

1775 艹 方 3k 4h

芳

HŌ – fragrance; (honorific prefix); ***kanba(shii)*** – sweetsmelling; favorable, fair

芳香	*hōkō*	fragrance, perfume, aroma	1682
芳名	*hōmei*	good name/reputation; your name	82
(来客)芳名録	*(raikyaku) hōmeiroku*	visitor's book	69, 641, 82, 538
芳紀	*hōki*	age (of a young lady)	372

芳 芳 芳

1776 亻 方 攵 2a 4h 4i

倣

HŌ, nara(u) – imitate, follow

模倣	*mohō*	imitation	1425
先例に倣う	*senrei ni narau*	follow precedent	50, 612

倣 倣 倣

1777 日 艹 ノ 4c 3k 1c

昇

SHŌ, nobo(ru) – rise, be promoted

上昇	*jōshō*	rise, ascent; upward trend	32
昇進	*shōshin*	promotion, advancement	437
昇格	*shōkaku*	promotion to a higher status, upgrading	643
昇給	*shōkyū*	pay raise	346
昇級	*shōkyū*	promotion to a higher grade	568

昇 昇 昇

1778 馬 攵 艹 10a 4i 3k

驚

KYŌ, odoro(ku) – be surprised, astonished; be frightened; ***odoro(kasu)*** – surprise, astonish; frighten

驚嘆	*kyōtan*	admiration, wonder	1246
驚異	*kyōi*	wonder, miracle, marvel	1061
驚がく	*kyōgaku*	astonishment; alarm, consternation	

驚 驚 驚

1779 月 言 亻 4b 7a 2a

謄

TŌ – copy

謄写	*tōsha*	copy, duplication	540
謄写器	*tōshaki*	mimeograph machine	540, 527
謄写版	*tōshaban*	mimeograph	540, 1046
謄本	*tōhon*	transcript, copy	25

謄 謄 謄

1780 月 馬 亻 4b 10a 2a

騰

TŌ – rise (in prices)

(物価)騰貴	*(bukka) tōki*	rise (in prices)	79, 421, 1171
暴騰	*bōtō*	sudden/sharp rise	1014
高騰	*kōtō*	sudden rise, jump (in prices)	190

騰 騰 騰

1781 巾 攵 ⺌ 3f 4i 3n2

幣

HEI – Shinto zigzag paper offerings; money

紙幣	*shihei*	paper money	180
貨幣	*kahei*	money; coin, coinage	752
貨幣価値	*kahei kachi*	the value of money currency	752, 421, 425
造幣局	*Zōheikyoku*	Mint Bureau	691, 170
幣制	*heisei*	monetary system	427

幣 幣 幣

1782 艹 攵 ⺌ 3k 4i 3n2

弊

HEI – evil, abuse, vice; (humble prefix) our

弊害	*heigai*	an evil, ill effect	518
疲弊	*hihei*	impoverishment, exhaustion	1321
旧弊	*kyūhei*	an old evil; old-fashioned	1216
弊社	*heisha*	our company, we	308

弊 弊 弊

1783	卩 土 ノ 2e 3b 1c	***KYAKU*** – pull back, withdraw			
却		却下	*kyakka*	reject, dismiss	31
		返却	*henkyaku*	return, repay	442
		退却	*taikyaku*	retreat	846
		売却	*baikyaku*	sale, disposal by sale	239
		忘却	*bōkyaku*	forget, lose sight of	1374

却 却 却

1784	月 土 卩 4b 3b 2e	***KYAKU, [KYA], ashi*** – leg			
脚		橋脚	*kyōkyaku*	bridge pier	597
		失脚	*shikkyaku*	lose one's position/standing	311
		脚注	*kyakuchū*	footnote	357
		脚本	*kyakuhon*	play, script	25
		脚色	*kyakushoku*	dramatization, stage/film adaptation	204

脚 脚 脚

1785	心 目 十 4k 5c 2k	***SHIN, tsutsushi(mu)*** – be discreet, careful; restrain oneself, refrain from			
慎		謹慎	*kinshin*	good behavior; house arrest	1247
		慎重	*shinchō*	cautious	227
		慎み深い	*tsutsushimibukai*	discreet, cautious	536

慎 慎 慎

1786	金 目 十 8a 5c 2k	***CHIN, shizu(meru)*** – calm, quell; ***shizu(maru)*** – calm down			
鎮		鎮静剤	*chinseizai*	a sedative	663, 550
		鎮痛剤	*chintsūzai*	pain-killer	1320, 550
		鎮圧	*chin'atsu*	suppression, quelling	1342
		鎮魂曲/歌	*chinkon-kyoku/ka*	requiem	1525, 366, 392
		鎮守	*chinju*	local/tutelary deity	490

鎮 鎮 鎮

1787 車 一 丨 7c 1a 1b

軌

KI – wheel track, rut, railway, orbit

軌道	*kidō*	railroad track; orbit	149
狭軌鉄道	*kyōki tetsudō*	narrow-gauge railway	1353, 312, 149
常軌	*jōki*	normal course of action	497
軌範	*kihan*	model, example	1092
軌跡	*kiseki*	(geometrical) locus	1569

軌 軌 軌

1788 車 欠 7c 4j

軟

NAN, yawa(rakai/raka) – soft

柔軟	*jūnan*	soft, pliable	774
軟化	*nanka*	become soft; relent	254
軟弱	*nanjaku*	weak, weak-kneed	218
軟骨	*nankotsu*	cartilage	1266
軟着陸	*nanchakuriku*	soft landing	657, 647

軟 軟 軟

1789 宀 王 火 3m 4f 4d

窯

YŌ, kama – kiln

窯業	*yōgyō*	ceramic industry, ceramics	279
窯元	*kamamoto*	place where pottery is made	137

窯 窯 窯

1790 火 戸 4d 4m

炉

RO – furnace, hearth

暖炉	*danro*	fireplace	635
溶鉱炉	*yōkōro*	smelting/blast furnace	1392, 1604
原子炉	*genshiro*	atomic reactor	136, 103
核反応炉	*kaku hannōro*	nuclear reactor	1212, 324, 827
増殖炉	*zōshokuro*	breeder reactor	712, 1506

炉 炉 炉

1791 火 欠 4d 4j

炊

SUI, ta(ku) – burn, light a fire; boil, cook

炊事	*suiji*	cooking	80
自炊	*jisui*	do one's own cooking	62
炊飯器	*suihanki*	rice cooker	325, 527
雑炊	*zōsui*	porridge of rice and vegetables	575
炊き出し	*takidashi*	emergency group cooking	53

炊 炊 炊

1792 氵 弓 丨 3a 3h 1b2

沸

FUTSU, wa(ku) – boil, seethe; ***wa(kasu)*** – (bring to a) boil

沸騰	*futtō*	boiling; excitement, agitation	1780
沸(騰)点	*fut(tō)ten*	boiling point	1780, 169
沸き立つ	*wakitatsu*	boil up, seethe	121
湯沸かし(器)	*yuwakashi(ki)*	hot-water heater	632, 527

沸 沸 沸

1793 氵 貝 土 3a 7b 3b

漬

tsu(keru) – soak, immerse; pickle, preserve; ***tsu(karu)*** – soak, steep, be submersed; be well seasoned

漬物	*tsukemono*	pickled vegetables	79
漬物石	*tsukemonoishi*	weight stone (used in making pickles)	79, 78
塩漬	*shiozuke*	food preserved with salt	1101

漬 漬 漬

1794 氵 十 3a 2k

汁

JŪ, shiru – juice, sap; soup, broth, gravy

(天然)果汁	*(tennen) kajū*	(natural) fruit juice	141, 651, 487
肉汁	*nikujū*	meat juices, gravy	223
墨汁	*bokujū*	India ink	1705
汁粉	*shiruko*	adzuki-bean soup with rice cake	1701
みそ汁	*misoshiru*	miso soup	

汁 汁 汁

1795 火 日 土 4d 4c 3b

煮

SHA, ni(eru/ru) – (intr./tr.) boil, cook

煮沸	*shafutsu*	boiling	1792
雑煮	*zōni*	rice-cake soup with vegetables	575
生煮え	*namanie*	half-cooked, underdone	44
煮返す	*nikaesu*	reboil, cook over again	442
業を煮やす	*gō o niyasu*	become exasperated	279

煮 煮 煮

1796 弓 丨 3h 1b

弔

CHŌ, tomura(u) – mourn, condole

弔意	*chōi*	condolence, sympathy	132
弔辞	*chōji*	words/message of condolence	688
弔電	*chōden*	telegram of condolence	108
弔問	*chōmon*	visit of condolence	162
慶弔	*keichō*	congratulations and condolences	1632

弔 弔 弔

1797 心 一 丨 4k 1a2 1b

忌

KI, i(mu) – hate, loathe; avoid, shun; ***i(mawashii)*** – abominable, disgusting, scandalous; ominous

忌中	*kichū*	in mourning	28
忌避	*kihi*	evasion, shirking; (legal) challenge	1491
忌み言葉	*imikotoba*	word taboo by superstition	66, 253

忌 忌 忌

1798 辶 十 一 2q 2k 1a

迅

JIN – fast

迅速	*jinsoku*	quick, rapid, speedy	502
迅雷	*jinrai*	thunderclap	952
奮迅	*funjin*	roused to powerful action	1309

迅 迅 迅

1799	日 ⺈ 一 (4c 2n 1a2)		
殉	***JUN*** – follow into death; lay down one's life		
殉教者	*junkyōsha*	martyr	245, 164
殉難	*junnan*	martyrdom	557
殉職	*junshoku*	die in the line of duty	385
殉国	*junkoku*	dying for one's country	40
殉死	*junshi*	kill oneself on the death of one's lord	85

殉 殉 殉

1800	扌 口 一 (3c 3d 1a)		
拘	***KŌ*** – seize, arrest; adhere to		
拘束	*kōsoku*	restriction, restraint	501
拘留	*kōryū*	detention, custody	761
拘置	*kōchi*	keep in detention, confine, hold	426
拘置所	*kōchisho*	house of detention, prison	426, 153
拘泥	*kōdei*	adhere (to), be a stickler (for)	1621

拘 拘 拘

1801	扌 山 丨 (3c 3o 1b2)		
拙	***SETSU*** – unskillful, clumsy		
拙劣	*setsuretsu*	clumsy, bungling, unskillful	1150
稚拙	*chisetsu*	artless, crude, naïve	1230
拙作	*sessaku*	poor policy, imprudent measure	880
拙速	*sessoku*	not elaborate but fast, rough-and-ready	502
巧拙	*kōsetsu*	skill, dexterity	1627

拙 拙 拙

1802	尸 山 丨 (3r 3o 1b2)		
屈	***KUTSU*** – bend; yield		
屈曲	*kukkyoku*	crookedness; refraction; curvature	366
不屈	*fukutsu*	indomitability, dauntlessness	94
屈辱	*kutsujoku*	humiliation, indignity	1738
卑屈	*hikutsu*	lack of moral courage, servility	1521
退屈	*taikutsu*	tedious, monotonous, boring	846

屈 屈 屈

1803 扌 尸 山 (3c 3r 3o)

掘

KUTSU, ho(ru) – dig

採掘	*saikutsu*	mining, digging	933
発掘	*hakkutsu*	excavation; exhumation	96
掘り出し物	*horidashimono*	treasure trove; lucky find; bargain	53, 79
掘り返す	*horikaesu*	dig up	442
掘り抜く	*horinuku*	dig through, bore	1713

掘 掘 掘

1804 土 尸 山 (3b 3r 3o)

堀

hori – moat; canal, ditch

堀割	*horiwari*	canal, waterway	519
堀江	*horie*	canal	821
堀川	*horikawa*	canal	33
内堀	*uchibori*	inner moat	84
外堀	*sotobori*	outer moat	83

堀 堀 堀

1805 土 尸 艹 (3b 3r 3k)

塀

HEI – wall, fence

板塀	*itabei*	board fence	1047
石塀	*ishibei*	stone fence	78
土塀	*dobei*	mud/earthen wall	24

塀 塀 塀

1806 氵 雨 尸 (3a 8d 3r)

漏

RŌ, mo(ru/reru) – leak, slip from; ***mo(rasu)*** – let leak, divulge

漏電	*rōden*	electric leakage, short circuit	108
脱漏	*datsurō*	be omitted, left out	1370
遺漏なく	*irōnaku*	without omission, exhaustively	1172
雨漏り	*amamori*	leak in the roof	30
聞き漏らす	*kikimorasu*	fail to hear, miss (a word)	64

漏 漏 漏

1807 貝 戈 十 7b 4n 2k

賊

ZOKU – rebel; robber

盗賊	*tōzoku*	thief, burglar, robber	1100
海賊	*kaizoku*	pirate	117
山賊	*sanzoku*	mountain robber, bandit	34
賊軍	*zokugun*	rebel army, rebels	438
国賊	*kokuzoku*	traitor	40

賊 賊 賊

1808 貝 戈 卜 7b 4n 2m

賦

FU – tribute; payment, installment; prose poem

月賦	*geppu*	monthly installment	17
賦税	*fuzei*	taxation	399
賦課	*fuka*	levy, assessment	488
賦役	*fueki*	compulsory labor, corvée	375
天賦	*tenpu*	inherent nature; inborn, natural	141

賦 賦 賦

1809 ネ 口 冂 4e 3d 2r2

禍

KA – calamity, misfortune

禍根	*kakon*	root of evil, source of calamity	314
災禍	*saika*	accident, disaster	1335
戦禍	*senka*	the ravages of war, war damage	301
禍福	*kafuku*	fortune and misfortune	1379
舌禍	*zekka*	unfortunate slip of the tongue	1259

禍 禍 禍

1810 氵 口 冂 3a 3d 2r2

渦

KA, uzu – swirl, vortex, whirlpool, eddy

渦流	*karyū*	eddy, whirlpool	247
渦中	*kachū*	maelstrom, vortex	28
戦渦	*senka*	the confusion of war	301
渦巻き	*uzumaki*	eddy, vortex, whirlpool; spiral	507

渦 渦 渦

1811 疒 禾 刂 (5i 5d 2f)

痢

RI – diarrhea

下痢	*geri*	diarrhea	31
赤痢	*sekiri*	dysentery	207
疫痢	*ekiri*	children's dysentery, infant diarrhea	1319

痢 痢 痢

1812 疒 亻 一 (5i 2a 1a2)

疾

SHITSU – illness, disease; fast

疾患	*shikkan*	disease, ailment	1315
悪疾	*akushitsu*	malignant disease	304
廃疾	*haishitsu*	disablement, disability	961
疾走	*shissō*	run at full speed	429
疾風	*shippū*	strong wind, gale	29

疾 疾 疾

1813 疒 口 亻 (5i 3d 2a)

痴

CHI – foolish

白痴	*hakuchi*	idiocy, idiot	205
痴漢	*chikan*	molester of women, masher	556
痴情	*chijō*	foolish passion, blind love; jealousy	209
音痴	*onchi*	tone-deaf	347
愚痴	*guchi*	idle complaint, grumbling	1642

痴 痴 痴

1814 忄 巾 厂 (4k 3f 2p)

怖

FU, kowa(i) – frightening, scary, dreadful; eerie, weird

恐怖	*kyōfu*	fear, terror	1602
恐怖政治	*kyōfu seiji*	reign of terror	1602, 483, 493
恐怖症	*kyōfushō*	phobia, morbid dread	1602, 1318
高所恐怖症	*kōsho kyōfushō*	acrophobia	190, 153, 1602, 1318

怖 怖 怖

1815 心 戈 口 (4k2 4n 3d)

憾

KAN – regret

遺憾	*ikan*	regrettable	1172

憾 憾 憾

1816 金 木 日 (8a 4a 4c)

錬

REN – forge, temper (iron); polish, refine; train, drill

精錬所	*seirensho*	refinery	659, 153
錬金術	*renkinjutsu*	alchemy	23, 187
錬成	*rensei*	training	261
修錬	*shūren*	training, discipline	945

錬 錬 錬

1817 金 几 又 (8a 2s 2h)

鍛

TAN, kita(eru) – forge, temper; train, drill, discipline

鍛工	*tankō*	metalworker, smith	139
鍛錬	*tanren*	temper, anneal; train, harden	1815
鍛え上げる	*kitaeageru*	become highly trained	32

鍛 鍛 鍛

1818 金 宀 ト (8a 3m 2m)

錠

JŌ – lock, padlock; pill, tablet

錠前	*jōmae*	a lock	47
組み合わせ錠	*kumiawasejō*	combination lock	418, 159
手錠	*tejō*	handcuffs	57
錠剤	*jōzai*	tablet, pill	550
一錠	*ichijō*	1 tablet/pill	2

錠 錠 錠

1819 鎖

金 貝 ⺍
8a 7b 3n

SA – close, shut; ***kusari*** – chain

封鎖	*fūsa*	blockade	1463
閉鎖	*heisa*	closing, shutdown, lockout	397
鎖国	*sakoku*	national isolation	40
連鎖反応	*rensa hannō*	chain reaction	440, 324, 827
金鎖	*kingusari*	gold chain	23

鎖 鎖 鎖

1820 鉢

金 木 一
8a 4a 1a

HACHI, [HATSU] – bowl, pot; brainpan, crown

火鉢	*hibachi*	hibachi, charcoal brazier	20
植木鉢	*uekibachi*	flowerpot	424, 22
衣鉢	*ihatsu*	the mantle, secrets (of one's master)	677
すり鉢	*suribachi*	(conical) earthenware mortar	
鉢巻き	*hachimaki*	cloth tied around one's head	507

鉢 鉢 鉢

1821 鐘

金 立 日
8a 5b 4c

SHŌ, kane – bell

晩鐘	*banshō*	evening bell	736
警鐘	*keishō*	alarm bell	706
半鐘	*hanshō*	fire bell	88
鐘乳洞	*shōnyūdō*	stalactite cave	939, 1301

鐘 鐘 鐘

1822 鈴

金 亻 一
8a 2a 1a2

REI, RIN, suzu – bell

電鈴	*denrei*	electric bell	108
呼び鈴	*yobirin*	doorbell, (hotel) service bell	1254
風鈴	*fūrin*	wind-bell	29
鈴虫	*suzumushi*	"bell-ring" insect	873
鈴木	*Suzuki*	(surname)	22

鈴 鈴 鈴

1823 雫亻一 8d 2a 1a2

零

REI – zero

零点	*reiten*	(a score of) zero	169
零時	*reiji*	12 o'clock	42
零度	*reido*	zero (degrees), the freezing point	377
零下	*reika*	below zero, subzero	31
零細	*reisai*	small, trifling	695

零 零 零

1824 雫亻刂 8d 2a 2f

雰

FUN – fog

雰囲気	*fun'iki*	atmosphere, ambience	1194, 134

雰 雰 雰

1825 木口宀 4a 3d2 3m

棺

KAN – coffin

棺おけ	*kan'oke*	coffin	
石棺	*sekkan*	stone coffin, sarcophagus	78
納棺	*nōkan*	place (a body) in the coffin	758
出棺	*shukkan*	start of a funeral procession	53

棺 棺 棺

1826 土日 3b2 4c

埋

MAI, u(maru) – be buried (under), filled up; ***u(meru)*** – bury, fill up; ***u(moreru)*** – be buried; sink into obscurity

埋葬	*maisō*	burial, interment	812
埋没	*maibotsu*	be buried; fall into oblivion	935
埋蔵	*maizō*	buried stores, underground reserves	1286
埋め立て	*umetate*	land reclamation	121

埋 埋 埋

1827	彡 立 日 3j 5b 4c	*SHŌ* – clear		
彰		顕彰	*kenshō*	manifest, exhibit, exalt 1170
		表彰	*hyōshō*	official commendation 272
		表彰状	*hyōshōjō*	certificate of commendation, citation 272, 626

1828	土 立 口 3b 5b 3d	*BAI, tsuchika(u)* – cultivate, foster		
培		栽培	*saibai*	cultivation, culture, growing 1125
		培養	*baiyō*	cultivation, culture 402
		培養液	*baiyōeki*	culture fluid/solution 402, 472
		純粋培養	*junsui baiyō*	pure culture 965, 1708, 402

1829	貝 立 口 7b 5b 3d	*BAI* – indemnify		
賠		賠償	*baishō*	reparation, indemnification 971
		賠償金	*baishōkin*	indemnities, reparations, damages 971, 23
		損害賠償	*songai baishō*	compensation for damages 350, 518, 971

1830	刂 立 口 2f 5b 3d	*BŌ* – divide		
剖		解剖	*kaibō*	dissection, autopsy, analysis 474
		解剖学	*kaibōgaku*	anatomy 474, 109
		生体解剖	*seitai kaibō*	vivisection 44, 61, 474

1831 貝 日 一 7b 4c 1a

賜

SHI, tamawa(ru) – grant, bestow, confer

下賜	*kashi*	imperial grant, donation	31
恩賜	*onshi*	imperial gift	555
賜暇	*shika*	leave of absence, furlough	1064

賜 賜 賜

1832 扌 尸 口 3c 3r 3d

据

su(eru) – set, place, put into position; **su(waru)** – sit, be set

据え付ける	*suetsukeru*	set into position, install	192
据え置く	*sueoku*	leave as is, let stand	426
腹を据える	*hara o sueru*	decide, make up one's mind	1271

据 据 据

1833 扌 石 3c 5a

拓

TAKU – open, clear, break up (land)

開拓	*kaitaku*	reclamation, clearing	396
開拓者	*kaitakusha*	settler, pioneer	396, 164
拓殖	*takushoku*	colonization, settlement	1506
干拓	*kantaku*	land reclamation by drainage	584
拓本	*takuhon*	a rubbing (of an inscription)	25

拓 拓 拓

1834 石 艹 丷 5a 3k 2o

碁

GO – (the board game) go

囲碁	*igo*	(the game of) go	1194
碁石	*goishi*	go stone	78
碁盤	*goban*	go board	1098
碁盤の目	*goban no me*	go-board grid, checkerboard layout	1098, 55
碁会所	*gokaisho, gokaijo*	go club	158, 153

碁 碁 碁

1835 木 艹 丷 4a 3k 2o

棋

KI – go; shogi, Japanese chess

将棋	*shōgi*	shogi, Japanese chess	627
将棋盤	*shōgiban*	shogi board	627, 1098
棋譜	*kifu*	record of a game of go/shogi	1167
棋士	*kishi*	(professional) go/shogi player	572
将棋倒し	*shōgidaoshi*	fall down (like dominoes)	627, 905

棋 棋 棋

1836 女 艹 亠 3e 3k 2j

嬢

JŌ – daughter; young lady

お嬢さん	*ojōsan*	(your) daughter; young lady	
(御)令嬢	*(go)reijō*	(your) daughter; young lady	708, 831
愛嬢	*aijō*	one's dear/favorite daughter	259

嬢 嬢 嬢

1837 酉 艹 亠 7e 3k 2j

醸

JŌ, kamo(su) – brew; bring about, give rise to

醸造所	*jōzōsho*	brewery, distillery	691, 153
醸成	*jōsei*	brew; cause, bring about	261

醸 醸 醸

1838 土 月 凵 3b 4b 3o

塑

SO – modeling, molding

塑像	*sozō*	modeling, molding	740
可塑性	*kasosei*	plasticity	388, 98
彫塑	*chōso*	carving and (clay) modeling, plastic arts	1149

塑 塑 塑

1839 壇

土 日 口
3b 4c 3s

DAN, [TAN] – rostrum, dais, podium

演壇	*endan*	(speaker's) platform, rostrum	344
祭壇	*saidan*	altar	617
文壇	*bundan*	the literary world	111
花壇	*kadan*	flower bed	255
土壇場	*dotanba*	last/critical moment; place of execution	24, 154

壇 壇 壇

1840 塔

土 艹 口
3b 3k 3d

TŌ – tower

監視塔	*kanshitō*	watchtower	1663, 606
管制塔	*kanseitō*	control tower	328, 427
広告塔	*kōkokutō*	poster column, advertising pillar	694, 690
象げの塔	*zōge no tō*	ivory tower	739
五重の塔	*gojū no tō*	5-story pagoda	7, 227

塔 塔 塔

1841 楼

木 米 女
4a 6b 3e

RŌ – tower, turret, lookout

鐘楼	*shōrō*	bell tower, belfry	1821
楼閣	*rōkaku*	many-storied building, castle	837
楼門	*rōmon*	2-story gate	161
摩天楼	*matenrō*	skyscraper	1530, 141

楼 楼 楼

1842 栓

木 王 亻
4a 4f 2a

SEN – stopper, cork, plug, spigot

消火栓	*shōkasen*	fire hydrant	845, 20
給水栓	*kyūsuisen*	water tap, hydrant	346, 21
水道栓	*suidōsen*	hydrant, tap	21, 149
ガス栓	*gasusen*	gas tap	
栓抜き	*sennuki*	bottle opener	1713

栓 栓 栓

1843	阝 亻 十 2d 2a 2k			
附	***FU*** – attach; accompany (cf. No. 192)			
	附属	*fuzoku*	belonging to, accessory	1637
	寄附	*kifu*	contribution, donation	1361
	附近	*fukin*	neighborhood, vicinity	445
	附録	*furoku*	supplement, appendix	538
	附随	*fuzui*	accompany, be entailed by	1741

附 附 附

1844	阝 夂 土 2d 4i 3b			
陵	***RYŌ, misasagi*** – imperial tomb, mausoleum			
	丘陵	*kyūryō*	hill	1357
	丘陵地帯	*kyūryō chitai*	hill area	1357, 118, 963
	御陵	*goryō*	tomb of the emperor/empress	708

陵 陵 陵

1845	亻 夂 丷 2a 4i 2o			
俊	***SHUN*** – excellence, genius			
	俊秀	*shunshū*	person of outstanding talent	1683
	俊英	*shun'ei*	talent, gifted person	353
	俊才	*shunsai*	genius, outstanding talent	551
	俊傑	*shunketsu*	great man	1731
	俊敏	*shunbin*	keen, quick-witted	1735

俊 俊 俊

1846	口 夂 丷 3d 4i 2o			
唆	***SA, sosonoka(su)*** – tempt, entice; incite, abet			
	示唆	*shisa*	suggestion	615
	教唆	*kyōsa*	instigation, incitement	245

唆 唆 唆

1847 頁⺌⺊ 9a 3n 2m

頻

HIN – occur repeatedly

頻度	*hindo*	frequency, rate of occurrence	377
頻発	*hinpatsu*	frequency, frequent occurrence	96
頻繁	*hinpan*	frequency, rapid succession	1292
頻々と	*hinpin to*	frequent, in rapid succession	

1848 頁⺌一 9a 2o 1a2

頑

GAN – stubborn, obstinate

頑固	*ganko*	stubborn, obstinate	972
頑迷	*ganmei*	bigoted, obstinate	967
頑強	*gankyō*	stubborn, obstinate, unyielding	217
頑健	*ganken*	strong and robust, in excellent health	893
頑張る	*ganbaru*	persist in, stick to it, hang in there	1106

1849 頁火 9a 4d

煩

HAN, [BON], wazura(u) – worry about; be ill, suffer from; ***wazura(wasu)*** – trouble, bother, annoy

煩雑	*hanzatsu*	complicated, troublesome	575
煩忙	*hanbō*	busy, pressed with business	1373
煩悩	*bonnō*	evil passions, carnal desires	1279
煩わしい	*wazurawashii*	troublesome, tangled	

1850 頁⺌刂 9a 2o 2f

頒

HAN – divide, distribute

頒布	*hanpu*	distribute, circulate	675

1851 宀 冂 刂 3m 2r 2f

寡

KA – alone, widowed; few, small

多寡	*taka*	quantity, number, amount	229
寡婦	*kafu*	widow	316
寡聞	*kabun*	little knowledge, ill-informed	64
寡黙	*kamoku*	taciturn, reticent	1578
寡占	*kasen*	oligopoly	1706

寡 寡 寡

1852 宀 貝 ⺍ 3m 7b 3n

賓

HIN – guest

賓客	*hinkaku, hinkyaku*	honored guest, visitor	641
貴賓	*kihin*	distinguished guest, guest of honor	1171
主賓	*shuhin*	guest of honor	155
来賓	*raihin*	guest, visitor	69
迎賓館	*geihinkan*	reception hall, guest mansion	1055, 327

賓 賓 賓

1853 ⺍ 口 冂 3n 3d 2r

尚

SHŌ – further; value, respect

高尚	*kōshō*	lofty, noble, refined	190
尚武	*shōbu*	militaristic, martial	1031
尚早	*shōsō*	premature, too early	248
時機尚早	*jiki-shōsō*	too soon, time is not ripe	42, 528, 248
和尚	*oshō*	Buddhist priest	124

尚 尚 尚

1854 宀 月 ⺍ 3m 4b 3n

宵

SHŌ, yoi – early evening

春宵	*shunshō*	spring evening	460
徹宵	*tesshō*	all night long	1422
宵越し	*yoigoshi*	(left over) from the previous evening	1001
宵っ張り	*yoippari*	staying up till late; night owling	1106
宵の口	*yoi no kuchi*	early evening	54

宵 宵 宵

1855	石 月 ⺌ 5a 4b 3n	***SHŌ*** – saltpeter		
硝				
	硝酸	*shōsan*	nitric acid	516
	硝石	*shōseki*	saltpeter	78
	硝煙	*shōen*	gunpowder smoke	919

硝 硝 硝

1856	石 亠 丨 5a 2j 1b3	***RYŪ*** – sulfur		
硫				
	硫酸	*ryūsan*	sulfuric acid	516
	硫化水素	*ryūka suiso*	hydrogen sulfide	254, 21, 271
	硫黄	*iō*	sulfur	780

硫 硫 硫

1857	月 方 4b 4h	***BŌ*** – (animal) fat		
肪				
	脂肪	*shibō*	fat	1042
	皮下脂肪	*hika shibō*	subcutaneous fat	975, 31, 1042
	脂肪ぶとり	*shibōbutori*	fat, obese	1042
	脂肪層	*shibōsō*	layer of fat	1042, 1367
	植物性脂肪	*shokubutsusei shibō*	vegetable fat	424, 79, 98, 1042

肪 肪 肪

1858	土 方 3b 4h	***BŌ, [BO']*** – priest's residence; Buddhist priest; boy		
坊				
	坊主	*bōzu*	Buddhist priest; bonze	155
	朝寝坊	*asanebō*	a late riser	469, 1079
	けちん坊	*kechinbō*	stingy person, tightwad	
	赤ん坊	*akanbō*	baby	207
	坊ちゃん	*botchan*	(your) son, young master, boy	

坊 坊 坊

1859 糸 方 6a 4h

紡

BŌ, tsumu(gu) – spin, make yarn

紡績	*bōseki*	spinning	1117
紡績工場	*bōseki kōjō*	spinning mill	1117, 139, 154
紡織	*bōshoku*	spinning and weaving	680
混紡	*konbō*	mixed/blended spinning	799

紡 紡 紡

1860 罒 隹 糸 5g 8c 6a

羅

RA – silk gauze, thin silk

羅列	*raretsu*	enumerate, cite	611
羅針	*rashin*	compass needle	341
羅針盤	*rashinban*	compass	341, 1098
網羅	*mōra*	be all-inclusive, comprehensive	1612
一張羅	*itchōra*	one's best/only clothes	2, 1106

羅 羅 羅

1861 罒 月 ト 5g 4b 2m2

罷

HI – end, discontinue, stop; leave, withdraw

罷免	*himen*	dismissal (from one's post)	733
罷業	*higyō*	strike, walkout	279

罷 罷 罷

1862 金 一 ノ 8a 1a 1c

釣

CHŌ, tsu(ru) – fish, angle; decoy, allure, take in

釣り道具	*tsuridōgu*	fishing tackle	149, 420
釣り針	*tsuribari*	fishhook	341
釣り堀	*tsuribori*	fishing pond	1804
釣り合い	*tsuriai*	balance, equilibrium, proportion	159
釣り銭	*tsurisen*	(make) change	648

釣 釣 釣

1863	酉 一 ノ 7e 1a 1c	*SHAKU* – pour (wine), serve at table		
酌				
	媒酌	*baishaku*	matchmaking	1496
	媒酌人	*baishakunin*	matchmaker, go-between	1496, 1
	晩酌	*banshaku*	evening drink	736
	独酌	*dokushaku*	drinking alone	219
	しん酌	*shinshaku*	take into consideration	

酌 酌 酌

1864	酉 丨 丶 7e 1b3 1d3	*SHŪ* – reward, compensation		
酬				
	報酬	*hōshū*	remuneration	685
	無報酬	*muhōshū*	without remuneration, free of charge	93, 685
	応酬	*ōshū*	reply, response, retort	827

酬 酬 酬

1865	酉 夂 口 7e 4i 3d	*RAKU* – whey		
酪				
	酪農(場)	*rakunō(jō)*	dairy, dairy farm	369, 154
	酪製品	*rakuseihin*	dairy products	428, 230
	酪農家	*rakunōka*	dairy farmer, dairyman	369, 165

酪 酪 酪

1866	酉 土 子 7e 3b 2c	*KŌ* – fermentation; yeast		
酵				
	酵母	*kōbo*	yeast	112
	酵母菌	*kōbokin*	yeast fungus	112, 1222
	酵素	*kōso*	enzyme	271
	発酵	*hakkō*	fermentation	96

酵 酵 酵

1867 酉 ⺊ 一 (7e 2m 1a2)

酢

SAKU, su – vinegar

酢酸	*sakusan*	acetic acid	516
酢漬け	*suzuke*	pickling in vinegar	1793
酢の物	*su no mono*	vinegared dish	79
甘酢	*amazu*	sweet vinegar	1492

1868 尸 一 丨 (3r 1a2 1b)

尾

BI, o – tail

末尾	*matsubi*	the end	305
首尾	*shubi*	beginning and end; result, outcome	148
尾行	*bikō*	shadow, tail (someone)	68
尾灯	*bitō*	taillight	1333
徹頭徹尾	*tettō-tetsubi*	thoroughly	1422, 276

1869 尸 氵 (3r 3a)

尿

NYŌ – urine

尿素	*nyōso*	urea	271
尿酸	*nyōsan*	uric acid	516
排尿	*hainyō*	urination	1036
夜尿症	*yanyōshō*	nocturnal enuresis, bedwetting	471, 1318
糖尿病	*tōnyōbyō*	diabetes	1698, 380

1870 氵 心 ノ (3a 4k 1c)

泌

HITSU, HI – flow, secrete

分泌	*bunpitsu, bunpi*	secretion	38
内分泌	*naibunpi*	internal secretion	84, 38
分泌物	*bunpitsubutsu*	a secretion	38, 79
泌尿器	*hinyōki*	urinary organs	1869, 527
泌尿器科	*hinyōkika*	urology	1869, 527, 320

1871 木 卩 丨 4a 2e 1b

柳

RYŪ, yanagi – willow tree

川柳	*senryū*	humorous 17-syllable Japanese poem	33
花柳界	*karyūkai*	demimonde, red-light district	255, 454
柳び	*ryūbi*	beautiful eyebrows	
枝垂れ柳	*shidare yanagi*	weeping willow	870, 1070
柳腰	*yanagi-goshi*	slender graceful hips	1298

1872 木 彡 4a 3j

杉

sugi – Japanese cedar

杉並木	*suginamiki*	avenue of *sugi* trees	1165, 22
杉並区	*Suginami-ku*	Suginami Ward (Tokyo)	1165, 183

1873 叒木 2h3 4a

桑

SŌ, kuwa – mulberry tree

桑門	*sōmon*	Buddhist priest/monk	161
桑園	*sōen*	mulberry farm/orchard	447
桑田	*sōden*	mulberry orchard	35
桑畑	*kuwabatake*	mulberry field	36
桑原桑原	*kuwabara-kuwabara*	Heaven forbid! Thank God!	136

1874 日 ト 4c 2m2

昆

KON – elder brother; later; insect

昆虫	*konchū*	insect	873
昆虫学	*konchūgaku*	entomology	873, 109
昆虫採集	*konchū saishū*	insect collecting	873, 933, 436
昆布	*konbu, kobu*	sea tangle, tang, kelp	675
昆布茶	*kobucha*	tang tea	675, 251

1875 蛇

虫 宀 ト (6d 3m 2m)

JA, DA, hebi – snake

蛇の目	*janome*	bull's-eye design (on oilpaper umbrella)	55
蛇腹	*jabara*	accordion-like folds, bellows; cornice	1271
蛇行	*dakō*	meander, zigzag, fishtail	68
蛇足	*dasoku*	superfluous (like legs on a snake)	58
長蛇の列	*chōda no retsu*	long queue/line of people	95, 611

蛇 蛇 蛇

1876 蚊

虫 亠 ノ (6d 2j 1c)

ka – mosquito

蚊帳/屋	*kaya*	mosquito net	1107, 167
蚊取り線香	*katori senkō*	mosquito-repellent incense	65, 299, 1682
蚊柱	*kabashira*	column of swarming mosquitoes	598

蚊 蚊 蚊

1877 蚕

虫 亻 一 (6d 2a 1a2)

SAN, kaiko – silkworm

養蚕	*yōsan*	sericulture, silkworm raising	402
蚕糸	*sanshi*	silk thread/yarn	242
蚕食	*sanshoku*	encroachment, inroads	322

蚕 蚕 蚕

1878 蛍

⺍ 虫 冖 (3n 6d 2i)

KEI, hotaru – firefly, glowworm

蛍光灯	*keikōtō*	fluorescent lamp	138, 1333
蛍光塗料	*keikō-toryō*	fluorescent paint	138, 1073, 319
蛍雪の功	*keisetsu no kō*	the fruits of diligent study	949, 818
蛍狩り	*hotarugari*	firefly catching	1581

蛍 蛍 蛍

1879 亠 虫 丨 2j 6d 1b2

蛮

BAN – barbarian

(野)蛮人	*(ya)banjin*	barbarian, savage	236, 1
南蛮	*nanban*	southern barbarian, European (hist.)	74
蛮風	*banpū*	barbarous ways/customs	29
蛮行	*bankō*	act of barbarity, brutality	68
蛮勇	*ban'yū*	recklessness; brute force	1386

蛮 蛮 蛮

1880 馬 亻 一 10a 2a 1a

駄

DA – pack horse; footwear; of poor quality

駄賃	*dachin*	reward, recompense, tip	751
駄菓子	*dagashi*	cheap candy	1535, 103
駄作	*dasaku*	poor work, worthless stuff	360
無駄	*muda*	futile, useless, in vain	93
下駄	*geta*	geta, Japanese wooden clogs	31

駄 駄 駄

1881 馬 口 亻 10a 3d 2a

騎

KI – horse riding; (counter for horsemen)

騎手	*kishu*	rider, jockey	57
騎士	*kishi*	rider, horseman	572
騎兵	*kihei*	cavalry soldier	784
騎馬	*kiba*	on horseback, mounted	283
一騎打ち	*ikkiuchi*	single combat, man-to-man fight	2, 1020

騎 騎 騎

1882 馬 匚 ノ 10a 2t 1c

駆

KU, ka(keru) – gallop; run, rush; ***ka(ru)*** – drive, spur on

先駆	*senku*	forerunner, pioneer	50
駆逐	*kuchiku*	drive away, expel, get rid of	1134
駆除	*kujo*	exterminate	1065
駆け回る	*kakemawaru*	run around	90
駆け足	*kakeashi*	running, galloping	58

駆 駆 駆

1883	⺮ 馬 6f 10a	**TOKU** – serious; cordial			
	篤	危篤	*kitoku*	critically ill	534
		篤行	*tokkō*	good deed, act of charity	68
		篤志家	*tokushika*	benefactor, volunteer	573, 165
		篤農家	*tokunōka*	exemplary farmer	369, 165
		篤学	*tokugaku*	love of learning, diligence in studies	109

篤 篤 篤

1884	氵 ⺍ 亻 3a 3n 2a	**KEI** – valley			
	渓	渓谷	*keikoku*	ravine, gorge, valley	653
		渓流	*keiryū*	mountain stream, torrent	247
		雪渓	*sekkei*	snowy valley/ravine	949
		渓間	*keikan*	ravine; in the valley	43

渓 渓 渓

1885	言 口 刂 7a 3d 2f	**SHŌ, mikotonori** – imperial edict			
	詔	大詔	*taishō*	imperial rescript	26
		詔書	*shōsho*	imperial edict/rescript	131

詔 詔 詔

1886	力 木 口 2g 4a 3s	**CHOKU** – imperial decree			
	勅	勅語	*chokugo*	imperial message, speech from the throne	67
		勅命	*chokumei*	imperial order/commission	578
		詔勅	*shōchoku*	imperial proclamation	1885
		勅使	*chokushi*	imperial messenger/envoy	331

勅 勅 勅

1887 王 丷 冂 4f 2o 2r

璽

JI – imperial seal

国璽	*kokuji*	great seal, seal of state	40
御璽	*gyoji*	imperial/privy seal	708
玉璽	*gyokuji*	imperial seal	295
璽書	*jisho*	document with the imperial seal	131

1888 亻 丷 一 2a2 2o 1a4

僕

BOKU – I (in masculine speech); manservant

従僕	*jūboku*	servant, attendant	1482
家僕	*kaboku*	manservant	165
僕ら	*bokura*	we (in masculine speech)	

1889 扌 丷 亻 3c 2o 2a

撲

BOKU – hit, strike

打撲傷	*dabokushō*	bruise, contusion	1020, 633
撲滅	*bokumetsu*	eradication, extermination	1338
相撲	*sumō*	sumo wrestling	146
相撲取り	*sumōtori*	sumo wrestler	146, 65
大相撲	*ōzumō*	grand sumo tournament; exciting bout	26, 146

1890 亻 衤 一 2a 5e 1a2

俵

HYŌ, tawara – straw bag/sack

土俵	*dohyō*	sandbag; sumo ring	24
米俵	*komedawara*	straw rice-sack; bag of/for rice	224
炭俵	*sumidawara*	sack for charcoal	1344
一俵	*ippyō*	1 bag/sack	2

1891	亻 山 2a 3o	**SEN** – hermit; wizard		
	仙人	*sennin*	mountain wizard; hermit, settler	1
	仙女	*sennyo*	fairy, nymph	102
	酒仙	*shusen*	heavy drinker	517
	水仙	*suisen*	narcissus	21
	仙台	*Sendai*	(city in Tohoku)	492

1892	一 丨 1a3 1b2	**TOTSU** – protruding, convex		
	凸レンズ	*totsurenzu*	convex lens	
	凸面	*totsumen*	convex (surface)	274
	両凸	*ryōtotsu*	biconvex	200
	凸版 (印刷)	*toppan (insatsu)*	letterpress, relief printing	1046, 1043, 1044

1893	一 丨 1a3 1b2	**Ō** – indentation, hollowed out, sunken in, concave		
	凹凸	*ōtotsu*	uneven, jagged, rough	1892
	凹面鏡	*ōmenkyō*	concave mirror	274, 863
	凹レンズ	*ōrenzu*	concave lens	

1894	十 丶 2k 1d	**SUN** – (unit of length, about 3 cm)		
	寸法	*sunpō*	measurements; plan	123
	寸評	*sunpyō*	brief comment	1028
	寸暇	*sunka*	a moment's leisure, spare moments	1064
	寸前	*sunzen*	immediately/right before	47
	寸断	*sundan*	cut/tear to pieces	1024

1895 尸 丶 (3r 1d)

尺

SHAKU – (unit of length, about 30 cm); measure, length

尺貫法	*shakkanhō*	old Japanese system of weights and measures	914, 123
巻き尺	*makijaku*	tape measure, surveying tape	507
縮尺	*shukushaku*	reduced scale (map)	1110
尺八	*shakuhachi*	Japanese end-blown bamboo flute	10

尺 尺 尺

1896 土 十 一 (3b 2k 1a)

坪

tsubo – (unit of area, about 3.3 m²)

坪数	*tsubosū*	number of *tsubo*, area	225
延べ坪(数)	*nobetsubo(sū)*	total area (of all floors)	1115, 225
建坪	*tatetsubo*	floor space/area	892
坪二万円	*tsubo niman'en*	20,000 yen per *tsubo*	3, 16, 13
坪当たり	*tsuboatari*	per *tsubo*	77

坪 坪 坪

1897 厂 一 丨 (2p 1a 1b)

斤

KIN – (unit of weight, about 600 g)

一斤	*ikkin*	1 *kin*	2
斤量	*kinryō*	weight	411

斤 斤 斤

1898 卄 ノ (3k 1c)

升

SHŌ, masu – (unit of volume, 1.8 liters)

一升	*isshō*	1 *shō*	2
一升瓶	*isshōbin*	1.8-liter bottle	2, 1161

升 升 升

1899 十 丶 2k 1d2

斗

TO – (unit of volume, 18 liters)

一斗	*itto*	1 *to*	2
斗酒	*toshu*	kegs of saké	517
北斗(七)星	*hokuto(shichi)sei*	the Big Dipper	73, 9, 730

1900 厂 日 土 2p 4c 3b

厘

RIN – (old unit of currency, 1/1,000 yen); (unit of length, about 0.3 mm)

二銭五厘	*nisen gorin*	2 *sen* 5 *rin*, 2.5 *sen*	3, 648, 7
一分一厘	*ichibu ichirin*	1 *bu* 1 *rin*, 1.1 *bu*; some, little, slight	2, 38
厘毛	*rinmō*	a trifle; unimportant, insignificant	287

1901 田 亠 ⺈ 5f 2j 2n

畝

se – (unit of area, about 1 are); ***une*** – ridge (between furrows); rib (in fabric)

畝間	*unema*	space between ridges, furrow	43
畝織	*uneori*	rep, ribbed fabric	680

1902 刂 丿 丶 2f 1c 1d

匁

monme – (unit of weight, about 3.75 g)

1903	一 ノ 丶 (1a 1c 1d)
勺	*SHAKU* – (unit of volume, about 18 ml)

勺 勺 勺

1904	金 土 艹 (8a 3b 3k)			
錘	***SUI, tsumu*** – spindle			
	紡錘	*bōsui*	spindle	1859
	錘状	*suijō*	spindle-shaped	626

錘 錘 錘

1905	金 土 丷 (8a 3b 2o)			
銑	***SEN*** – pig iron			
	銑鉄	*sentetsu*	pig iron	312

銑 銑 銑

1906	木 戈 一 (4a 4n 1a2)			
桟	***SAN*** – crosspiece, frame, bolt (of a door)			
	桟橋	*sanbashi*	wharf, jetty	597
		sankyō	wharf; bridge	
	桟道	*sandō*	plank bridge	149

桟 桟 桟

1907 木 十 一 (4a 2k 1a)

枠

waku – frame, framework; limit, confines

窓枠	*madowaku*	window frame	698
枠内	*wakunai*	within the limits	84
枠組	*wakugumi*	frame, framework; framing	418

枠 枠 枠

1908 木 月 (4a 4b2)

棚

tana – shelf

本棚	*hondana*	bookshelf	25
戸棚	*todana*	cupboard	152
棚上げ	*tanaage*	put on the shelf, shelve	32
大陸棚	*tairikudana*	continental shelf	26, 647
棚卸	*tanaoroshi*	inventory, stock taking	707

棚 棚 棚

1909 艹 十 一 (3k 2k 1a)

芋

imo – potato

じゃが芋	*jagaimo*	(white) potato	
焼き芋	*yakiimo*	baked sweet potato	920
里芋	*satoimo*	taro	142
芋掘り	*imohori*	digging sweet potatoes	1803

芋 芋 芋

1910 艹 立 木 (3k 5b 4a)

薪

SHIN, takigi – firewood

薪水	*shinsui*	firewood and water	21
薪炭	*shintan*	firewood and charcoal, fuel	1344

薪 薪 薪

1911	艹 糸 虫 3k 6a 6d	**KEN, mayu** – cocoon			
繭		繭糸	*kenshi*	cocoon and (silk) thread; silk thread	242
		繭玉	*mayudama*	(type of New Year's decoration)	295

1912	土 艹 亠 3b 3k 2j	**JŌ** – soil			
壌		土壌	*dojō*	soil	24

1913	土 艹 丷 3b 3k 2o	**KAN, ta(eru)** – endure			
堪		堪忍	*kannin*	patience, forbearance; forgiveness	1414
		堪え忍ぶ	*taeshinobu*	bear patiently	1414
		堪えかねる	*taekaneru*	cannot bear	

1914	扌 木 一 3c 4a 1a	**MATSU** – erase, expunge			
抹		抹殺	*massatsu*	expunge; deny; ignore	576
		抹消	*masshō*	erase, cross out	845
		一抹	*ichimatsu*	a tinge of	2

1915 扌 艹 口
3c 3k 3d

搭

TŌ – ride

搭乗	*tōjō*	board, get on	523
搭乗券	*tōjōken*	boarding pass	523, 506
搭載	*tōsai*	load, embark	1124

搭 搭 搭

1916 扌 口 刂
3c 3d 2f

拐

KAI – kidnap

誘拐	*yūkai*	kidnap	1684
拐帯	*kaitai*	abscond with money	963

拐 拐 拐

1917 口 艹 冂
3d2 3k 2r

嗣

SHI – heir

嗣子	*shishi*	heir	103
後嗣	*kōshi*	heir	48

嗣 嗣 嗣

1918 口 土 丨
3d 3b2 1b4

嚇

KAKU – threat

威嚇	*ikaku*	threat, menace	1339

嚇 嚇 嚇

1919	口 日 ⺊ 3d 4c 2m	***KATSU*** – scold		
喝		恐喝 *kyōkatsu*	threaten, blackmail	1602
		喝破 *kappa*	declare, proclaim	665

喝 喝 喝

1920	言 日 ⺊ 7a 4c 2m	***ETSU*** – audience (with someone)		
謁		謁見 *ekken*	have an audience (with)	63
		拝謁 *haietsu*	have an audience (with)	1201
		謁する *essuru*	have an audience (with)	

謁 謁 謁

1921	月 丷 亻 4b 2o 2a	***CHIN*** – (imperial) we
朕		

朕 朕 朕

1922	月 ⺊ 一 4b 2m 1a3	***CHŌ*** – swell		
脹		膨脹 *bōchō*	expansion	1145

脹 脹 脹

1923	罒 日 ⺍ 5g 4c 3n	***SHAKU*** – peerage, court rank			
爵		男爵	*danshaku*	baron	101
		公爵	*kōshaku*	prince, duke	126
		伯爵	*hakushaku*	count, earl	1176
		爵位	*shakui*	peerage, court rank	122
		授爵	*jushaku*	elevate to the peerage, create a peer	602

1924	亻 一 ノ 2a2 1a4 1c	***KŌ*** – marquis			
侯		王侯	*ōkō*	royalty	294
		諸侯	*shokō*	feudal lords	861
		侯爵	*kōshaku*	marquis	1923

1925	口 亻 冂 3d2 2a2 2r	***KYŌ, ta(meru)*** – straighten; correct			
矯		矯正	*kyōsei*	correct, reform	275
		矯激	*kyōgeki*	radical, extreme	1017
		奇矯	*kikyō*	eccentric conduct	1360
		矯め直す	*tamenaosu*	set up again, correct, reform, cure	423

1926	冂 一 2r 1a3	***ka(tsu)*** – and			
且		且つ又	*katsumata*	and	1593

1927 亻 日 一 (2a 4c 1a)

但

tada(shi) – but, however, provided

但し書き	*tadashigaki*	proviso	131

但 但 但

1928 亻 貝 ト (2a 7b 2m)

偵

TEI – spy

探偵	*tantei*	detective	535
探偵小説	*tantei shōsetsu*	detective story, whodunit	535, 27, 400
偵察	*teisatsu*	reconnaissance	619
内偵	*naitei*	scouting; private inquiry	84

偵 偵 偵

1929 日 艹 (4c2 3k)

曹

SŌ – friend

法曹	*hōsō*	the legal profession; lawyer	123
法曹界	*hōsōkai*	legal circles, the bench and bar	123, 454

曹 曹 曹

1930 丷 冫 一 (2o 2b2 1a2)

翁

Ō – old man

老翁	*rōō*	old man	543

翁 翁 翁

1931 女 氵 厂 3e 3a 2p

婆

BA – old woman

老 婆	*rōba*	old woman	543
産 婆	*sanba*	midwife	278
お 転 婆	*otenba*	tomboy	433
塔 婆	*tōba*	wooden grave tablet	1840

婆 婆 婆

1932 女 口 亠 3e 3d 2j

嫡

CHAKU – legitimate

嫡 (出) 子	*chaku(shutsu)shi*	legitimate child	53, 103
嫡 嗣	*chakushi*	legitimate heir	1917
嫡 流	*chakuryū*	lineage of the eldest son	247
嫡 男	*chakunan*	eldest son, heir, legitimate son	101
嫡 孫	*chakuson*	eldest son of one's son and heir	910

嫡 嫡 嫡

1933 女 又 3e 2h

奴

DO – servant, slave, fellow

守 銭 奴	*shusendo*	miser	490, 648
農 奴	*nōdo*	serf	369
売 国 奴	*baikokudo*	traitor	239, 40

奴 奴 奴

1934 ネ 士 氵 4e 3p 3a

隷

REI – servant

奴 隷	*dorei*	slave	1933
隷 従	*reijū*	slavery	1482
隷 属	*reizoku*	be subordinate (to)	1637
隷 書	*reisho*	(ancient squared style of kanji)	131

隷 隷 隷

1935	巾 口 丿 3f 3d2 1c

師

SUI – leading troops

元帥	*gensui*	field marshal	137
総帥	*sōsui*	commander in chief	697
統帥	*tōsui*	supreme/high command	830

師 師 師

1936	丨 丿 1b3 1c

屯

TON – barracks

駐屯	*chūton*	be stationed	599
駐屯地	*chūtonchi*	military post	599, 118

屯 屯 屯

1937	辶 巾 厂 2q 3f 2p

逓

TEI – in turn; send

逓信	*teishin*	communications	157
逓送	*teisō*	convey, send by mail, forward	441
逓減	*teigen*	successive diminution	715
逓増	*teizō*	gradual increase	712

逓 逓 逓

1938	辶 酉 丷 2q 7e 2o

遵

JUN – follow, obey

遵守	*junshu*	obey, comply with	490
遵奉	*junpō*	observe, adhere to, abide by	1541
遵法	*junpō*	law abiding; work-to-rule (tactics)	123

遵 遵 遵

1939 力亠亻 2g 2j 2a

劾

GAI – criminal investigation

弾劾	*dangai*	impeachment	1539

劾 劾 劾

1940 匚几又 2t 2s 2h

殴

Ō, nagu(ru) – beat, hit, strike

殴打	*ōda*	assault (and battery)	1020
殴り殺す	*nagurikorosu*	beat to death, strike dead	576
殴り付ける	*naguritsukeru*	strike, beat, thrash	192
殴り込み	*nagurikomi*	an attack, raid	776
ぶん殴る	*bunnaguru*	give a good whaling/thrashing	

殴 殴 殴

1941 ⺊口厂 2m 3d 2p

虞

osore – fear, danger, risk

虞 虞 虞

1942 疒口丷 5i 3d 2o

痘

TŌ – smallpox

種痘	*shutō*	vaccination	228
痘苗	*tōbyō*	vaccine	1468
天然痘	*tennentō*	smallpox	141, 651
水痘	*suitō*	chickenpox	21

痘 痘 痘

1943	阝 立 口 2d 5b 3d

陪

BAI – follow, accompany, attend on

陪審	*baishin*	jury	1383
陪席	*baiseki*	sitting as an associate (judge)	379
陪食	*baishoku*	dining with a superior	322

陪 陪 陪

1944	氵 皿 匚 3a 5h 2t

濫

RAN – overflow

濫用	*ran'yō*	abuse, misuse, misappropriation	107
濫費	*ranpi*	waste, extravagance	749
濫作	*ransaku*	overproduction	360
濫伐	*ranbatsu*	reckless deforestation	1509
濫獲	*rankaku*	overfishing, overhunting	1313

濫 濫 濫

1945	田 十 一 5f 2k 1a

畔

HAN – rice-paddy ridge, levee

湖畔	*kohan*	lakeshore	467
河畔	*kahan*	riverside	389

畔 畔 畔

GENERAL INDEX by Readings

(Kanji 1 - 1,945)

– N –

– O –

– R –

– T –

– U –

– W –